FINANCIAL STATEMENT ANALYSIS

FINANCIAL STATEMENT ANALYSIS

An International Perspective

Peter Walton

Business Press
Thomson Learning™

Australia • Canada • Denmark • Japan • Mexico • New Zealand • Philippines
Puerto Rico • Singapore • South Africa • Spain • United Kingdom • United States

Financial Statement Analysis

Copyright © 2000 Peter Walton

Business Press is a division of Thomson Learning. The Thomson Learning logo is a registered trademark used herein under license.

For more information, contact Business Press, Berkshire House, 168–173 High Holborn, London, WCIV 7 AA or visit us on the World Wide Web at: http://www.thomsonlearning.co.uk

British Library Cataloguing-in-Publication Data
A catalogue record for this book is available from the British Library

ISBN 1-86152-487-0

First edition published 2000 by Thomson Learning

Typeset by Saxon Graphics Ltd, Derby
Printed in Great Britain by TJ International, Padstow, Cornwall

Contents

Preface

This book was conceived as a support for MBA courses whose objective is to provide students with a working understanding of accounting and the meaning of accounting numbers. It does, however, aim to go beyond that in that it sets out to deal with a wide range of accounting-related issues of interest to the business manager and to provide background knowledge usually absent from a textbook. It aims therefore to fulfil the typical requirements of an MBA accounting course but in addition provide further material so that the book is a stand-alone text which provides a *vade mecum* for managers which can be used – and useful – beyond the confines of the MBA class.

The book is sited emphatically in an intuitive approach to understanding accounting and concerns itself with the underlying logic of the corporate accounting database and its exploitation in financial reports. It is absolutely not a book-keeping course, and there is hardly a debit or credit in sight. The book does not situate itself in any one national regulatory base, and is intended to be usable in any national context and applicable to most multinational companies. The technical regulations of reference are the standards of the International Accounting Standards Committee and the examples are drawn from many different countries.

Feedback from teachers and students is very welcome.

Peter Walton
Rochefort sur Loire
peter.walton@wanadoo.fr

Acknowledgements

This book has evolved out of teaching materials drawn from a wide range of teaching experiences in the UK, Switzerland, France and the US. As a result, many people, students and colleagues, have influenced the content indirectly, and I am grateful for their help over the years. I should like to thank Jennifer Pegg at International Thomson Business Press for pursuing the idea and for her very effective support.

The text contains quotations from published material and I should like to thank the following for permission to use these: International Accounting Standards Committee, The Association of Chartered Certified Accountants/ *Accounting & Business*, the International Federation of Accountants, the United Nations Conference on Trade and Development, the Organization for Economic Cooperation and Development, the US Securities and Exchange Commission, the Institute of Chartered Accountants in England and Wales/*Accountancy*, Stanley Thornes (Publishers).

Part One

The accounting and business environment

1 Financial reporting and regulation

This chapter lays out the structure of the book, and the approach to mastering accounting information. The first step is a review of what financial information is for and how it is controlled by governments, the stock exchanges and other institutions.

Introduction

The ultimate objective of this book is to enable you to use accounting information effectively. Accounting reports are the only way presently available of getting a picture of what a company is doing, how it is structured and so on. Photographs can show you the company's physical locations, and if it manufactures or sells physical products, what these look like. Words can describe the company and its products, but only accounting data can tell you about a company's profitability, its size and its financial structure in a format which is more or less comparable with other companies and carries with it an assurance that this is the whole of the company, warts and all, that you are looking at, and not just the good-looking parts.

Financial accounting is intimately linked with business, and as Karl Marx was the first to point out, business cannot exist, except in very primitive forms, without accounting. Accounting data makes the business visible, and makes it possible to manage the business and understand it. Accounting makes it possible for the business to work in many locations, directed by a central team. Multinational companies can only work because accounting is there to control what is going on in distant places, to monitor this and to provide information back to centre.

If you look at developing countries and those in transition to a market economy, the lack of accounting skills and the lack of reliable and independent auditors to verify data and ensure that resources are used as intended are a major obstacle to economic progress.

On the whole, most managers meet accounting in the form of financial reports, and are rarely concerned with the day-to-day running of the accounting department. However, they do interface with this in areas like salaries, expense refunds, authorizing payment of invoices and so on. Financial reports and understanding them are the central issue in this book, although we will certainly pass by the accounting department to see what is going on there, as well as review audit, both internal and external. We will focus also on *published* financial reports. The calculation and dissemination of *internal* reports is itself a long and complicated subject, usually dealt with as *management accounting* or *managerial accounting*, and calling for adaptation of standard accounting data for internal purposes. In order to understand that, you need to know about standard accounting data, and that is the purpose of this book. What you learn here will enable you to understand the annual financial statements published by companies but also the basis of most internal reports as well, since they use the same source data.

Using this book

The book is organized to take you into the accounting world in a series of steps, which do not involve learning how to be an accountant. In Part One, we will look at the environment within which financial reporting takes place – how it is regulated, what an accounts department in a company does, how the accounting records are checked. In Part Two, we will go on to basic accounting techniques used by a reasonably simple individual company and the preparation of annual financial statements from the database. This presentation will be based on using worksheets to show what is happening in the company's accounting database, rather than the formal book-keeping techniques which involve the famous debits and credits. Part Three will then discuss how financial statements are interpreted.

We then move on to look at larger companies. In Part Four, we see how groups of companies prepare consolidated accounts in order to be able to present a worldwide picture of their economic situation. We will then go on to consider related issues of international taxation, audit of a group and dissemination of information to stock exchanges. Part Five will come back to the financial analysis of statements and review more sophisticated techniques such as Z scores, shareholder value and growth calculations.

While the structure of the book has been designed to lead you logically through a potential minefield as comfortably as possible, you can, of course, choose to omit some chapters. Our intention is not merely to teach you to understand the nature of accounting information but also to enable you to understand the interactions between accounting and management in a wider sense, and see how intimately accounting links with the life of the company, both internally and in helping manage relations with the outside environment in which the company operates.

Annual financial statements

All commercial companies produce annual financial statements (also known as the annual report, the annual accounts). Generally these have to be filed with the government, either centrally or in regional offices, and they have to be sent to shareholders. In many countries, the government file is available to the public, so the financial statements are in effect public and available to competitors or customers or suppliers, and are regularly consulted by these. Equally there are credit information companies, such as Dun & Bradstreet, which collect financial information and sell it to interested parties.

Many small companies do not like this exposure, but large companies generally welcome it and indeed publish the data widely, including on their website. Large companies are well aware that this is the only independently confirmed information on the company which is widely available, and is a major tool in engendering confidence in those with whom the company wishes to do business.

The annual accounts typically consist of the following elements:

- *The profit and loss account* (or 'income statement' in American English) reports on the sales, costs and profits of the company for the year and consequently is the main performance indicator as far as profitability is concerned.
- *The balance sheet* (sometimes 'statement of financial position' in North America) gives a picture at a given moment – the last day of the financial year – of how the company has been financed and how that money has been invested in productive capacity (plant, buildings, computers, stocks etc.).
- *The notes to the accounts* can be anything from two or three pages to forty or fifty – the notes provide detailed analysis of some of the figures in the balance sheet and profit and loss account, such as the dates when loans fall due for repayment, or the different constituents of the total stock. Importantly, the notes also contain a statement of the different accounting policies followed by the company. They are increasingly a means of conveying non-accounting information, such as commitments to honour futures contracts, to interested outsiders. The notes are subject to audit.
- *The cash flow statement* is an analysis of the main cash movements through the company in the previous twelve months – cash created by the company through profitable trading, cash spent on acquiring new capacity, cash repaid to lenders and new borrowings. This statement is obligatory in most developed countries but not all.
- *The audit report* is the statement by the independent auditors of their opinion on the other statements.

For a large multinational, these reports are usually bundled together with a lot of voluntary disclosures about group activities. Typically the published 'annual report' of a company will start with a chairman's statement, thanking the management team and saying what a good (mostly, but just occasionally bad or indifferent) year it has been and so on. This is followed by many pages of photographs of managers, products and plant, as well as lots of charts, graphs and other data which show how individual divisions in the group have behaved. None of this data is subject to independent checking – but it is nonetheless very useful information which no one should neglect. It very often gives a more detailed picture of the deeds behind the numbers, and helps an analyst get a feel for the company.

We will discuss corporate governance issues in more detail in another chapter, but between the operating information and the hard accounting information, many companies put in disclosures, which stock exchanges and other regulators have encouraged, about company policy in what are perceived as key areas – above all, future prospects, but also things like the company's continuing viability, the nature of the control systems which enable the management to believe that they know what is going on in the company worldwide, and how the company deals with sensitive issues like relations between the management and the auditors, and the award of salary increases to senior management.

If you've never seen the hard copy of a company's annual report, you should get at least one and preferably several. Generally all you need do is phone up the national office of a multinational you are interested in, and ask for a copy of the current annual report. Most companies will be only too happy to provide this by return mail. Most also have the information on their website, but this method of publication varies quite a lot from company to company, so the mix of analysis and hard accounting is probably different. You should certainly consult company websites (for example: www.nestle.com), but make sure that you have a look at least one traditional hard copy at at an early stage.

It may have occurred to you that publishing the annual report is an extremely expensive business – it is. Aside from the cost of creating the accounts in the first place and indeed having them audited, the cost of producing the photographs, artwork and analytical copy, plus running them past your company lawyers and your public relations advisers, is very high, before you even get into the cost of printing probably several million copies and having translations made if, like many multinationals, your report is available in several languages. Internally the annual report will involve the accounting managers, the legal and company secretarial specialists, the investor relations staff and public relations – apart from the chief executive, chairman and the board. Also note that companies try to publish their annual report as soon as possible after the financial year end – certainly in less than three months for the US.

Uses of financial statements

It is a standard question to ask who uses company financial statements, but curiously it is a very difficult question to answer. It is surprising, but despite the fact that so much money goes into producing these documents, and so many regulations are created to control their content, and so many people read them, there is a good deal of uncertainty about exactly what use is made of them. Broadly, very many people inside and outside the company look at these documents – as we have said already, they constitute the only performance indicator available. So we can be confident that they are used. What no one has been able to prove incontestably is how financial data is integrated into decision-making and how different accounting scenarios influence users. Accounting data is, or should be, only one of several sources of information about a company and its future prospects; it is concerned with past performance which is not in all circumstances a guide to future performance; many people prefer to let a specialist (a broker or financial journalist) look at the data and then provide an opinion.

The International Accounting Standards Committee (IASC) – of whom more later – say the following:

> *The objective of financial statements is to provide information about the financial position, performance and changes in financial position of an enterprise that is useful to a wide range of users in making economic decisions.*

> *Source:* IASC Framework for the preparation and presentation of financial statements
> (para. 12)

While this is a useful statement, it needs to be put into context. There are two major different traditions in accounting which affect not only how accounting is regulated but also how it is done and how it is used. These are the *Anglo-Saxon* tradition and the *Continental European* tradition, and we will need to come back to these ideas time and again to explain how accounting works.

IASC Framework

9. The users of financial statements include present and potential investors, employees, lenders, suppliers and other trade creditors, customers, governments and their agencies and the public. They use financial statements in order to satisfy some of their different needs for information. These needs include the following:

   (a) *Investors*   The providers of risk capital and their advisers are concerned with the risk inherent in, and return provided by, their investments. They need information to help them determine whether they should buy, hold or sell. Shareholders are also interested in information which enables them to assess the ability of the enterprise to pay dividends.

   (b) *Employees*   Employees and their representative groups are interested in information about the stability and profitability of their employers. They are also interested in information which enables them to assess the ability of the enterprise to provide remuneration, retirement benefits and employment opportunities.

   (c) *Lenders*   Lenders are interested in information that enables them to determine whether their loans, and the interest attaching to them, will be paid when due.

   (d) *Suppliers and other trade creditors*   Suppliers and other creditors are interested in information that enables them to determine whether amounts owing to them will be paid when due. Trade creditors are likely to be interested in an enterprise over a shorter period than lenders unless they are dependent upon the continuation of the enterprise as a major customer.

   (e) *Customers*   Customers have an interest in information about the continuation of an enterprise, especially when they have a long-term involvement with, or are dependent on, the enterprise.

   (f) *Governments and their agencies*   Governments and their agencies are interested in the allocation of resources and, therefore, the activities of enterprises. They also require information in order to regulate the activities of enterprises, determine taxation policies and as the basis for national income and similar statistics.

   (g) *Public*   Enterprises affect members of the public in a variety of ways. For example, enterprises may make a substantial contribution to the local economy in many ways including the number of people they employ and their patronage of local suppliers. Financial statements may assist the public by providing information about the trends and recent developments in the prosperity of the enterprise and the range of its activities.

   Source: IASC Framework, para 9

Anglo-Saxon accounting

The IASC statement owes more to the Anglo-Saxon tradition. Anglo-Saxon is the term widely used, but 'anglophone' would be more appropriate. In this tradition, countries (US, UK, Australia, Canada, New Zealand etc.) have no *free-standing* accounting regulations on their statute book (although they have traffic laws, tax laws, etc.). Instead businesses have been left to work out their own accounting rules (but alongside disclosure requirements enshrined in company or stock exchange law), and this has often proceeded alongside the development of a powerful accounting profession. You could call this a market solution – to the extent that companies need to communicate understandably, such as to raise finance, they use understandable common measures, but no one obliges them to do so.

What has happened is that the government has reinforced the market from time to time, so that the legal obligation to provide information has grown over time. The regulations have generally been made heavier following on from some market abuse – such as the Maxwell frauds recently in the UK, or historically the Wall Street crash of 1929. The last was blamed on adventurous accounting, and the Securities and Exchange Commission (SEC), which is the world's leading stock market regulator, was created by the US government as a response. Accounting regulation in these countries is a function of the legal vehicle used, not a function of the kind of activity carried on by the business. So if you are a US company that wants to be listed on the New York Stock Exchange, you will need to meet stringent SEC accounting requirements, but if you want to run the same business with no public offering of shares, there are hardly any formal accounting requirements which apply in the US. Similarly, if you want to constitute your business as a public limited company (plc – not necessarily listed on the London Stock Exchange) in the UK, you will have to comply with many corporate accounting rules, but if you constitute it as a partnership, there are no statutory requirements for accounting.

In an Anglo-Saxon accounting context, the financial statements are traditionally a function of the financing of the company. They derive from the Industrial Revolution when technology first transformed business and entrepreneurs started looking for vehicles through which they could raise capital to start industrial ventures. Prior to the Industrial Revolution most business investment was made by owner-managers and was inevitably relatively small scale. But from this point on, the managers of companies were less and less often the source of finance for those companies, and financial reports developed as a means of informing outside financiers (shareholders principally but also banks) as to what had been done with their money. We have the start of a split between management and capital: professional managers started to run 'companies' in which several investors, eventually many, had put money.

The annual accounts were a necessary means of informing the investors (shareholders) and creating an atmosphere of confidence, which in turn would encourage investors to reward the managers – in conditions of uncertainty, the investors would reduce the reward to managers because they could not be sure that it had been earned. At the same time, the idea of independent audit developed as a means of increasing the degree of confidence which shareholders might have in the financial statements. In more recent times, companies have simply extended this principle to customers, suppliers, staff and the general public, as these have become more sophisticated in their understanding of financial data.

Continental Europe

The *continental European* accounting tradition has its roots much earlier in business history than Anglo-Saxon accounting. The main model for European systems started out in 1673 as a French government statute (known as the 'Savary Ordonnance'), which was borrowed by other countries in this form or in its later form as Napoleon's Commercial Code (1807). The French required all businesses (in whatever legal form, but companies as such were rare at that time) to calculate an annual 'inventory' – in effect a balance sheet. The French model was subsequently borrowed by many countries, one way and another, and in particular by Belgium, Spain, Germany and Italy (but this is not to suggest that accounting regulation in those countries is exactly the same in modern times – regulation is constantly evolving).

The main reason for its introduction in France is believed to have been government regulation of the economy. The government was concerned at the large number of business bankruptcies. Apart from causing people to lose money, they also damage confidence in the market, which you will appreciate is essential if the market is to function correctly – you have only to think of the Asian crisis as an example of the flight of capital when confidence is lost. This is often a key trigger of regulation – government concern to strengthen the operation of the market, and thus the national economy.

The effect in continental Europe has been to create a tradition where *all* businesses are subject to accounting rules (with extra rules for limited liability companies and listed ones), and for accounting regulation to be primarily the concern of the government rather than the accounting profession or companies themselves. This remains broadly the case in these countries still.

Link with taxation

These different historical roots can probably also explain another important aspect of accounting regulation – the link between measuring performance for shareholders and measuring profits for tax purposes. This link is looser in Anglo-Saxon countries than in continental European ones. In the United Kingdom, income tax was introduced first in 1799 – well before there was any accounting regulation as such. There grew up a tradition, therefore, where measurement of profit for tax purposes was seen as a legal matter, with its own statutes and jurisprudence which were separate from company regulation. In continental Europe, however, income taxes were mostly introduced in the early twentieth century (Germany was a little ahead of this) but well after the introduction of accounting regulation by the state. Not surprisingly, measurement of profit for tax purposes became closely intertwined with other accounting needs, and the formal link between reporting to the tax authorities and reporting to shareholders is much closer than in Anglo-Saxon jurisdictions.

It should be said that the relationship between these two reporting streams is constantly evolving, and that the widespread use of consolidated accounts has introduced a new element into the equation. Consolidated accounts are produced by large groups of companies for their shareholders. They consist, as we shall see later, of aggregate figures for all the individual companies making up the group. Tax assessment is done only through the individual companies, and the group accounts therefore have no tax implications. This means that larger companies, at least, are able to separate out to some degree the measurement of profit for tax purposes, and the measurement of economic performance for shareholders and others. You will appreciate that in theory there should perhaps be no difference between the two concepts, but in practice governments distort economic behaviour through taxation, partly to counter tax avoidance, and partly to give companies incentives to behave in a way that the government wishes to encourage (e.g. installing environmentally friendly processes, maintaining employment etc.).

This usually means that tax considerations enter into company strategic choices (or should – individual companies differ quite widely in the extent to which they integrate tax into their planning) and also play a significant role in accounting regulation. For example, tax rules may well fix maximum limits on some expenses, which encourages companies to charge the maximum in their accounts. The rules may also refuse to accept other types of expenditure as a deduction from taxable profits, with the consequence that companies restrict some kinds of activity. We will look at this later in a chapter on taxation.

The extent to which taxation impacts upon company accounting is not only a function of the regulatory environment, but also depends on the ownership of the company, which is in turn an issue frequently linked to size. Many small and medium-sized companies do not operate as a group of companies and their ownership is in the hands of the managers, or of a family. This may mean that the shareholders do not depend upon the annual accounts as their only source of information about the company – they work in the company or they can ask, or even just go along and have a look.

This means that there is no point in producing sophisticated economic measurements for the shareholders. Annual reports are consequently influenced most heavily by tax considerations – reducing the profit in order to reduce tax becomes the main objective in making accounting choices. This may also mean that managers of small companies have only a hazy idea of their profitability, because they believe the reported figure to be artificially low as a result of tax manipulations, but they have no means of knowing the extent of the difference. This is not particularly useful for management decision-making!

Accounting choices

Some people come to accounting believing that it is a set of precise measurement rules which permit the exact measurement of company profit and the value of the company. In fact accounting rules are anything but precise, the measurement of profit can never be anything but an estimate and the accounts do not under any circumstances show what a company is 'worth' (we should also bear in mind that value is a subjective notion and must always be defined when used – for example, the value of something as between buyer and seller is usually different, there are different calculation bases such as economic value, cost etc.).

If we first look at choices, you will soon appreciate as you go through this book that accounting measurement is full of choices. We can distinguish between three types of encounter between choice and rules:

1. The rules are quite specific and there is no choice (maybe the law specifies what must be done).
2. There are accounting rules, but we have freedom to make a choice between two or more alternative sets of rules, each of which is acceptable to regulators (the most common case).
3. There are no rules so we must decide for ourselves how to deal with a problem (maybe by reference to what other people in the same line of business generally do, or after consultation with our auditors).

The existence of these choices is something that makes accounting comparisons difficult within the same jurisdiction, and also leads to different accounting rules being used in different countries. Companies are generally required, therefore, to state clearly in their annual accounts what choices they have made in key areas. Large companies typically have two pages devoted to 'accounting principles' alongside their financial statements.

Consolidated Accounts of the Nestlé Group

➤ Consolidated Income Statement for the Year Ended 31st December 1998
➤ Consolidated Balance Sheet as at 31st December 1998
➤ Consolidated cash Flow Statement for the Year Ended 31st December 1998

Annex
• Accounting Policies
• Valuation Methods and Definitions
• Changes in Accounting Policies and Modification of the Scope of Consolidation
• Notes
• Principal Exchange Rates

➤ Report of the Group Auditors
➤ Financial Information – Ten Year Review
➤ Companies of the Nestlé Group

Extract from Nestlé website
Source: Nestlé Management Report 1998
www.nestle.com/mr1998/consolaccts/index.htm
© 1999 Nestlé SA

The variability of accounting principles is often criticized by the financial press, and it is one reason why those who design MBA courses insist upon a significant accounting component in the degree. As we advance through the accounting territory we will highlight areas where there are choices and show how these impact measurement.

Profit as estimate

There is a conundrum in accounting which is that the most reliable information is necessarily old information, since all the facts can be established incontrovertibly only after the elapse of some time. Against this, the most useful information is that which concerns the immediate past because we use it to know what we need to improve or change in managing the future. There is, in the words of the conceptual framework of the main US accounting standard-setter, a conflict between *reliability* and *relevance*.

The 'real' profit of a company can only be measured absolutely when the company has ceased trading, all its assets have been sold, its debts paid off and all its money distributed to its owners. To illustrate, suppose a company builds a factory, equips it with sophisticated machinery and then uses it to manufacture a product which it sells. Say the factory and equipment cost $100m, and the factory closes down after ten years and is sold for $10m; we can say that, in addition to raw materials, staffing, power and so on, the company had a net cost of $90m ($100m to set up, less final exit receipt of $10m) for the factory, which should be taken into account in measuring profit for each of the ten years in which the factory was operating. We only know this for sure when the factory has been sold. If, though, we ignore the cost of the factory in measuring profit in the years when the factory is operating, we will be overstating the profit. Overstating the profit will mislead those who lend to or invest in the firm, and potentially lead to paying out too much in tax and dividends so that the company eventually fails. To avoid this we are obliged to include an estimate of this expense, so the annual profit during those years is necessarily based in part on an unprovable estimate.

IASC Framework

Relevance

26. To be useful, information must be relevant to the decision-making needs of users. Information has the quality of relevance when it influences the economic decisions of users by helping them evaluate past, present or future events or confirming, or correcting, their past evaluations.

27. The predictive and confirmatory roles of information are interrelated. For example, information about the current level and structure of asset holdings has value to users when they endeavour to predict the ability of the enterprise to take advantage of opportunities and its ability to react to adverse situations. The same information plays a confirmatory role in respect of past predictions about, for example, the way in which the enterprise would be structured or the outcome of planned operations.

28. Information about financial position and past performance is frequently used as the basis for predicting future financial position and performance and other matters in which users are directly interested, such as dividend and wage payments, security price movements and the ability of the enterprise to meet its commitments as they fall due. To have predictive value, information need not be in the form of an explicit forecast. The ability to make predictions from financial statements is enhanced, however, by the manner in which information on past transactions and events is displayed. For example, the predictive value of the income statement is enhanced if unusual, abnormal and infrequent items of income or expense are separately disclosed.

Reliability

31. To be useful, information must also be reliable. Information has the quality of reliability when it is free from material error and bias and can be depended upon by users to represent faithfully that which it either purports to represent or could reasonably be expected to represent.

32. Information may be relevant but so unreliable in nature or representation that its recognition may be potentially misleading. For example, if the validity and amount of a claim for damages under a legal action are disputed, it may be inappropriate for the enterprise to recognise the full amount of the claim in the balance sheet, although it may be appropriate to disclose the amount and circumstances of the claim.

Accounting regulation

The existence of choices in accounting is one very good reason to have regulation. Of course, choice is not of itself necessarily a bad thing: it is only a problem in accounting where some people use accounting choice to deceive others. This explains why governments become involved in accounting regulation. As tax collectors they naturally want reliable figures for income. As managers of the national economy they want that economy to function efficiently and produce wealth. Its functioning, and particularly that of the capital markets, is at least slowed down if not stalled entirely, if investors, customers and suppliers do not know whether they can rely on the financial statements of companies with which they wish to do business. Investors either do not invest or demand much higher returns to compensate for the uncertainty, clients may go elsewhere or be prepared to pay only a low price, while suppliers may refuse to supply on credit. If the financial stability of a company cannot be judged reliably, others are reluctant to deal with it.

This leads to another argument, which is that, given that the markets cease to function without reliable information, surely market pressures will force competitive companies to adopt reliable, comparable accounting in order to reduce financing costs and help business relations generally. This is also valid, and is supported by the way in which many large companies have voluntarily adopted International Accounting Standards for their group accounts and use an international audit firm to attest the validity of these. However, the market is not necessarily that efficient, and there are failures, notably in recent times in the Asian crisis, which in part derive from unclear accounting causing people to make wrong decisions.

The world functions on a complex mixture of regulation and market forces. Given that this book is intended to be used outside of any one specific legal environment, we propose to present below the different types of regulation which are to be found. International managers should make a note that there will be a different mix of regulators in different countries and they may need to familiarize themselves with the local situation.

Types of regulation

It may be worth pointing out that the reasons why a change in regulation takes place are a fruitful field of research in accounting. The model that we will use here suggests that, starting from an equilibrium position where there is no obvious pressure for change, there is a cycle:

1. Equilibrium
2. Shock (which destroys the equilibrium)
3. Search for an acceptable solution
4. Articulation of regulation
5. New equilibrium

The shock to the system could come from any one of a multitude of sources. Individual financial scandals have in the past been a common source of disequilibrium, but other possibilities are economic changes such as the introduction of new techniques (e.g. derivatives and financial instruments generally), legal changes in the national economy (e.g. joining the European Union, moving from a communist regime to a market economy) etc. The search for a solution often involves seeking consensus, which will involve different people on different issues, leading to some inconsistencies in regulation. The method of articulating the solution is also subject to local cultural differences – some countries prefer legal regulation, others codes of best practice and so on. The result of all this is that accounting rules are different in different countries in some of their details, even if the main lines tend to converge.

We would distinguish the following types of regulatory body:

- government – for economic management;
- government – for tax purposes;
- stock exchange;
- private sector body;
- professional accountants;
- specialist industry organizations.

We should also point out that the regulation of the accounts of banks and insurance companies, while typically linked to that of commercial companies, is nonetheless usually subject to separate rules, because governments wish to control the financial health of banks much more closely than that of commercial companies, and impose limits on their activities based on balance sheet figures.

Government

As we have discussed, the government is interested in the efficient functioning of the economy, and this leads to regulation designed to ensure that the markets can operate as far as possible free from fraud and misrepresentation. This form of regulation may be articulated through laws which address accounting, commercial codes and government regulatory agencies. An example of this kind of approach would be France where there are laws governing accounting, but also two government-sponsored committees which operate (Conseil National de la Comptabilité and Comité de Réglementation de Comptabilité) under the aegis of the ministry of finance and issue detailed regulations on specific accounting issues.

The government is also active in regulating accounting for tax purposes. This is often done through individual measures contained in annual finance laws or similar instruments. In some countries jurisprudence, the decisions of tax courts on specific cases, can also be very important in determining some accounting issues. This is notably the case in Germany and to a lesser extent in the UK.

The stock exchange usually regulates the financial information that has to be provided by companies listed on it. In some countries there is a government regulator that does this, such as the Securities and Exchange Commission (SEC) in the US, while the exchange itself is run by private sector bodies. In other countries there is no split between those who run the stock exchange on a day-to-day basis (generally the members of the exchange) and those who regulate admission to it. This is the case, for example, in Switzerland, where therefore regulation of listed companies is done by the private sector (although subject to a limited legal framework).

Private sector

In most countries there is some input into accounting best practice from the private sector in the form of standard-setting committees of one kind or another. In the US, although the SEC controls listings on the various stock exchanges, and is therefore responsible for specifying what accounting rules they should use, in practice it delegates the responsibility for writing detailed rules (accounting standards) to a private sector body, the Financial Accounting Standards Board (FASB). The FASB is financed by contributions from companies, the audit industry etc. and is a free-standing body without any special rights other than what it derives from the SEC's endorsement of its standards.

This is typical of the modern form of detailed rule-making – the rules do not have to go through a long drawn out statutory process, and can be changed at any time if they appear to be ineffective or become irrelevant. The flexibility and rapidity of this form and the high level of technicality of its pronouncements are the major argument for using a private sector body rather than relying solely on statutes or government agencies, where accounting regulation would have to compete for parliamentary time with other important issues and be debated by those with no knowledge of accounting.

In many countries that have this kind of private sector regulatory body, it developed from advisory committees run by the accounting profession, and most developed professional accounting bodies have technical committees which make recommendations as to best practice. Such a committee may be the only private sector source of national standards in a particular country, but even so does not necessarily command the automatic acceptance of its pronouncements. An example would be the technical committee of the Ordre des Experts Comptables in France.

Another source of private sector rules is industry associations. Their activity varies very much from sector to sector and country to country, but sometimes such organizations agree special rules which apply to their members and are intended to address accounting for transactions which are specific to their industry, or lead to a higher comparability in presentation or valuation of balance sheet and profit and loss account items. Evidently such arrangements are voluntary but in some countries they may also be endorsed by official regulatory committees – the UK standard-setter approves 'statements of recommended practice' which are prepared by industry groups such as banks or insurers, and France's Conseil National de la Comptabilité confirms industry-specific applications of its accounting plan.

Different combinations of these kinds of regulatory organizations exist in each developed country, and the diverse sources of regulation are one reason why expert local advice is needed.

International

Apart from the national regulators, there are also international bodies which provide important rules. The most well known is the International Accounting Standards Committee (IASC). This was launched in 1973 as a recognition that there was much diversity in accounting rules and that the globalization of commerce meant that some of this diversity should be removed. The IASC was set up by the professional accountancy bodies in nine countries, and has come to be the accepted international source of best practice. Its rules are primarily oriented towards the needs of large companies and the financial markets; it specifically excludes tax measurement as an objective in accounting. Its rules are the rules of reference for accounting debate and are used by many companies for their consolidated accounts, and by many countries as a source of national regulation. We shall use their rules as the main source of reference in this book.

In the past few years the IASC has been working out a joint plan with the International Organization of Securities Commissions (IOSCO) which represents the world's stock exchange regulators. IOSCO wants to arrive at a situation where companies listed on a stock exchange that is a member of IOSCO may list their securities on any foreign stock exchange by using a single, uniform set of disclosures (which is not the case right now). Such a facility would probably open up worldwide stock exchange activity and certainly simplify the question of raising money around the world, but requires that national regulators all accept the same standards.

This acceptance is particularly hard for Americans, where the SEC believes it has the best financial market in the world and the toughest financial transparency requirements. Some Americans believe that adoption of IASC standards for foreign issuers (non-US companies issuing securities on the US markets) would result in lower standards of reporting, which would in turn lead to pressure from US companies to lighten national requirements. Against this, there is no possibility that national governments elsewhere would accept US or any other national standards as a basis for worldwide listing requirements. In the long term, therefore, a single international approach is likely to be put in place. The current IOSCO/IASC programme is not complete, but has had a dramatic effect on the IASC, motivating it to tighten up its standards and putting it into a position where it should become the world's leading accounting regulator.

There are no other bodies writing international accounting standards for private sector companies, but we should mention that the UN has an annual accounting conference where government regulators meet. This takes place under the auspices of the UN Conference on Trade and Development (UNCTAD) and is called the intergovernmental working group of experts on international standards of accounting and reporting (ISAR for short). The ISAR group commissions research reports into current accounting problems. These are debated at the annual conference and recommendations made to help governments develop their regulatory and professional structures. ISAR supports the IASC and helps involve governments, particularly of developing countries, in discussions about the utility and implementation of IASC standards.

There is also an international representative of the accounting profession; this is called the International Federation of Accountants (IFAC), based in New York, and we will come back to it in the chapter on the accounting profession. It has committees which publish recommendations on auditing, education and other matters. However, of relevance here is that it also has a committee (Public Sector Committee) which issues standards for governmental organizations.

Public sector

This is probably a good point to mention that accounting in the public sector is generally very different from that in the private sector, although governments are beginning to turn to private sector techniques. Basically, private sector accounting is concerned with measuring profit and the sources of finance for an enterprise. It produces annual reports which are in effect a series of interim reports on a business which is intended to have long or limitless time horizons.

Public sector accounting on the other hand has traditionally had short horizons where the object is primarily to explain what has been done with the money available to spend in any one year. Reports typically focus on a particular source of revenue (e.g. government grants for road improvement) and explain how it has been spent, or a particular activity (e.g. primary school education). Any particular public sector unit, say a municipality or a government ministry, does not therefore present a single coherent report on its activities for the year, but rather a whole series of individual reports. Equally, the public sector makes little or no distinction between short-term (sometimes known as current) and long-term (sometimes called capital) expenditure – money in a particular year might be spent on building a hospital, and other money on paying the running costs of a hospital, but for traditional public sector accounting these are just two 'funds' like any others. The hospital is in effect treated as a current year expense and does not appear on any kind of government 'balance sheet'.

In the 1990s the desire for performance evaluation measures in the public sector has caused a number of countries, led by New Zealand, to move towards private sector techniques where long-lived purchases remain on the books, and where 'revenues' are determined or, put another way, outputs are assigned financial values, so that the efficiency of the use of resources can be measured. It would be a mistake to think that such a revolution in public sector accounting will be either widespread or rapid. Firstly, it involves a desire on the part of government for transparency in their financial dealings, which is not something too many governments necessarily see as a policy objective. Secondly, the change-over involves massive re-education, not only of accounting staff but also all those who use financial information, and also complete reform of accounting systems, which is both costly and time-consuming.

For the moment it would be better to think of public sector accounting as a different subject from that of private sector (and one which will not be taken further in this book), albeit changes can be expected.

Summary

The object of this chapter was to start to explain the environment of accounting. It has looked at the main financial statements published by companies and discussed the framework through which these are regulated. It has noted that governments need to regulate accounting to ensure the efficient running of the economy and the financial markets in particular, since business relies heavily on accurate information about other businesses. Government also wants to collect taxes and accounting is linked directly with the calculation of taxable profits. Apart from this, there are other bodies with an interest, notably stock exchanges, specialist standard-setting agencies and bodies organized by the accounting profession or industry sectors.

In the international field there is a growing movement to the use of international standards which are promulgated by the IASC. These enable company reports to be compared across national boundaries and help smooth management decision-making in the context of global business.

Questions

1. What are the annual financial statements of a company?
2. Contrast broadly the regulatory traditions in continental Europe as opposed to the anglophone countries.
3. Are the financial accounting requirements of entities in the public sector different from those of business in the private sector?
4. Compare and contrast the different types of accounting regulation that exist.

2 Accounting and accountants

This chapter discusses the work of the company accounting department and the system called 'internal control' which is used to ensure accuracy and security. It will also introduce independent accountants and the auditing profession, as well as discussing the external audit.

We are going to start off this chapter by looking at the accounting system within a company and how it maintains its records. If your interest is only to be able to read financial statements, you may not want to learn about the processes through which the data is collected. On the other hand, a successful manager in a multinational is bound to have responsibility at some point for a free-standing operating unit and therefore for oversight of its accounting system. Apart from that, understanding where the information comes from is always going to help understand the information.

Accounting function

All businesses need a financial accounting system with the object of tracking all the economic transactions that the business undertakes and recording them logically in a database. This system is a prime resource of the business, and should provide:

- controls to ensure that only legitimate expenses are paid;
- systems to ensure that debts to suppliers are well tracked and paid when due;
- systems to calculate salary payments to employees and deduct social security and other charges;
- controls to ensure that all customers are correctly invoiced, and that customers in turn pay what they owe;
- controls to safeguard the company's assets;
- information to management on a regular basis to enable them to run the business efficiently;
- information to the authorities to support payment of taxes;
- information to shareholders on the health of the company and to help determine dividends;

- information and measurements to others with whom the company has performance-related contracts (debt covenants, employee bonus schemes, joint ventures, franchises, licences etc.);
- information to those who lend money to the company, and to suppliers;
- information that represents the company to all outside interests and all stakeholders.

Notice that while the first six objectives are wholly internal to the operation of the company, the other five involve providing information to those who are external to the company. We could describe the first six functions as being those of financial control and the others as financial reporting.

Different companies have different needs – in a large, publicly held company the shareholders will usually be remote from the management, whereas in a small, family company, the managers are often also major shareholders. We will generally assume that the typical company we are dealing with is a large multinational, but will point out differences for smaller businesses as we go along. In this case, a small, family business will often want to keep information secret, while a multinational will generally be keen to give information (often accounting reports are on the group's website).

The accounts department of a company needs to meet these objectives, and this is mostly done through feeding the company's database, and then using the aggregate data to prepare reports about the company's activities. The nature of the accounts department will vary enormously depending upon the size of the company. A very small business may simply use a part-time book-keeper to process transactions and maintain the database, or use an outside accounting firm to do this. The largest global groups will have enormous accounting departments in each operating unit together with a large head office unit to gather together data from throughout the group. In an international group, the management of the group is controlled mostly through uniform accounting systems which involve subsidiaries in sending data regularly to head office (or via regional offices) to enable central and regional management to know what is happening. In this sense it would be impossible to manage an international group without accounting.

Usually such a group will have an internal accounting manual which lays out the procedures to be followed in accounting for typical transactions in order to ensure a uniform treatment of operations worldwide, without which management would have difficulty in interpreting the accounting information. The accounting manual may run to several volumes, and is usually available in several languages.

In fact global companies have problems because national accounting rules differ from country to country. The national rules should normally be followed for tax purposes, so the group has to have a reporting system which is capable of delivering uniform data worldwide for management purposes and for the group accounts, while also providing potentially different data in each country to suit local tax requirements. Too much should not be made of these differences in that they centre on one or two areas of accounting, and generally therefore the transition from one set of accounts to the other is not that complicated. At the same time, this is a problem that multinationals have to address, and one that is costly in terms of hiring professionals to deal with it. Very often a multinational will choose to have uniform internal systems, and then ask its accounting advisers in each country, who are familiar with the subtleties of the local regulations, to liaise with the local tax officials and prepare a revised set of accounts for local reporting purposes (see Figure 2.1).

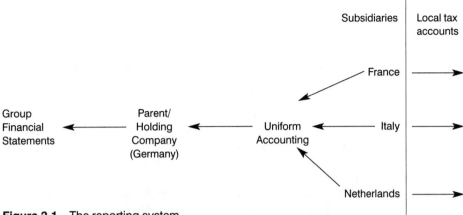

Figure 2.1 The reporting system

In principle the company's accounting function should provide systems that capture all the transactions that the company undertakes. The main categories of this are:

- trading sales;
- trading purchases;
- payroll;
- treasury;
- investment in long-term capacity.

These transactions involve an interaction with other departments, and the exact split of responsibility between the accounting function and the operating department will vary according to the nature of the business and the technology used.

In the *sales* area, there are many combinations possible. In a hotel, for example, the reception desk ('front office') generally also operates customer billing and cash collection, and then passes the transactions on to the accounting function ('back office'). In retailing, very often sales representatives call on retailers and take orders in person. The sales person then transmits the order to the company where the system will capture it as an instruction to the warehouse, and a linked instruction to the accounts department to issue an invoice. Increasingly companies are enabling their customers to access their intranet to place orders directly into the company system, which are then, through the computer, translated into delivery instructions and an invoice.

The accounts department will normally have a data file for each customer, will control credit levels, and will send out monthly statements of account to the customer and track payment when that is due. The issue of credit control is occasionally a problematic one which gives liaison difficulties between accounting staff and sales staff. The accounting department will want to make sure that where credit is given, the customer does pay the bills in due course. The sales department on the other hand want to sell as many units as possible, and easy credit helps them to do this, so they may be less demanding in their assessments of creditworthiness.

The capture of *purchases* has its own problems. Here the company will often have a system of purchase orders or requisitions where a manager with authority to purchase supplies must sign a requisition, a copy of which goes to the accounts department to alert them to the fact that a purchase is in hand. Later, when the goods are received, a delivery document should be sent to the accounts department and then the invoice. The accounts department should marry all these together and put them into the system. The supplier data file should then be checked with the monthly statement sent by the supplier to check that all invoices have been recorded.

Finally the account will be authorized and paid. In a small company this is relatively straightforward, but in a big operation, this can be very complicated and the potential for error is considerable. This explains why there are specialist companies who review purchases, particularly for large stores, and often recover large amounts of money. Equally, this explains the success of scams where a fraudster sends out invoices for small sums for, say, listing in an Internet directory or something like that, and some large companies will pay the invoice, although no order was ever placed and the directory does not exist.

The *payroll* is usually a specialist function within accounting. It calls for special knowledge in that in many countries the employer is responsible for deducting social security charges from the employee, sometimes the employee's income tax is deducted by the employer, and then there may be pension schemes to which the employee contributes, and other voluntary schemes such as savings or membership of a staff social club etc. This means that each employee's pay file is individual and probably quite complex. Small companies will often sub-contract this function to an accounting firm or a specialist service company. The possibilities for error are considerable, and where government deductions are involved, there may be fines for making mistakes. The accounting involved is also quite complex in that the company deducts money from the individual's pay packet and then has to pay this to government departments, pension funds and so on.

The *treasury* function is one where all the others meet up: treasury controls all the receipts and payments into the company's bank accounts, as well as any cash tills that might exist (company accountants do not like cash floating around). Evidently this is the area where authorizations are most stringently required, and also where accurate coding of transactions is essential. The treasury unit works very closely with the company's bankers. In fact in a large company, the treasury may well be able to access the bank's accounting system to interrogate the records of the company's account in real time. Apart from anything else, this enables the treasury to know exactly how much money is in each account at the close of banking business, and then lend out any surplus, perhaps on the overnight market (yes, you can lend money just overnight, provided you have enough of it to do so in large quantities).

The accounting system is organized with separate data files for each bank account, so that the company's information can be checked directly against the statement put out by the bank. This provides a regular control on the accuracy of the company's records – all charges and revenues that have gone through the bank should also be in the company's records. The company regularly (ideally at least once a month) prepares a 'bank reconciliation'. This is a document which compares the balance on the bank account as seen by the bank, with the balance on the corresponding data file within the company. These two will rarely agree, because of time lags in transactions going through the bank account, but the differences can and must be identified as a check on the accuracy of both sets of records (in a large company this can involve cross-checking hundreds of transactions). One way of conducting a fraud is to make payments without entering them in the company's accounting records. These payments will show up as differences on the bank reconciliation, but if nobody reviews the reconciliation, they will stay outside the company records.

You can see that the accounting unit has a quite complex set of tasks and objectives. Its prime function is to capture information for the company and to ensure that customers pay their bills and that suppliers are paid – it is a service function to help the company to operate efficiently. However, most company frauds are going to involve obtaining money via the accounting department, so the staff and systems have to be organized to prevent this. Therefore they seem less than keen on giving a service and rather inclined to demand bits of paper, and signatures, which appear to be obstacles to the free running of the company.

Database

Coming back to the central issue of accumulating information, a company's financial accounting system is organized to provide data for a central database (the nominal ledger, US: general ledger) which is then used as the source of information used by management and given to outsiders. The system normally looks as shown in Figure 2.2.

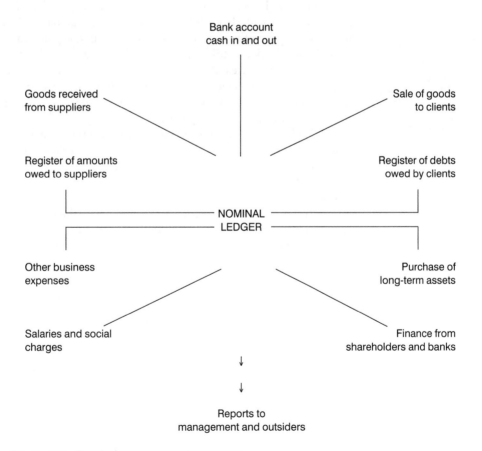

Figure 2.2 The financial accounting system

Recording transactions

Information flows into the database through several layers of preparation which summarize and resummarize transactions to build up to aggregates for the year's activities (Figure 2.3).

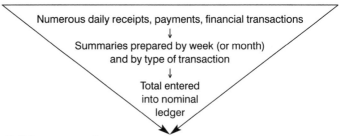

Figure 2.3 Building aggregates

'Journals' are used to build up the periodic summaries and feed aggregated data into the nominal ledger. The nominal ledger is then used as a source for the preparation of periodic profit and loss accounts (or income statements) and balance sheets. This kind of approach was particularly useful when all entries in the database were made by hand, and is still used even though virtually all systems in companies are computerized. The essential idea is that while aggregated data is needed in the ledger, to enable management summaries to be prepared, the system must be capable of being interrogated to confirm that a particular transaction has or has not taken place, so it must be possible later to go from the monthly figure in the ledger, for example, back through the journals to the individual payment.

This is both because accounts departments have regularly to deal with queries, and because the transactions are subject to checking by internal or external auditors. There must be what is called an 'audit trail' to show the links and provide evidence that the initial transaction was authorized. Computerized systems may very well carry out the intermediate stage between the individual transaction (known as a 'prime entry' in the trade) and the ledger total. Once the first entry has been keyed in, the system will organize a batch of similar transactions and 'post' this to the ledger, but it is normally organized also to provide a printout of each batch, which becomes the bridge between prime entry and ledger. Of course, there could be several intermediate levels.

Some decisions have to be taken as to what level of detail is going to be useful within an accounting system. At one extreme an accounting system might record every single transaction separately so that its annual profit and loss account was a detailed list of every transaction that had taken place over the year. At the other extreme the profit and loss account could be one figure representing the net difference (profit or loss) of the whole year's revenue and expenses.

The exact point at which one makes a decision about the degree of detail to be kept will vary with the precise circumstances of each company, its size and the nature of the business being carried out. However, as guidelines, the final records should obviously, as a minimum, keep information aggregated for a whole accounting year on each of the separate categories (of the income statement and balance sheet) which will appear in the annual accounts. Normally, though, the database will be much more detailed. It will need to be capable of delivering information about each individual operating unit within a company, so that an analysis which shows the profitability of each unit for management purposes can be produced without difficulty. This information is aggregated for the purposes of the published accounts.

The precise form taken by the nominal ledger and the journals will vary from one system to another. In some countries (e.g. France, Belgium, Greece, Spain) there is a state-mandated system, generally known as a 'chart of accounts' or accounting plan. In other countries (e.g. Germany, Switzerland, Austria) there are widely used standard charts whose adoption is voluntary. Generally anglophone countries do not use standard charts of this kind, but large companies with uniform systems worldwide must develop in effect their own chart of accounts. A nationally standardized chart has certain advantages in terms of staff training, lower audit costs and cheaper software, but has typically been rejected by anglophone professions as being too restrictive.

In large companies the system may well be partitioned to enable the major operations (sales, purchases, treasury and payroll) to operate independently of each other – with links to the central ledger to ensure the integrity of the system. In this way the specialist functions can operate dedicated systems which not only maintain the ledger but issue invoices or bank transfers, issue monthly statements to customers, provide analysis of outstanding items etc.

Organization of data within the nominal ledger

When the data about the financial transactions of the company reach the nominal ledger they will be stored according to a system which has been in existence for hundreds of years: the double entry system. The first written account of the system appeared in 1494 (Luca Pacioli) and the fact that the system is still in use today will give you some idea of its practical effectiveness.

First, the nominal ledger is organized into a series of 'accounts' – data files – each of which is used to record transactions of a particular type. For example, if your business is selling books, you would need one account in which to record sales, another to record the cost of the books sold, and a series of accounts to record the various different types of expense incurred in the business (advertising, rent of premises, heat etc.), as well as accounts for financing and investments in property, stock etc. (This is the minimum – if more analysis were useful, then more accounts would be used.)

Each account within the nominal ledger is organized in a particular (peculiar?) way. The account has two columns for figures and some space to write in explanatory remarks and cross-referencing details. The left-hand column is always referred to as the debit column and the right-hand column is called the credit column (there seems to be no satisfactory explanation for the derivation of these words). Debit and credit are also used as verbs, so one says 'debit insurance expense' to mean a figure should be entered into the left-hand column of the insurance expense account. In formal, manual book-keeping there are no plus or minus signs; the value of an account is the difference between the debit and credit columns, and can be either a debit balance (more left hand than right) or a credit balance (more right hand than left).

A traditional manual ledger account would look as shown in Figure 2.4.

Account number: Account name:				
Date	Narrative	Ref.	Debit	Credit

Figure 2.4   A manual ledger account

A computerized printout often preserves the same format, but may also provide a running balance perhaps in a third column out to the right, or elsewhere on the printout.

The exact form in which the accounts are kept is not of essential interest for our purposes – what is important is how the figures are arrived at and what they mean, rather than the detail of the methodology of the data file. However, one normally comes across accounting statements, notably one's bank statement, from time to time, and knowledge of the notation system is useful to that extent.

This is what my bank statement looks like:

CREDIT
SUISSE
Genève

Compte privé

Date	Narrative	In our favour	In your favour	Balance	
170799	Balance brought forward			2,726.50	C
260799	receipt IIM		348.00	3,074.50	C
270799	Credit card settlement	1,791.65		1,282.85	C
280799	receipt DIP		7,589.70	8,872.55	C
300799	Monthly payments	3,700.70		5,171.85	C
090899	Cash – ATM	500.00		4,671.85	C
160899	Cash – ATM	500.00		4,171.85	C

C = in your favour
D = in our favour

If you were looking at an accounting textbook intended for accountants, then the whole of the discussion of accounting technique would involve notation involving debits and credits – making entries in left-hand and right-hand columns. This notation system is largely redundant for our purposes, and we will use non-specialist signs, and tools such as worksheets to explain what is going on. Since you are not going to run an accounting system, a detailed knowledge of the notation is not useful and tends to divert attention from the reality of what is actually going on.

Control and audit

The accounting system, as we have seen, fulfils a number of different functions, being both an information system and a security system. In both cases it is essential that the system is efficient. Without an efficient system, central management (a) do not know reliably what is going on in the company, and (b) cannot safeguard the shareholders' money. In recent years, this issue has come to be seen as more and more important – the well-known corporate embarrassments, such as the fall of Barings Bank, the copper trading scandal and so on, would not have been possible with tighter systems – in the jargon, tighter internal control. Public concern has grown to the point where many companies publish a statement in their annual report to the effect that the directors are satisfied that they have in place an adequate system of internal control. The internal control system provides for automatic checking of transactions and is relied upon by external auditors in assessing the viability of the company's records. In this section we will look at internal control and its links, through internal audit, to the external audit.

Internal control

The main objective of internal control is to ensure the integrity of the information system and the security of the company's assets. The internal control system is a way of organizing the company's data processing so that all transactions are checked automatically as they progress through the company administration.

While all of the accounting process is centralized ultimately on the nominal ledger, it is good management practice to split up the way accounting transactions are processed into different units, partly to allow for the development of specialist skills and partly to provide an environment where fraud is difficult. This is known as 'separation of functions'. A simple example would be that where a payment has to be made, the payment is authorized by one person, the cheque drawn by another person, the cheque signed by a third, and the nominal ledger entry made by a fourth. Each person is responsible for ensuring that they process nothing which is not correctly supported by documents and authorizations, and therefore in theory at least four people would need to be in collusion for a fraudulent payment to be made. Equally, at least four people should have checked that the transaction has been correctly categorized.

This is obviously easier in a large company than in a small one, and it also has the effect of increasing the costs of each transaction. There is therefore a difficult trade-off between the costs and the level of security. There is also the psychological problem that people get used to routines and after a while do not check efficiently. Indeed, a system where everyone knows there are five other people checking the transaction leads to a failure to check adequately because each link in the chain may start to rely on someone else doing the job properly.

Aside from the separation of functions, the internal control system should include routine checks such as inspection of the monthly bank reconciliation and outstanding client and supplier accounts, all of which provide areas where fraudulent items can be kept outside the system but also where company records can to an extent be checked against the records of outside organizations with which the company deals. Many companies keep asset registers where lists of computers and desks and so on (to say nothing of cars, plant etc.) are maintained and these should be checked periodically against the physical existence of these items. Equally, where staff have access to large quantities of goods (supermarket staff, factory workers etc.) it is usual to have security systems which control what goods the employees are taking in and out of the business.

> Why should you check goods being taken *in* to a company? It is not always relevant, but a sophisticated fraud is easy to operate in something like a bar where the barman takes in, for example, a bottle of whisky, then when a customer asks for a measure of whisky, the barman serves the customer from his private stock and then keeps the money. This way the customer is not cheated, and the bar owner does not necessarily have any idea anything is wrong. The barman is robbing the business by using its infrastructure, but the main internal controls generally focus on the relationship between the value of sales and the value of the liquor consumed, and the barman is circumventing these controls by bringing in liquor.

Internal audit

Most large companies have an internal audit department. Typically this consists of a team of several people whose job is to visit the group's different sites and check whether accounting procedures are being followed correctly. The objective, as ever, is to ensure the integrity of the group's accounting and control system. Partly the task is psychological: if people know that at any time in the year the internal audit department may call in to check the accounting transactions and see whether the procedures in the group manual have been followed, this encourages them to apply the procedures more thoroughly, and also discourages anyone who was contemplating fraud.

The internal audit department can help create a culture within the group that says the accounting function has a vital role to play, and members of it are valued for their technical knowledge and their skill in handling the sometimes difficult interpersonal situations that can arise. Equally, this unit can provide important feedback about applications problems to those who design and maintain the procedures. A difficulty in operating group-wide systems is that not all operating units are the same size (and therefore may have quite different accounting structures and personnel) and not all have the same type of operations.

By way of example of the problems that can arise when trying to install uniform systems, I once worked in a group which had both electronics and entertainment interests. Within the entertainment division was a sub-group which ran London theatres and produced live theatrical shows. The head office internal audit department were conducting an exercise to fix levels of expenditure authority within operating units, as part of the internal control structure. They said that the chief executive of this sub-group could sign contracts only up to an individual value of $500,000. Beyond that he should seek authority from the chief executive of the entertainment division. The chief accountant of the theatrical sub-group said this was not possible because the group did not know the value of many contracts which were signed. The internal audit manager was dumbfounded – how could the chief executive sign contracts without knowing their value? Should he not be replaced at once (and maybe the chief accountant too)?

The chief accountant explained that theatre contracts in the West End of London are usually open-ended. They provide for a minimum weekly rental (generally against a percentage of sales), and as long as the minima are exceeded, the contract can run indefinitely. Indeed, the object of the exercise is to find a single production that could potentially run for years. So while the minimum weekly rental might be (say) $50,000, the show could run for two or three years, or only two or three weeks, so the value of the contract could be anything from $200,000 to $20m or more. The internal audit manager then understood, but pointed out that the chief executive of the worldwide group could only sign contracts up to $10m without the approval of the board of directors. In the end, they agreed to write a special authority for the theatre sub-group, based on maximum weekly figures.

Getting the 'control environment' right is a very tricky problem in a large group. Ideally you want the accounting departments of the different units to be efficient and useful contributors to the team, who are willing to provide a high quality of service to help with the efficient running of the unit. On the other hand, the integrity of the group system and the necessity to provide inputs whose justification can be demonstrated, if necessary years after the event in a tax investigation, demand that accounting staff insist on the presentation of the appropriate paperwork and the required authorizations. Accounting staff in remote subsidiaries sometimes have a particularly difficult time since they have a line responsibility to the chief executive of their subsidiary, but a functional responsibility to the head office accounting managers. Locally employed staff, particularly in areas where unemployment is high, may fear losing their job if they upset the local chief executive, and may therefore not apply systems correctly.

The internal audit team should make frequent but unscheduled visits to subsidiaries to make spot checks on recent transactions but also to reinforce the local accounting unit if there are problems. The internal audit team should have a reporting responsibility within the head office, and not to local managers, although of course they should discuss local problems with operational management on site.

> *Internal auditing is an independent, objective assurance and consulting activity designed to add value and improve an organisation's operations. It helps an organisation accomplish its objectives by bringing a systematic, disciplined approach to evaluate and improve the effectiveness of risk management, control and governance processes.*
>
> *Source:* Institute of Internal Auditors

It follows from this that working in internal audit is not a particularly easy job. It is necessary to have a wide knowledge of the group's operations and accounting systems. A great deal of time is spent away from home visiting remote subsidiaries and often either working in foreign languages or with people who are obliged to use their second or third language, and who, of course, have different cultural backgrounds and therefore different understandings about their role and responsibilities. People in either accounting or operational roles often resent also what they perceive as an intrusion from head office, without understanding that without effective accounting systems the group cannot continue to exist for very long.

External audit

In most jurisdictions the accounts of medium and large companies must be submitted to an independent audit. This is often referred to as 'statutory audit' and is usually carried out by independent firms of auditors. Audit has evolved differently in different countries, and the object of the audit is not uniform. In some countries, the auditor has a quasi-legal role to check for the legality of the company's activities and its annual statements, whereas in other countries the auditor is checking the accounts on behalf of the shareholders. In both cases the audit firm is usually appointed in fact by the management of the company.

In both cases, too, the responsibility both for keeping accounts and for preparing the annual statements is that of the management of the company, not that of the auditors. Generally, while auditors should certainly report fraud if they spot it, and they will normally comment on the adequacy of the internal control system to prevent fraud, their job is not to search for fraud, even if many people think that it is. In a modern multinational, the management are looking to the statutory auditor to provide reassurance to outside stakeholders that the accounts of the company are a valid representation of the company's financial position. This is part of the very broad role played by financial statements, and the fact that the information is independently verified is probably one reason why the role is so broad. Nearly all multinationals have their accounts audited by one of the five international audit networks which dominate the business:

Pricewaterhouse Coopers
KPMG
Ernst & Young
Deloitte & Touche
Arthur Andersen

These five firms are probably better known than many of their clients, and their logo on the audit report (published within the accounts) carries a high level of reassurance to users in general and the financial markets in particular. As a consequence, any company with ambitions is likely to use one of these firms. In addition, they have worldwide networks, and are capable of delivering an audit anywhere in the world. This is quite important in that the multinational generally prefers to have a single firm responsible for all its subsidiaries, not least because this reduces the risk of lack of coordination between countries. This tends to reinforce the dominant position of the 'Big Five', as they are known, since other audit firms cannot offer the global service.

The basic statutory audit consists of two tasks:

1. to check that the accounting database effectively picks up all the company's activities and is correct;
2. to check that the financial statements drawn up from it are a correct representation of what is in the database, use appropriate accounting policies and are a reasonable representation of the company's real state (but this last aspect may not always be part of local audit requirements).

The audit firm maintains a master file on the company, and in this is collated all the relevant information necessary for the annual audit. This includes items left outstanding from the previous audit for subsequent management action, and an analysis of the company's systems. When starting a new audit, the first requirement is to check the accuracy of the systems chart. Having established the current system and internal controls in place, the next step is to check how well these work. This is done by sampling the transactions of a particular (short) period. If this checking reveals that the internal control system is correctly applied, the auditor can go on to carry out verifications of things like stock valuations, bank reconciliations (comparing the client's bank records with the statements provided by the bank), client accounts, supplier accounts and so on.

Only if the internal control system is thought to be ineffective will more detailed checking be done.

Once satisfied with the database, the auditor looks at the financial statements and the interpretation of the database which has been made in these. The nature of the company's business does not necessarily change every year, so there need not be any queries at this point, but as new transactions appear, so there may well be disagreement about how these are represented. Such disagreements are usually resolved more or less amicably between the audit staff and the chief accountant, but occasionally there can be substantial disagreement – usually because a change in treatment would diminish profits (we will look at some cases later). In such circumstances things can be very tense, and large companies have been known to bring in legal opinion, or consult another firm of auditors, when trying to insist on their view of the accounts. The auditor can, in some countries, even be replaced, but this generally sends a bad signal to the market. The auditor's only threat is to refuse to sign the audit report at all (very extreme) or (more normally) to say that they will be obliged to include a reservation in their audit report which details the matter in dispute.

Nestlé

Report of the Group Auditors

As group auditors we have audited the group accounts (balance sheet, income statement, cash flow statement and annex) of the Nestlé group for the year ended 31 December 1998.

These group accounts are the responsibility of the Board of Directors. Our responsibility is to express an opinion on these group accounts based on our audit. We confirm that we meet the legal requirements concerning professional qualification and independence.

Our audit was conducted in accordance with auditing standards promulgated by the profession, and with International Standards on Auditing issued by the International Federation of Accountants (IFAC), which require that an audit be planned and performed to obtain reasonable assurance about whether the Group accounts are free from material misstatement. We have examined on a test basis evidence supporting the amounts and disclosures in the Group accounts. We have assessed the accounting principles used, significant estimates made and the overall Group accounts presentation. We believe that our audit provides a reasonable basis for our opinion.

In our opinion, the group accounts give a true and fair view of the financial position, the net profit and cash flows and comply in all respects with International Accounting Standards (IAS), the Listing Rules of the Swiss Exchange and the law.

We recommend that the Group accounts submitted to you be approved.

KPMG Klynveld Peat Marwick Goerdeler SA
25 March 1999
Source: Nestlé Management Report 1998 © 1999 Nestlé SA
www.nestle.com/mr1998/cansolaccts/ii/

Although the auditor signs a public report, there is also usually a private report which is given to the management, and is known as a 'management letter'. This, unlike the published report, does not follow any prescribed formula but rather comments on the audit findings for the year, highlights potential areas of weakness and makes recommendations. This is something which the following year's audit will revisit to see what action has been taken.

The conduct of the audit is regulated in three ways. Firstly, the statutory audit, by definition, is mandated by a government statute (such as a Companies Law or a Commercial Code) which will prescribe the objects of the audit and normally specify whether client confidentiality applies or not. In the second place there will normally be a national professional association for auditors which will provide detailed audit regulations. Finally the audit firm itself will have its own internal procedures which all its staff follow – for reasons of efficiency and also to enable the firm's management to assess the degree of risk in the audit and similar issues.

The audit firm has a potentially difficult relationship with its client because on the one hand the outside world depends upon the rigour of the audit firm to ensure that the company maintains proper accounts and gives adequate reports. On the other hand, the audit firm is in effect appointed by the management, must negotiate with the management, and in many countries, hopes to be able to sell supplementary services such as tax advice and management consultancy to the audit client. This problem is known as the issue of 'independence'. Regulators are concerned that, since auditors are at the front line of corporate regulation, they should be independent of management and provide an appropriate control on management. The SEC in the US recently set up an Independence Standards Board with a view to addressing this problem.

Companies listed on the New York Stock Exchange are obliged to appoint an *audit committee*, which should normally consist on independent directors of the company who liaise with the statutory auditors. The idea is that this committee provides a forum free from the influence of operating management where shareholder representatives can discuss audit problems. The role of the audit committee is growing in a context where society is becoming more and more concerned with corporate governance issues.

Corporate governance

In recent years, more and more government and shareholder attention has been given to the question of how management's freedom of action may be limited by outside interests – a topic known as *corporate governance*. There are many issues in this area which cause concern to investors and governments. Abuses by management are not necessarily widespread but sometimes the remuneration of top executives seems out of all proportion to the effort put in, and again, sometimes managers are either implicated in or not aware of frauds taking place within the company, or indeed of risk-taking by middle management. Some company bosses are thought to be able to operate virtually as dictators, with no effective monitoring of their activity within the company.

Criticism in this area, for example articulated in the financial press, has produced a number of different outcomes. At a general level, most companies are not insensitive to the views of the outside world, and make at least a token response by disclosing in their annual report some details of their activities in sensitive areas. Notably, companies are increasingly making voluntary disclosures about their interaction with the environment, their involvement with their employees and the wider community, and their policy on issues such as the use of child labour by sub-contractors etc. In addition, institutional investors such as insurance companies and pension funds increasingly provide a checklist of corporate governance matters to the directors of the companies in which they plan to invest. Only if the board can satisfy them on these points will they go ahead and make an investment.

Concerns in this area have also resulted in a number of government or quasi-official reports in different countries (Viénot in France, Cadbury in the UK, OECD) which tend to recommend the installation of supplementary controls on management and the distancing of management from the audit. The first plank of such an approach calls for companies to appoint a chairman who is not also the chief executive, and for the board to include 'non-executive' or independent directors who can bring experience and independence to the board room. The non-executive directors, aside from normal board meetings, are then called upon to form two key committees, the compensation committee (fixes directors' pay packages) and the audit committee. The audit committee should provide a forum where external and internal auditors can discuss audit issues without line management being present.

The basic idea is that the non-executive directors have no role in the day-to-day running of the company but are there to safeguard investors' interests and to provide ethical controls. Of course, for this to work, the individuals must be experienced in business matters and be willing to take a strong line within the board. It is not clear that this always works, not least because appointment of non-executive directors generally falls to the chairman or chief executive. However, in principle, the non-executives should be in a position to determine what is a fair pay package for senior executives by reference to market conditions. Equally, they should prove some protection for staff who wish to express concerns in the context of internal controls and audit. A frequently encountered problem in large companies is that even if staff are aware that some fraud or abuse is taking place, they are reluctant to report it because they fear that no action will be taken, but their position will be made untenable. The existence of an audit committee should make it possible for staff to raise issues which are passed up the audit chain, and not discussed with operational management until an investigation has taken place.

In some countries, notably Germany, large companies have a two-tier board system where a management board runs the company on a day-to-day basis, but this reports to a supervisory board. The supervisory board represents investors and staff and receives regular reports on corporate activity and can replace the management board if they wish.

Government also reacts sometimes by creating penalties for abusive behaviour. For example, in the USA in the 1970s government became aware that some corporations were involved in paying substantial bribes to foreign governments to enter into equipment and service contracts. This resulted in the Foreign Corrupt Practices Act (1976) which provided criminal penalties for managers involved in such behaviour and outlawed the use of so-called slush funds to finance such activity.

The accounting profession

It is worth spending a few moments to look at the accounting profession as such. In the anglophone world we tend to use the terms 'accountant' and 'auditor' interchangeably, and we tend not to distinguish very clearly between those people who operate independent public accounting firms and those who work for companies or in the public sector. Not the least reason for this is that there is no clear worldwide definition of what an accountant does, and indeed the training and licensing arrangements and type of work done vary somewhat from country to country. For our purposes we will distinguish between the following categories:

1. Independent auditor
2. Independent accountant
3. Company accountant

Independent auditors are specialists who work in audit firms and are licensed either directly or indirectly by the government to carry out the 'statutory audit' (i.e. independent audit required by company law) of large companies. An individual who works in this way has generally done a university degree and then studied for professional exams. These exams are typically under the supervision of a professional organization (e.g. American Institute of Certified Public Accountants) and a candidate must also spend at least three years as a student in a public auditing firm. In some countries, such as the UK, success in the professional examination, allied with the necessary practical experience, confers an auditing licence automatically and this is issued by the professional body. In other countries (e.g. Germany) the auditor must register with a government supervisory body.

In fact many auditors leave public practice fairly early in their careers, either to undertake wider management careers or to work full time for a company. In anglophone countries, such accountants may well remain members of their professional body, but in many continental European countries, membership is linked to public practice and anyone leaving public practice leaves their professional body at the same time. This leads to professional bodies being quite different in size and nature. The Institut der Wirtschaftsprüfer (the only body for auditors of public companies in Germany) has approximately 18 000 members, while the Association of Chartered Certified Accountants (one of four bodies in the UK whose members may work as auditors) has 70 000 members.

The precise nature of the audit and the relationship between auditor and client vary from place to place. In France the auditor has a public responsibility to report to the public prosecutor any evidence of a client's failure to comply with the law, discovered during the audit. However, in most countries the company's information must be kept confidential by the auditor. There are also differences as to what the auditor is commenting on in the audit report – sometimes it is simply conformity with local accounting rules, while sometimes the auditor is saying that the image of the company given by the annual accounts is not misleading. This difference is quite important since the user of the accounts is being offered a different level of reassurance about the information.

It is relatively rare that audit firms offer only an audit service, although France and Germany in particular say that the auditor, for reasons of independence, may only provide audit services to an audit client, even if they may offer other services to non-audit clients. Anglo-Saxon audit firms generally offer a wide range of consulting services to their audit clients, and indeed provision of the audit is seen by some as the means of access to selling a wide range of consulting services.

Independent accountants are a related branch of the profession. In some countries there has developed a network of firms which offer accounting services to (generally small) businesses. In France there are, for example, the Experts Comptables, in Germany the Steuerberater, and in the Netherlands the Accountants Administratieconsulenten. These firms specifically do not offer statutory audit for large companies, and their principal role is in providing the accounting function for companies that are either too small to have an in-house service or that prefer to outsource the function. They may also provide tax and general business advice.

Company accountant on the other hand is a function not necessarily covered by any professional organization, and indeed many company accountants do not have any specific accounting training. At the management end of company accounting, the larger companies tend to engage former auditors or others with specialized professional training to run their accounting function. However, it is commonplace in both North America and continental Europe for people to study business at university, perhaps with an accounting specialization, and then go directly into a company and work in the accounting, internal audit and finance areas, building up a store of practical experience in that way.

Professional accounting bodies exist in most countries, but their nature may vary quite a lot depending on the nature of the economy within which they operate. In the developed world, the standards of professional exams for auditors are comparable, and indeed in the European Union are the subject of a harmonization statute (Eighth Company Law Directive), but in the developing world and in countries in transition to a market economy this is not necessarily so. Not all professional bodies have examination requirements for entry, and not all are independent associations. For example, the Chinese Institute of Certified Public Accountants is an agency of the Chinese Ministry of Finance.

There are some regional bodies to which national bodies may belong, such as the Fédération des Experts Comptables Européens (European Accountants' Federation) or the Confederation of Asia Pacific Accountants. Finally there is, at a world level, the International Federation of Accountants (IFAC) which represents the profession worldwide and issues auditing standards and public sector accounting standards, as well as providing guidance on education and ethical matters.

Summary

In this chapter we have looked at the functioning of the company accounting unit, and seen that its objectives are to provide accurate financial data about the company but also to provide controls which prevent the possibility of fraud. The company runs a permanent accounting database into which all transactions are summarized, and from which one may at any point produce reports about the company's performance and financial position. The processing of transactions follows the same principles irrespective of whether it is computerized or not, but computers are widespread and permit of efficient accounting and sophisticated analysis.

The way in which transactions are processed is organized so as to reduce the possibility of loss or fraud. Companies have a system of 'internal control' which operates to ensure that necessary authorities are obtained before transactions take place and managers sign for the transactions under their responsibility. In larger companies this system is backed up by an 'internal audit' function: dedicated staff check the work of accounts departments to ensure that internal controls are applied. Finally all public companies, and many private ones, are subject to independent audit by external auditors. These professionals also rely upon the internal control system and run sample checks on it in order to form an opinion on the accuracy of the company's financial records. They also give an opinion on the validity of the annual accounts.

The external audit is a major part of a wider system of 'corporate governance', through which investors and other interested parties aim to monitor and control the behaviour of corporate managers, a subject which we will revisit later in the book. This involves the use of disclosures, adhesion to codes of behaviour and the use of board members who represent investor interests. The term accountant or auditor is used fairly freely and there are a number of professional structures and education patterns which occur in different countries. Generally, statutory auditors must be licensed by government and have completed suitable professional training and minimum periods of internship.

Questions

1. What are the objectives which a company's accounting department should be aiming to achieve?
2. How is the company's accounting database organized and from where does it get its data?
3. What is 'internal control'?
4. What is the purpose of external audit, and who carries this out?

Part Two

Basic financial statements

3 Measurement concepts and the balance sheet equation

This part goes through the main techniques which are used to prepare the basic financial statements – income statement and balance sheet – of individual companies. These are the basic building blocks of financial reporting.

   Chapter 3 introduces two of the three main financial statements. It then goes on to explain the basic assumptions which are applied to financial accounting and therefore provide the framework which both limits and informs accounting information. The chapter introduces the balance sheet equation, which is the fundamental logic on which accounting is based.

Introduction

In general terms the annual financial statements produced by a business for external consumption (also known as the annual accounts, annual report etc.) are the single public source of economic data on the company and represent a prime communication between the company and its external constituents. The statements of larger companies are usually subject to verification by external experts (auditors) and are sent automatically to shareholders. They form the starting point for tax assessment. They are usually of prime interest to all main trading partners: banks, other lenders, suppliers of goods and services, major customers. They are often, particularly in large companies, an important device used to monitor contracts (bank covenants, profit shares in joint ventures, employee bonuses, royalties).

   In most jurisdictions there is a requirement for the accounts to be filed at a public registry so that, even if the company does not provide a copy of the accounts directly to an interested party, access to them is still readily possible (for example, in the UK there is a single government office which holds all company files, in Belgium they are held by the Banque Nationale de Belgique and in France they are filed at local commercial courts, but in Switzerland access is restricted, while in Germany many small and medium-sized companies deliberately do not file their accounts – the fine is minimal).

   In practice, large companies frequently now put their accounts on their website and generally make physical copies of their annual report available to anyone who cares to telephone and ask for it, and indeed see it as a major public relations document, while small, privately owned companies will give up information only when the law or their trading interest decrees it.

The annual accounts consist of two primary statements, the profit and loss account and the balance sheet, together with explanatory notes as a sort of appendix (as discussed in Chapter 1). The profit and loss account sets out the result of the company's trading operations for the year, while the balance sheet shows, at a given date, where the company's finance comes from (banks, shareholders etc. – liabilities and equity) and what assets such as factories, equipment and so on have been bought by the company.

The balance sheet does not, though, purport to show what the company is worth

This issue crops up from time to time in MBA courses and is obviously a key question if one's main interest in looking at the annual accounts is to form an opinion on the economic health and prospects of the company. Usually, when we ask what a company is 'worth', this means what would we have to pay to acquire the company, and this in turn is linked to the value of the future benefits which one would gain by buying the company. If Company X will deliver a dividend of $10,000 a year for ten years, its total value over ten years is $100,000. Since, if you buy the company, you cannot enjoy all the benefits at once, you would normally be willing to pay less than $100,000 for it – you would deduct a discount equivalent to interest costs at least. The price agreed is a compromise between the value to the purchaser and what the seller is willing to sell for. In fact takeover situations typically arise because Company A believes that it can reorganize Company X (maybe there are savings to be made by combining operations) and deliver more than $10,000 a year from it. In this case the owners of Company X will value it on the basis of $10,000 a year but Company A will make a bid at a higher price, so there is a basis for a deal.

The point is that company value, from a market perspective, is (a) based on future earnings, and (b) these earnings may well be different in different situations. Financial statements give certain economic information about a company's past activities, drawn up according to a fairly flexible set of rules. They give partial information, and anyone wanting to make serious use of the statements needs to know (a) what are the rules, (b) to what extent are they flexible, and (c) how this impacts upon interpretation of the information. On top of that, anyone looking across national boundaries needs to know how the rules differ from one jurisdiction to another, where different flexibilities arise and so forth. Once the analyst has decoded the accounting information, then he or she can make a forecast of future earnings from that information (and other external factors) and come to a view about the company's worth.

Environment

This brings us to another major point: while the bulk of accounting rules for commercial companies are the same in all developed countries, there are differences at a detailed level from one country to another (as discussed in Chapter 1); also, the way the rules are applied may differ from one company to another within the same country. While the way companies record and track their transactions in their accounting systems does not vary substantially, the way these are presented in annual reports may be subject to significant variations. Financial reporting is not a precise measurement tool and is deeply embedded in the culture and traditions of each country, even if following, in developed market economies, the same basic model.

Looking first at businesses within one country, there are many differences which impact upon reporting, such as the nature of their ownership, their objectives, their legal form and their size. Most European market economies are in fact mixed economies with a large slice of activity in the hands of commercial companies, but also a significant element owned by the state. Where a business is owned by the state, its management may be under different pressures from those of an ordinary commercial concern; for example, it may not be politically acceptable to show too much profit, or again, the government may want to fatten the company up for privatization. State-owned enterprises may not operate under the same regulations as private sector firms.

In the private sector, it is easy to see two extremes, the large, multinational company, listed on several stock exchanges, and the small company owned entirely by its chief executive. A company whose securities are traded on the capital markets has a major concern in terms of maintaining the buoyancy of the share price and this is likely to lead the company either to release good news as soon as possible and hide bad news as long as possible, or to make an attempt to smooth profits so that the company appears to go from one successful year to another in a reliable progression. For these companies the capital market is a privileged user of their financial information and the rules are likely to be applied by such companies in ways that will influence the market reaction. The management of the company and its owners are separate and distinct from each other, and the annual report plays a significant role in the conduct of that relationship.

The small company at the other extreme has no external shareholders to whom to report. The manager is also the main shareholder and so the reporting pressures are likely to be different. Such a manager might be more concerned about keeping reported profits as low as possible in order to reduce tax liability. Or again, if it is perhaps a family company, the manager may want to keep profits low so that relatives will not demand high dividends, and cash can be kept in the business to finance expansion.

Financial Reporting Standard for Smaller Companies

The objective of this Financial Reporting Standard for Smaller Entities (FRSSE) is to ensure that reporting entities falling within its scope provide in their financial statements information about the financial position, performance and adaptability of the entity that is useful to users in assessing the stewardship of management and for making economic decisions, recognising that the balance between users' needs in respect of stewardship and economic decision-making in respect of smaller entities is different from that for other reporting entities.

Source: Accounting Standards Board (UK)

These are archetypes and there exist many variants. There are, for example, large, family-owned companies which are not listed on stock exchanges (e.g Firmenich, Bosch, Mars). There are particularly many of these in Germany and Switzerland, and here there is another issue, which is the extent to which the community calls for businesses of significant economic size to make financial disclosures purely because their size may cause them to impact upon the public interest.

The nature of a company's ownership generally impacts upon its objectives. A state or other public sector entity probably has objectives other than profit generation, a listed company may want to angle towards maximizing declared short-term profits (or not – it depends upon the culture of the capital markets where it operates), a privately held company might want to minimize profits in order to minimize tax and dividends. On the other hand, a privately held company that planned to be listed on the capital markets in the future might choose to maximize profits. A commercial company listed on stock exchanges (a publicly held company) might be looking for long-term growth and be quite willing to take low profits while it builds market share. So while ownership and objectives are often closely inter-linked, this is not always the case.

Company activity is another variable. This is at its most obvious in regulations that affect banks and insurance companies. All jurisdictions have separate regulatory mechanisms for the accounting and disclosure requirements for financial institutions. These may relate to requirements for ordinary commercial companies (the Fourth Directive – a major accounting statute of the European Union – has banking and insurance variants) but usually go beyond them because of the different nature of the assets and liabilities of such companies and the profound effects on society of the failure of financial institutions. In this book we shall concentrate on the accounts of ordinary commercial companies.

Another significant variable in financial reporting within most countries is that of legal form. The major difference is generally between limited liability companies and entities that do not enjoy limited liability. For example, the European Fourth and Seventh Company Law Directives, which are the main common source of accounting regulations within the European Union, are based on legal form (and then size). Limited liability companies are those whose owners risk only the capital they put into a company – if the company makes a loss, the owners cannot be pursued for more money than they originally agreed to subscribe. Such limited liability vehicles are split in the Fourth Directive between public limited companies (which issue shares of equal value and may be listed on stock exchanges) such as the Aktiengesellschaft in Germany or the Société Anonyme in France, and private limited companies (Gesellschaft mit beschränkter Haftung, Société à responsabilité limitée etc.) whose capital cannot be publicly traded and which do not necessarily issue shares as such – a Société à responsabilité limitée has 'company parts'.

In anglophone countries, absence of limited liability may also go with absence of regulation in financial reporting terms. In Britain there are large auditing and consultancy firms employing thousands of people and with sales running into millions of pounds sterling which are constituted as partnerships where partners are personally liable for the full amount of all debts of the partnership, but there is no legal obligation to publish any accounts. The Church of England is probably the biggest landowner in the country, but publishes no accounts.

In continental Europe accounting regulations tend to run with the nature of the business (a commercial business follows the same basic accounting rules irrespective of size) but disclosures are modified according to size. The European accounting directives recognize three tiers of size, which are subject to change from time to time:

- small company – must not exceed two out of: sales euro 2m, total assets euro 1m, employees 50;
- medium company – must not exceed two out of: sales euro 16m, total assets euro 8m, employees 250;
- large company – any listed entity, and all that exceed medium size criteria.

Small companies may benefit from limited public disclosure and freedom from audit. These size criteria are built into reporting regulations within the European Union and outside it. There is nothing self-evidently 'right' about the EU's criteria, but they do give recognition to the idea that small, privately held companies need not disclose as much as large companies, which is a view expressed in many countries, even if the precise cut-off between 'small' and 'not small' is necessarily arbitrary.

In overall terms, it is true to say that published financial statements are aimed at a wide range of potential users, including (actual or potential) shareholders, lenders, trade suppliers, tax authorities, customers, employees etc. However, the company faces a need to present a different face for different users. It can only provide the one, general purpose, set of statements but where accounting rules provide any choices (and there are many instances) different companies will choose measurements that give priority to different sub-sets of users. Some will maximize profit, others will minimize it and so on. These factors have to be considered when evaluating any particular company's statements.

Content of financial statements

The core financial reporting process involves preparing an annual profit and loss account and a balance sheet. The profit and loss account brings together aggregated information about a company's trading performance during a twelve-month period (most often the calendar year, but in some countries not necessarily that). The balance sheet shows the state of the company's finances at the end of that year. Both statements are usually published with comparative data from the previous year (Figure 3.1). Accounting uses the terms stocks and flows to describe the kind of information that different reports provide. In this context the profit and loss account might be said to be reporting a 'flow' (trading activities during a period) while the balance sheet is reporting a 'stock' – a static inventory of the company's position at a given moment.

Balance sheet		Balance sheet		Balance sheet		Balance sheet
31/12/X1		31/12/X2		31/12/X3		31/12/X4
	Profit and Loss ← 20X2 →		Profit and Loss ← 20X3 →		Profit and Loss ← 20X4 →	

Figure 3.1   Time periods covered by the balance sheet and profit and loss account

While the published data usually only shows two years (although the SEC asks for three years of profit and loss accounts for publicly listed companies in the US), analysts need a longer time series, and therefore build up collections of annual reports or use inputs from commercial company data services so that they can look at five- and ten-year runs of data and get a wider picture of the progression of a company's economic state.

Obviously we are going to look in some detail at the content of these statements during this course. However, the intention here is just to introduce them and you should concentrate on the broad lines and picking up the vocabulary.

The structure of a profit and loss account is as follows:

		$'000
Sales		5,356
Raw materials	1,739	
Salaries and wages	783	
Depreciation	462	
External services	873	(3,857)
Profit before interest and tax		1,499
Interest		(362)
Profit before taxation		1,137
Taxation		(384)
Profit available for shareholders		753

You can see that this format can be split into two different sections, of which the main distinctions are:

- trading result;
- returns to interested parties other than the owners (providers of loan finance and government).

Looking at the trading or operational result, the approach to costs shown in this format is known as the value-added one: it shows inputs and outputs and enables the analyst to calculate the value added by the company in transforming raw materials into finished goods (assuming it is a manufacturing company). This is the most common approach in mainland Europe.

The alternative approach to presenting trading data is that used more often in the UK and USA, which splits costs not by type of cost, but by the activity to which the cost was assigned (in the technical jargon we refer to a value-added presentation as showing costs by nature while the alternative shows costs by function). The Anglo-Saxon style of format is shown below:

		$'000
Sales		5,356
Cost of sales		(2,601)
		2,755
Distribution costs	382	
Administration expense	874	(1,256)
Profit before tax and interest		1,499
Interest		(362)
Profit before taxation		1,137
Taxation		(384)
Profit available for shareholders		753

This kind of disclosure approach involves allocating raw materials, salaries, depreciation and other costs against the three functional areas of cost of sales (manufacturing cost in this case), distribution (marketing, advertising, warehousing and other selling costs) and administration (accounting, legal, general management costs). In our example, the costs are being presented in one of two ways:

Nature			Function		
		$'000			$'000
Raw materials		1,739	Cost of sales		2,601
Salaries and wages		783	Distribution		382
Depreciation		462	Administration		874
Other costs		873			
Total		3,857	Total		3,857

Opinions differ as to which is the more useful form for analysts (the IASC says there is a case for providing both). Some would say that showing costs by function enables a clearer comparison of efficiency between one company and another in the same industry. For example, if comparing two companies which both manufactured similar fork lift trucks, you could compare cost of sales as a percentage of sales revenue to see who was manufacturing more cheaply – or who was making the largest difference (gross margin) between selling price and manufacturing cost. However, many companies do not have just a single product, and so the opportunity for extremely precise comparisons does not usually occur. In addition, the allocation of expenses across functions must up to a point be subjective – if a canteen is used by both manufacturing and administrative staff, how much do you allocate to each function? Different companies might have different views.

In any event, this first part of the profit and loss account deals with a company's trading operations and provides a basis for comparisons with other years and other companies, irrespective of their financial structure or other considerations. The lower part of the profit and loss account, on the other hand, shows how the profit generated by the company is split up:

- taxation paid to government (society's share);
- interest (payment to those who have provided the company's loan capital);
- profit retained in the company (to pay dividends to shareholders and to finance future expansion etc.) and which is in effect the wealth generated by the company in that year.

The taxation identified here is tax on profits or income, and does not include elements such as value-added tax (excluded from the profit and loss account), import taxes (included under relevant cost headings such as raw materials) and social security charges (included in personnel costs).

The level of interest charges is a function of the degree to which the company has been financed by debt.

The balance sheet presents a picture of the company's finances at the end of the financial year, and the assets (factories, machinery, patents, brands etc.) which it has acquired and which have not yet been consumed within the business. The presentation of information in the balance sheet follows precise rules, although the detail again may vary from one jurisdiction to another. One of two formats offered by the Fourth Directive is known as a horizontal balance sheet and this is probably the format most commonly used in mainland Europe. This would look as follows:

	$'000		$'000
Fixed assets		**Capital**	
Intangible assets	943	Ordinary shares	2,455
Tangible assets	1,988	Reserves	982
Investments	_213_	Retained profit	_947_
	3,144	Shareholders' equity	4,384
Stocks	1,589	Provisions	520
Debtors	973	Financial	
Cash at bank	881	liabilities	1,500
		Trade liabilities	359
Deferred charges	_176_		
Total	6,763		6,763

Some US companies use the horizontal format, but with the elements presented in the reverse order:

Assets		**Liabilities and equity**	
Cash at bank	881	Trade payables	359
Deferred charges	176	Debt	1,500
Receivables	973	Provisions	520
Inventory	1,589		
Fixed assets		**Equity**	
Investments	213	Ordinary stock	2,455
Tangible assets	1,988	Reserves	982
Intangible assets	_943_	Retained profit	_947_
	6,763		6,763

The left-hand side of the balance sheet shows the company's assets, split into those which will be used up over a period of more than one year (fixed assets), typically physical plant (tangible assets), patents, brand names, licences (intangible assets) and investments (shares or loans to other companies, often made for strategic purposes to cement a trading relationship, investments in subsidiary companies). The remaining assets are usually constantly changing, and are generated by the company's trading activities. Stocks are being diminished every day as sales take place, but also are being increased as new stock is bought or manufactured. Amounts due from customers (debtors – *receivables* in US terminology) would normally also be changing day to day: a company will normally always have stocks and debtors, but the individual items which make up the total are constantly changing.

The right-hand side of the balance sheet shows the company's financing. This is split into capital (which is a word to be wary of in accounting because it has different meanings in different contexts, but here means money put into the company by the owners: shares or in US: *stock*), provisions (the company has a liability to pay something in the future, although the precise amount may be uncertain), financial liabilities (loans made by banks, the financial markets etc.) and trade liabilities (US: *payables*, debts due to suppliers – of raw materials, finished goods etc.).

The Fourth Directive offers a second balance sheet format, known as the vertical balance sheet. This shows the same information but presents it in a different way: liabilities are shown as a deduction from assets, and are split according to when they are due for payment, while the horizontal format shows them according to whether they are financing or for trade. The balance sheet data presented in the horizontal format would look like this:

	$'000	$'000
Fixed assets		
Intangibles	943	
Tangible assets	1,988	
Investments	213	3,144
Current assets		
Stocks	1,589	
Debtors and prepaid[1]	1,149	
Cash at bank	881	
	3,619	
Creditors due in less than one year	(359)	
Net current assets		3,260
Creditors due in more than one year		(1,500)
Provisions		(520)
		4,384
Capital		
Ordinary shares		2,455
Reserves		982
Retained profits		947
		4,384

In a published set of accounts, the shareholders (and other users) receive not only this information but several pages of explanatory notes which amplify the information and analyse certain categories such as fixed assets. Part of this extra detail is sometimes included in the basic statements themselves ('on the face of the accounts', as accountants would say). This additional information is regulated and many of the insights that an analyst wants from the annual report are gained from a thorough review of the notes rather than the primary statements.

For the most part the same information is given in the balance sheet whichever way it is presented. The horizontal presentation gives a picture of the whole company: total assets and the total financing which has been used to acquire those assets. This is sometimes called an *entity* approach, treating the company as an economic whole and not distinguishing between different providers of finance. This is summed up as:

$$\text{Assets} = \text{Equity and liabilities}$$

This contrasts with the vertical presentation which focuses on the interest of the owners, and is known as a *proprietary* approach. This second approach says the owners' interest is measured by starting with the value of the assets and deducting loans from this amount:

$$\text{Assets } less \text{ liabilities} = \text{equity}$$

---

1 This is the debtor figure of 973 plus deferred charges of 176 – there is no separate line for deferred charges in the horizontal format.

What is left is the owners' equity. This approach is often used in measuring personal wealth, but using a current market value: a family who bought a house with a loan might calculate (a) the current value of the house, and (b) the amount of loan outstanding, and would arrive at the current value of their interest by deducting (b) from (a). Traditional accounting does not use current values, of course, so the value of the 'equity' number in the balance sheet does not equate to a current or market value of the company.

The basics of accounting measurement

In this section we going to review the conventions by which accounting statements are prepared. We will do this in the following stages:

- a consideration of the underlying measurement assumptions;
- a review of the data recording process within companies;
- an analysis of the balance sheet equation;
- a practical exercise in tracking transactions using the balance sheet equation;
- preparing simple financial statements.

Some knowledge of the accounts preparation process is essential for any sensible interpretation of the end product: the financial statements. The reason for this is that the statements are today highly technical documents which make many assumptions about the state of knowledge of the reader. It is quite impossible for an untrained reader to make much sense of the accounts; for example, just the technical terms (accruals? reserves? provisions?) immediately put the general reader at a disadvantage.

In fact the problems go a lot further than that. Accounting measurement does not purport to provide a total measurement system which gives a rounded economic picture of the company, even if the general public is inclined to believe that it does. The measurement system is based on a series of conventions which automatically limit the information taken into it, and which then demand that accounts preparers use many estimates in allocating revenues and expenses to one year rather than another. Accounting measurement is a very subjective process, giving a partial picture.

In a sense the only absolutely accurate measure of profit is only available once the company has ceased to exist and its assets have been sold and its liabilities paid off – at that point you can calculate all the inputs to the business from its start-up to its final liquidation and arrive at a precise profit for its whole life. This, however, is not very useful in managing the company, and accounting is the art of estimating what proportion of the life profit of the company has been earned in a particular (usually twelve month) period. In order to arrive at this estimate the accountant has to make many assumptions about the future of the company and the uncertainties that surround it. While most accounting information is clear and exactly quantifiable, the profit measure also includes allocations of expenses (and less frequently revenues) between years. No allocation is incontestable, and the published profit figure is therefore an estimate, not a matter of fact, and is subject to correction in subsequent years.

This does not mean that the information is no use – quite the contrary – but it does mean that the user needs to be clear exactly what is the nature of the information given in accounts, and therefore needs to understand the essentials of the measurement process. It is rather like driving a car: you look most of the time at the road immediately ahead of you, because that is where the most important decisions lie. It is a convention that traffic driving in the opposite direction to you will use the opposite side of the road, so you need not watch that side so intently, even if to have a complete picture you should be looking at both sides, as well as behind you.

Accounting information is subject to constraints, which you need to know in order to interpret it, but it is also subject to estimate, which makes it flexible and open to manipulation.

Measurement assumptions

One of the most dubious assumptions is that of the true and fair view. Most accounting regimes specify some general qualitative objective of accounting: in France this was that the accounts should be sincere and regular, while in Germany they should conform to the principles of good book-keeping. The European Fourth Directive specifies two objectives: the accounts should conform to generally accepted accounting principles (GAAP), and should give a true and fair view of the financial state of the company. The IASC also recommends that accounts should give a true and fair view, while US regulators require that the accounts 'present fairly in accordance with generally accepted accounting principles'.

This idea of the true and fair view derives from British accounting, and there is endless discussion about what it actually means – it has not been defined in law, by standard-setters, or even through court decisions (although a French court did rule on a particular case in 1994 to the effect that reliance on complying with accounting rules does not automatically ensure a true and fair view). The unwary reader of accounts might think that it means the accounts are both true and fair, or perhaps that the accounts are not misleading. This would be a dangerous position. The safer assumption is that the term merely means that the accounts have been prepared by respecting all the technical rules in force at the time of their preparation. In theory, if application of the rules does not give a clear picture (or perhaps would be positively misleading), further explanation should be given in the notes, which was the thrust of the French case in 1994.

IASC Framework

46. Financial statements are frequently described as showing a true and fair view of, or as presenting fairly, the financial position, performance and changes in financial position of an enterprise. Although this Framework does not deal directly with such concepts, the application of the principal qualitative characteristics and of appropriate accounting standards normally results in financial statements that convey what is generally understood as a true and fair view of, or as presenting fairly such information.

If you think about it, for accounts to be useful and comparable, they need to follow some kind of generally agreed rules. However, as soon as you start to measure according to pre-specified rules, you automatically limit what can be shown in the accounts.

If the confusion about true and fair is common in the UK, where the formula originated, the picture becomes much more complicated in Europe generally, after implementation of the Fourth Directive and the attempt to transplant a very unclear concept into different cultural environments. If you wish to pursue this discussion, there is a useful review of true and fair in a European context in *The European Accounting Review* of May 1993 (Vol. 2 No. 1) and further discussion in Vol. 6 No. 3 1997. For our purposes, you should be sceptical as to whether its existence improves the quality of accounts, and rely rather more heavily on the other Fourth Directive requirement that the statements should use generally accepted accounting principles. The auditor's report will normally confirm that these have been followed. In the US, the expression 'present fairly in accordance with GAAP' is to be interpreted in this sense.

At a more practical level, accounting measurement follows some key basic assumptions, which can be found in IAS 1 and which are also now enshrined in the Fourth Directive:

- *consistency;*
- *accruals* and *matching;*
- *prudence;*
- *going concern.*

The significance of these assumptions is not conveyed merely by reciting what is understood by them – that is something which comes out in the context of looking at their application to particular accounting problems. However, we need to start somewhere, so we will look at the meaning of these assumptions as applied to financial reporting.

Consistency is fairly straightforward. It means that accounting measurement practices should be used by a company consistently both from one year to another, and within the same year in relation to similar transactions. It could be argued that from an analyst's point of view, consistency is the most important characteristic needed in accounting. If the analyst is looking to put together several years' data to produce a forecast of future performance, each year needs to be prepared on a basis consistent with that in the other years. For predictive purposes the rate and direction of change of the indicators is more important than their absolute values, so a set of indicators, even if only partial in terms of the overall economic picture, if it is produced consistently will provide useful information.

The extent to which accounts actually are consistent is open to question. Most jurisdictions require companies to explain any change in accounting methods in the notes to the accounts, and to provide, where a change takes place, alternative figures showing the effects of the change. However, there is often a grey area between changing estimates or assumptions upon which allocations were based, and actually changing the accounting method.

For example, suppose it has been assumed that a certain piece of plant, costing $10m, will last for ten years, and therefore its cost should be allocated against profits on the basis of $1m a year. After three years the company decides that the plant will really last 20 years, so the annual charge goes down from $1m to $0.5m. In addition, since $3m have already been expensed in the first three years, while only $1.5m was appropriate under the new estimate, the excess of $1.5m can be released to the profit and loss account. Generally this manoeuvre would not be classified as a change in accounting policy, but only a change in estimates, and would not call for any explanation in the notes, even though the profit in year 4 is inflated by the adjustment.

Accruals is the name of the approach which distinguishes accounting from a simple record of cash transactions. The accruals convention is that accounting aims to measure business transactions at the time they take place, rather than when cash changes hands. For example, a department store offers credit to its regular customers, and it also is given credit by its suppliers. Suppose that the store agrees to take a special consignment of video cameras from a manufacturer. The cameras are delivered on 15 December; the store runs a special advertising campaign at 1 January. You go into the store on 10 January and buy a camera, charging it to your account. On 31 January the store pays its camera supplier, and bills you. You settle your account on 26 February (see Figure 3.2.)

Transactions:

15 December: delivery

10 January: you buy camera

31 January: store pays supplier

26 February: you pay store

Figure 3.2 Transactions

Under a simple cash recording system, there would be a stock purchase on 31 January and a sale on 26 February, and yet we know that you actually went into the store and took the goods on 10 January. The accruals convention is that transactions are recorded as they take place, not only when there is cash involved. So the accruals system would log the incoming stock on 15 December, the sale on 10 January and so on.

This brings us to the related convention of *matching*. This says that all costs and revenues associated with a particular transaction should be brought together when the sale takes place. This means that, in our example, when the store buys the stock of cameras, they are treated as an asset (an item of value owned by the company) and shown in the balance sheet as stock (not taken to the profit and loss account as an expense). Only when the individual camera is sold does it move from being stock to being an expense. Otherwise in the example the expense would fall into December and the related revenue into January. If the store's financial year ended on 31 December, this would cause the first year's profit to be reduced and the second year's to be inflated. The matching convention requires us to put both revenue and expense in the same financial period (the one where the revenue was earned – see prudence).

In the example it is clear when each transaction takes place and there is no ambiguity about any of the transactions. However, there can be problems in this kind of area. For example, what if the camera turns out to be faulty and you return it, demanding your money back? Should the store not account for any sale until sufficient time has elapsed to be sure that the customer is satisfied?

Ambiguities and uncertainties bring about conflicts with the next convention, that of *prudence*. Basically the prudence convention requires that revenues are only recognized in the accounts when they are certain, while expenses should be recognized if they are probable. In the jargon, revenues should only be recognized when *realized*, that is, when these are sufficiently concrete to be in cash or a form near to cash (an agreement to pay on which the company can go to court). Unrecoverable expenses, though, should be recognized even if not yet realized – for example, you have spent $5,000 working on a contract to design software for a client and you hear that the client may be having financial difficulties. Matching would require that you carry the costs forward (as a current asset) until you can invoice the client, but a prudent view would be to treat the work as a loss because the client's situation is open to question. This also has the effect of diminishing current year profit (and therefore tax), with the possibility of higher profit the following year. Tax management is mostly about deferring tax payments for as long as possible rather than escaping them altogether. While everyone would like to escape tax, if the accounts are accurate this is generally not possible (outside of sophisticated, often cross-border, sets of linked companies etc.), and the tax manager's objective is to defer tax as long as possible and thereby conserve the company's cash and reduce its financing needs.

At a theoretical level, there is a clear conflict between the application of matching and that of prudence, and the extent to which the one has priority over the other is one of the major differences in the application of accounting between one jurisdiction and another. Germany and Switzerland are famous for very prudent accounting (anticipating expenses, building secret reserves), while the UK is equally so for giving priority to the matching convention (deferring expenses, building hidden losses ...).

Fraudulent revenue recognition

By now, most of you are aware that the Commission announced the filing of 30 enforcement actions just last week against 68 individuals and companies for engaging in fraudulent misconduct in the accounting, reporting and disclosure of financial results.

... The companies involved in last week's announcements run the gamut from small microcap companies to large sophisticated companies traded on the New York Stock Exchange. The actions allege a veritable cookbook of recipes for fraudulent accounting and reporting, including:

- recognition of revenue on shipments that never occurred or for products not yet manufactured;
- hidden "side letters" giving customers the right to return product;
- characterization of consignment sales as final sales;
- premature recognition of sales that occurred after the end of the fiscal period;
- shipment of unfinished product;
- shipment of product before customers wanted or agreed to delivery;
- creation of fictitious invoices;
- backdating of agreements;
- the list goes on and on.

Unquestionably ... as these cases confirm, fraudulent revenue recognition is the recipe of choice for cooking the books.

Extract from remarks to the Panel on Audit Effectiveness made in New York on 9 October 1999 by Richard H Walker, Director, Division of Enforcement, Securities and Exchange Commission.

At a practical level, the degree to which prudence is given a priority has also something to do with tax regulations. In the UK, tax rules only allow the recognition of an expense when that expense has become concrete – a prudent anticipation of an expense is disregarded for tax purposes, with the result that a company that follows very prudent accounting also appears to pay proportionately higher taxes. In France or Germany some anticipation of expenses in the form of provisions is acceptable for tax, provided that it appears in the company accounts, thereby encouraging companies to be prudent in their accounting because that defers their taxes.

The *going concern* convention specifies that in preparing the accounts it is assumed that the company will continue in business for the foreseeable future. This is a critical assumption because much of accrual accounting measurement is based on allocating expenses over different future time periods, as we have already touched upon. If the business is unlikely to be there in the future, this approach is not valid and prudence would require many items to be written off at once as valueless. This is, of course, often a bone of contention with auditors when a company whose accounts they have signed then goes out of business a few months later. People who have relied on the accounts find the figures become meaningless when the company is no longer in business. The going concern assumption is used to justify the valuation procedures and is therefore a major assumption which should be considered by anyone analysing the accounts.

Moving on from these, there is also a cost convention, known as *historical cost*.

Historical cost

Financial accounting, as currently practised, is based on historical cost, i.e. the past cost of items. In essence it works by tracking and recording all transactions of a company which have a financial value (book-keeping) and then categorizing these transactions into different classes (accounting) such as assets, liabilities, revenue, expenses. The categorizing process usually involves allocating the effect of transactions to different time periods.

As we have seen, financial accounting takes a starting statement of financial position (the balance sheet at the beginning of a year), and during the course of the year all financial transactions are recorded and classified. The classification will involve a first choice between the profit and loss account (revenue and expense from trading operations during the year) and the closing balance sheet (statement of items owned and items owed to third parties). Thus the closing wealth is a summary of the effect of financial transactions of the year past, rather than any independent valuation. The profit and loss account is a summary of trading operations, whose net effect will be to increase or decrease the ending wealth.

The relationship between the profit and loss account and the balance sheet is one that you will need to think about as you progress through the book. Under historical cost, the profit and loss account is the key document where revenue and expenses are stated, while the balance sheet value of assets is a residual of the profit measurement process. From this are deducted claims by third parties (liabilities) and the residual is equity.

This is a long way from an independent measure of value in an economic sense. For example, imagine that you bought shares in a listed company, say IBM, on 1 January for $50,000. During the year you receive dividend payments of $1,000. Under historical cost accounting, you have made a profit of $1,000 for the year, and your ending balance sheet will show assets of $50,000 (investment) and $1,000 (cash). However, it might be that the stock exchange valued your shares on 31 December at $55,000. Using market value as the measurement criterion, you are worth $56,000 (investment and cash), and your gain for the year is $6,000. Different measurement rules give different results, and historical cost accounting uses initial cost as the fundamental measurement criterion and only takes in 'realized' revenues – i.e. where cash or a reliable undertaking to pay cash has been obtained. In the example, the $5,000 gain in market value has not been realized – the shares have not been sold – so historical cost accounting disregards the gain. Of course, if you sold your shares at the end of the year, the gain would be part of your profit for the year – in the jargon the gain had been realized and could therefore be 'recognized'.

Measurement units

Most transactions carried out by a company involve money, and therefore can be translated into money values easily, provided that the basis of the recorded value is the value at which the transaction took place – hence historical cost. In essence, historical cost accounting uses money values to attach labels to economic events. The event of you buying a book becomes in accounting terms (from your perspective): assets: books +$50.00; Cash –$50.00. So the physical item, the specific book with a specific title and content, becomes asset $50.00. While at a personal level you might regard the purchase as an 'expense', from an economic perspective, you presumably bought it in order to use it, therefore it has a utility for you and remains part of your wealth. You have simply chosen to convert a cash asset into a book asset, and under a historical cost convention we say that the accounting value of the book is its cost value, although there are other possible ways of valuing the book (e.g. how much could you sell it for?). This is how accounting works, and when the book has no further use, it should become an expense, but not before. This process is akin to that of language in tying word labels to objects and there are numerous analogies between the process of communicating by accounting and that of communicating by language.

The use of money and historical cost as the measurement base poses two problems: what happens to values that cannot be expressed in financial terms, and what happens when the value of the money itself changes?

Here too we can see the language analogy. There are some concepts that cannot be expressed by language, or indeed some concepts for which there is an expression in one language but not another. In accounting there are some values not expressed – for example, a company may spend a lot of money advertising a new product. If the product is successful its trade name can become quite valuable in itself (Coca-Cola? Nestlé?) but the future sales value of an established trade name does not normally appear in the balance sheet since it was not bought. Similarly, efficient production depends to an extent on harmonious labour relations and good staff training, but neither value is expressed in accounting. It is difficult to say to what extent these omissions matter, but it is necessary to bear them in mind when reviewing balance sheet values. It is necessary to remember that the data is organized on these assumptions and values are not in any sense absolute, but are relative to a framework – change the framework and the values will change too.

The other major problem in historical cost accounting is that of changes in the value of the measuring unit – inflation. The measurement system records a transaction at the nominal value in currency which is paid for that transaction, and takes no account of the change in value of the unit which is being used for measurement. For example, supposing that we were measuring physical size, we could talk about something in terms of centimetres and metres. Two metres of cloth implies exactly the same length of cloth today as it did in 1900, but $5.00 worth of cloth is very much less today than it would have been in 1900 because the value of the dollar, the measuring unit, is much smaller today than it was in 1900.

This means that the values expressed in historical cost accounting may not always be what they appear to be. For example, supposing a bookseller buys for stock a book which cost him $37.50 and retails at $55.00 in 20X1. Over the next three years the publishers, reflecting the inflation of prices generally, increase their wholesale selling price to $45.00 and the retail price to $75.00. If the bookseller has not sold the copy he originally bought, it will appear in his accounts as stock worth $37.50 – the historical cost. But if he wanted to buy another copy it would now cost $45.00. The book itself is virtually the same, it is the underlying value of the measurement unit that has changed (and as a consequence, if the book is sold for $75.00, it is not clear that the difference of $7.50

between the original stock price and the replacement cost of the stock should necessarily be treated as 'profit'). Many attempts have been made to deal with this change in the underlying value of the measurement unit, none so far with any success.

Accounting for transactions

We are now going to focus in on the processes of accounting with a view to establishing a simple model of how accounting works.

The balance sheet equation

One way of approaching this is to look at the company as an artificial and empty vehicle constructed to carry out a particular project; finance is put into the vehicle, and this is used to buy productive capacity (factories, warehouses, vehicles, computers, retail premises, offices etc.). The production unit operates, its output is sold, and profit is generated. The profit belongs to the owners of the company, and they will either take it out of the company as a dividend, or leave it in as additional financing. The accounting unit must track what finance comes into the company and what is done with it and prepare periodic reports to the owners (Figure 3.3).

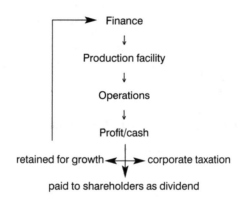

Figure 3.3 Tracking finance

The nature of the vehicle is such that, at the beginning, it can only have as much 'value' as is put into it:

Debt and equity (sources of finance) = Assets (use of finance)

This is called the balance sheet equation, and is usually stated as

Assets (uses of finance) = Debt and equity (sources of finance)

If the company is successful, it will generate value, but this belongs to the owners, and adds to the 'equity' part of the equation; if it is unsuccessful it will diminish the equity:

$$\Delta \text{ Assets} = \Delta \text{ Equity}$$

Respecting this fundamental approach, any accounting transaction must preserve the equilibrium between sources and uses, and will involve either a change in both, or a reallocation within one side of the equation. This is the origin of the term double entry book-keeping: any transaction must be reflected in (at least) two accounts.

Debt and equity

The sources of finance fall into two major categories: the finance put forward by the owners (equity), and the loans and other finance raised from outside which do not attract an ownership share (debt). The distinction between the two is that the owners take on all the risks of loss from the company's activities and gain from all profits, while loans are made purely in return for interest, which must be paid before arriving at any profit for the owners.

The difference between these two categories is fundamental. The suppliers of a loan are entering into a financial commitment with the company where the return they will receive, and therefore the cost to the company, is fixed in relation to the amount borrowed. The amount borrowed must be repaid at a fixed date and the lenders' risk is simply that the company may not have the means to repay (and bankers try to cover this kind of risk by asking for a legal link to company or shareholder assets – 'security' – in the event of default). The lenders' return is not affected by the company's profitability, except in the extreme of the company ceasing to trade.

The owners, on the other hand, are the people with the last claim upon the company's assets. They take the risk that the company will make a loss, but also reap the rewards if the company makes a profit. (The IASC talks about the 'risks and benefits' of ownership.) We can then recognize two basic categories of sources of finance – that deriving from the owner, and that representing financial liabilities to outside people. The owners' interest is variable, because the owners accept final responsibility (remember assets – debt = equity).

Constructing a balance sheet

Let us take a practical example to illustrate how that works out. We will do this using a simple spreadsheet, and we will continue to use this spreadsheet as a means of analysing accounting transactions. As indicated before, this is not how a book-keeper or accounting software would make the entries; it does, though, reproduce the principles behind the book-keeping, which are what are important. It is intended to simplify the learning process and put emphasis on the substance of the process rather than the form.

Note that the spreadsheet can have as many or as few rows as seems useful, but that overall it must be organized into two parts: assets and finance, and that, as the analysis proceeds, it is probably useful to split the assets side into 'cash' (i.e. bank account in accounting terms) and other assets, while other assets might equally split into short-term trading items and long-term ones (current and fixed assets). The financing side can also usefully be split between debt and equity, with debt subdividing into long-term debt and trading liabilities, and equity into initial shareholders' capital and profits.

$$\text{Assets} = \text{Debt and equity}$$

$$\text{Cash} + \text{Current} + \text{Fixed} = (\text{Long-term debt} + \text{Trading liabilities}) + (\text{Share capital} + \text{Profit})$$

Example: supposing three friends decided to form a company (called Reliable Runner SA) which would sell cars. Jane put in $20,000, Alan put in $15,000 and Colin put in $15,000.

	1	2	3	4	*Situation*
Assets					
Cash	+20000 +15000 +15000	+30000	–55000	–18000	7000
Receivables					
Stock				+18000	18000
Property			+55000		55000
Total	+50000	+30000	0	0	80000
Liabilities/ Equity					
Long-term debt		+30000			30000
Payables					
Equity:					
Shares	+20000 +15000 +15000				50000
Profit					
Total	+50000	+30000	0	0	80000

1. The initial financing, assuming the money was paid into a bank account, would be accounted for by showing (a) the (historical cost) value of money in the bank, and (b) the (historical cost) value of the shareholders' capital.

2. Next, the company obtained a bank loan for $30,000. Let us assume that this money is put into the company's current account, so we have a similar transaction, increase in cash assets, increase in financing, but this time it is debt financing. The company now has total assets, all cash, of $80,000, while it has equity of $50,000 and liabilities of $30,000.

3. Its next step is to buy a small office with a car lot for $55,000. Up until now we have been looking at transactions which affected both sides of the balance sheet equation, but the new transaction will affect one side only. The company is exchanging one asset, cash, for another asset, property. The total value it owns will remain the same, but the composition of the value will be different. Reliable Runner SA now has assets worth $80,000 in the form of property and cash, while it has liabilities of $30,000 (loan from the bank) and equity of $50,000 (owners' initial capital subscribed).

4. The next move is to acquire some stock for trading, and the company buys $18,000 of second-hand cars for cash (i.e. by issuing a cheque – cash is usually used in accounting to mean liquid funds available immediately at the bank, not necessarily physical cash). Here again there is a swap between cash assets and other forms of asset – this time a current asset, stock or inventory. It is assumed in accounting that stocks (which may be goods for resale, but also raw materials and work in progress) will be sold in less than one year. Of course the longer the stock turnover period the more financing is required by the company, and hence the emphasis in modern management of 'just in time' stocks.

The company is ready to start trading. If we drew up a balance sheet at this point (drawn from the company's accounting database above, it would look like this:

Assets		Financing	
Fixed assets		*Equity*	
Tangible	55000	Share capital	50000
Current assets		*Liabilities*	
Stock	18000	LT debt	30000
Bank	7000		
	80000		80000

Now we are ready to start trading and see what is the effect of trading on the balance sheet equation.

The owners' interest, or equity, represents initially the finance put into the company by the shareholders. That finance can be increased at any time during the company's life by the issue of new shares, but aside from that, it changes regularly as a result of the company's trading activities. The shareholders are the ultimate recipients of the wealth generated or lost by the company. They bear all the risks of the company – if the company fails they will lose their investment, but they are also the people who benefit if the company is successful.

Gains or losses can arise in two main ways: first, through the trading activities of the company (any trading profit or loss will accrue to the benefit or cost of shareholders); second, through changes in the underlying values of the assets. For example, if a company has investments, and the value of these rises, then the shareholders own the increase in underlying values. An important difference between these two types of gain is that classical accounting only recognizes gains when they have been validated by a sale transaction (in the jargon, the gain must have been *realized* in order to be *recognized*). Consequently, many companies have value gains in their assets which are not reflected in the balance sheet (one form of hidden reserve). Trading activities though, by definition, involve a series of completed transactions.

If we concentrate on the trading activities, it follows that as the shareholders are the ultimate recipients of any losses or profits, then trading activities will have the effect of increasing or decreasing the shareholders' equity – in this sense, the profit and loss account is simply a summary of the trading transactions which have occurred during a period, and is drawn up to explain the net change during a period in the value of the equity. (This linkage between the profit and loss account and the balance sheet is known as the *iteration* between the two, and is a central building block of financial reporting.)

Let us now move on to seeing how the trading transaction works in a balance sheet context.

	Situation A	5	6	7	*Situation B*
Assets					
Cash	7000	(a) +5000			11750
		(c) −250			
Debtor			(a) +7000		7000
Stock	18000	(b) −4000	(b) −5500	+12000	20500
Property	55000				55000
Total	80000	+750	+1500	+12000	94250
Liabilities/ Equity					
Long-term debt	30000				30000
Trade creditor				+12000	12000
Equity:					
Share capital	50000				50000
Profit		(a) +5000	(a) +7000		2250
		(b) −4000	(b) −5500		
		(c) −250			
Total	80000	+750	+1500	+12000	94250

5. In our example, if a car was sold for $5,000 cash, we should be able to record the acquisition of a new asset ($5,000 cash) and also show an increase in equity of $5,000 (transaction 5a on the spreadsheet).

The sale increases the value of the owners' equity and the cash received increases the assets of the company. However, we have so far failed to record the other aspect of the transaction: the fact that we have given up part of our stock. We need to record the reduction of our assets by one vehicle. We have gained a cash asset of $5,000, but we have given up a car asset, which in this case we had previously bought for $4,000 (part of our stock of $18,000, which amount we need for profit measurement purposes to have allocated across the individual cars concerned – which could bring in an element of subjectivity). The real effect of the transaction is to create a profit of $1,000, and this is reflected in the accounts by *expensing* the stock against the sale. We cancel the stock value of the car sold by deducting this from the sale. In our balance sheet equation, we reduce stock by $4,000 and reduce profit by $4,000 (transaction 5b).

This highlights the relationship between assets and expenses. When a company pays its electricity bill it is easy to see that the expenditure involved relates to something which has already been consumed in the business – the electrical energy. The payment therefore involves an immediate expense in the trading operations of the company. It represents a value consumed. However, when a company makes a payment – as in the case of the acquisition of the car stock in our example – the transaction is not always an expense. The car stock represented an economic value which will be consumed in the future by the company and remains in the balance sheet until it is consumed. And that is what has now happened in the case of the car sale above: an asset has been consumed; turned into an expense ('expensed') as a trading transaction by the company.

Many assets represent simply a store of future economic value to be consumed by a business. Clearly a stock of goods for resale is going to be seen to be consumed relatively quickly. But in the same way, assets such as equipment are used up over a period, albeit several years, and are consumed in the business. Equally, when a company pays in advance for something like insurance or rent, the expenditure is made initially to acquire a future benefit. That benefit expires as the company moves through the time period for which it paid in advance – the asset becomes an expense through the economic benefits being consumed by the company.

We should therefore distinguish between expenditure – where the company simply pays out money – and the classification of that expenditure as an expense of an accounting period or as an asset to appear in the end-period balance sheet and be carried forward to become an expense in a future period.

Returning to the car example, let us also imagine that, as the new owner was driving away, a wing mirror fell off. The company arranged for a nearby repair shop to replace this and carry out one or two other minor repairs. Reliable Runner SA paid the repair shop $250 for this work. That expenditure would also be an expense since the car has been sold (transaction 5c).

During the course of the series of transactions we have just finished describing, the accounting value of the company has changed several times, so any balance sheet which we might have drawn up would also have changed as the transactions progressed. The net change in the equity over the period is, of course, the profit which has been made by the company during that period. Normally this would be analysed in the profit and loss account and only the net change shown in the published balance sheet within equity. A company can draw up a profit and loss account as often as it wishes; most companies do this monthly for internal management purposes, as well as annually for official reporting to shareholders and tax authorities.

Credit transactions

All the transactions which we have made so far have involved an exchange of cash. However, in business many transactions are made on credit, with the cash exchange following sometime later. The accounting treatment of such transactions follows exactly the same ideas which we have already explored: if a business sells some goods on credit, it gives up one asset in exchange for another, but where the asset received was cash in the earlier example, in a credit transaction the asset received will be a promise to pay. That promise or debt is just as valuable as the cash, as long as there is an expectation that the person who owes the debt will pay in due course (and why would you give credit in the first place if you were not sure you would be paid?). The account created is known as a debtor (a receivable in US accounting terminology).

Suppose that Reliable Runner SA sells another car, this time for $7,000, and allows the customer credit. The transaction would appear in the balance sheet equation as an increase in equity and an increase in a new form of current asset, the debtor (transaction 6a in the spreadsheet). Let us say the allocated cost of the car sold was $5,500 so we have acknowledged through the balance sheet equation the expensing of another car from our stock (transaction 6b).

Businesses also receive short-term credit from their suppliers – assets are purchased or other expenses incurred in exchange for a promise to pay in due course. In essence this is a transaction very similar to the bank loan, with the difference that the finance is normally available only for a short period, so would be presented differently on the balance sheet. A credit supply consists of the receipt by a business of goods or services against a liability to pay later. The supplier and the debt which is owed are described as trade creditors (payables in US accounting terminology).

If our company now decided that it should expand its car stock and bought two more cars for $12,000 but this time on credit, the company should record an increase in assets – the additional car stock, and an increase in financing – the short-term credit given by the supplier (transaction 7). (There is no limit to the number of rows which might be used – we are constrained slightly by the size of the printed page, but generally one would have as many rows as seemed useful in terms of enabling a relevant and efficient analysis of the figures into a profit and loss account and balance sheet.)

If we were to draw up a profit and loss account for the whole period since the commencement of the business, it would now look like this:

	$	$
Sales		12,000
Expenses		
Cars	9,500	
Repairs	250	9,750
Net income		2,250

The balance sheet at the end of the period would look like this:

	Assets		Liabilities
	$		$
Assets		**Financing**	
Fixed assets		Equity	
Tangibles	55,000	Share capital	50,000
Current assets		Profit for the year	2,250
Stock	20,500	*Liabilities*	
Debtor	7,000	LT Debt	30,000
Bank	11,750	Trade creditor	12,000
	94,250		94,250

This series of transactions represents the essence of how accounting tracks and reflects a company's financing and its operations. Essentially the balance sheet is a financial model of the company – but based on the money value of transactions which have taken place. The profit and loss account is an analysis of the wealth-creating (or wealth diminishing!) activities of the company. The profit and loss account can be drawn up for any period, but is generally drawn up for one year for external reporting purposes and in businesses of any size, at least once a month for internal management purposes. Equally a balance sheet can be drawn up at any moment, but is published once a year for shareholders and others, while it is produced internally at least quarterly for management purposes.

The spreadsheet represents the company's accounting database. In reality this will consist of potentially hundreds of 'accounts' – data files – which are constantly being updated as the accounting department tracks the company's transactions and indeed participates in them with issuing invoices to clients, paying suppliers and so on. The balance sheet is in fact a highly aggregated summary of the data files in the accounting database, and corresponds exactly with that database. The profit and loss account is also an aggregation of those data files which deal with the company's operations for a specific period. They represent a more detailed analysis than is provided by the one-line profit entry in the balance sheet.

You can see in the above example how (a) the balance sheet is a presentation of the latest position in the company's accounting database, and (b) how the profit and loss account is an analytical document which gives the detail behind the net change in equity over the period (but excluding any new capital introduced by investors or dividends paid to them).

You should also note that the increase in company cash during the trading period (transactions 5–7) was $4,750, while the profit was $2,250. This is generally the case in accruals accounting, since we are trying to present an economic assessment and while this translates itself into cash flows in the end, there are timing differences. In this case we can reconcile the two as follows:

Profit as calculated	2,250
Value of stock consumed (paid earlier)	9,500
Amount owed by credit customer (will be received later)	–7,000
Change in cash during this period	+4,750

We will build on this model in subsequent chapters to see how it deals with more complex transactions and situations. But all the essentials of how accounting tracks company operations are contained in the above example. If you get stuck later on, you should always come back to this introduction to refresh your understanding of how accounting records company activity.

Summary

In this chapter we have taken a major step forward in looking at the technical basis of accounting. This has involved looking at the basic conventions of accounting, particularly historical cost as the valuation base, but also conventions such as accruals (accounts try to record all economic events affecting the company when they take place, not just cash movements), matching, going concern (allocations of costs to future periods are only valid if we think the company is going to continue to exist), and consistency (the comparability of data is limited if the basis on which it is prepared changes over time).

We then looked at the accounting database and its fundamental concepts that accounting information records both where finance came from and what was done with it (the balance sheet equation) and that therefore all movements within the database will involve at least two changes, since they must deal with both sources and uses of finance (double entry). We used a spreadsheet as a model of the accounting database and plotted a series of transactions through it. As a result we were able to prepare a profit and loss account and balance sheet from the database.

Questions

1. Jennifer decides that she will go into the tourist industry on Lake Geneva, and buy a concession to hire out canoes on the lake. She borrows CHF40,000 from her parents and puts in CHF20,000 herself. The arrangement with the Canton is that she pays CHF50,000 at the start for the concession, which runs five years, but must also pay an annual rental of CHF10,000 at the end of the season in October.

    She negotiates a deal with a canoe supplier, who sells her 20 canoes for CHF30,000, but agrees that she should pay CHF15,000 on delivery and the rest a year later.

During the season she receives CHF90,000 (cash) in canoe rentals.

Making (and specifying) whatever assumptions you wish, you are asked to draw up a simple income statement for the first year and balance sheet at the end of the year.

2. James, on completing his MBA, sees a possibility to make a profit selling computers. He has the opportunity to buy a job lot of computers for $50,000, and he can buy a shop lease with two years to run for $5,000 and pay an annual rent of $6,000. He happens just to have inherited $60,000, so he starts a company and puts the money in as share capital.

   During the first year, he sells $30,000 of computers for $45,000. During the second year he sells no computers at all, and at the end of the year he sells the remaining stock for $1,000 and liquidates the company.

   1. Calculate his accounting profit for each of the two years of operations.
   2. Explain why the assumptions made at the end of the first year led to the wrong profit estimate.
   3. What are the consequences of the assumptions which proved to be incorrect?

3. George and Val set up a company together to trade as decorators. George owns a three-year-old van which he puts into the company instead of cash for share capital. Val puts in $2,000 in cash and they agree the van is worth $2,000. They have no premises as such; materials are stored in their home garage or left in the van. In the first month of business the following transactions take place:

   (a) They get an order worth $600 to decorate a small flat. The customer pays $300 in advance.
   (b) They buy materials worth $125 on credit from Tottenham Building Merchants which are used in this job.
   (c) When the job is finished the customer pays a further $100 but says they will have to wait another month for the balance of $200.
   (d) They get an order to decorate a large house for $1,200 plus materials. They buy $270 of materials on credit from the same builders' merchants.
   (e) At the end of the month they have done 80 per cent of the work on the house painting order and they pay themselves $500 each as salary.

   Prepare a spreadsheet to show the transactions and then draw up an profit and loss account for the month and a balance sheet as at the end of the month.

   Next month:

   (f) They complete the house job and receive $1,200 from the customer plus $270 for the materials.
   (g) They get a job painting some shop premises – the price is $500 including materials. They buy materials on credit from the usual supplier for $80.
   (h) They complete the job and receive $500 cash.
   (i) The next contract is to decorate a flat and they agree to do the job for $800 plus materials. They obtain $180 of materials, but the supplier says that they must clear their outstanding account before he will release the goods. They pay what was due at the end of the previous month.
   (j) The van breaks down and is repaired for $90 which is paid in cash.

(k) They complete the job and bill the customer for $980. The customer pays $600 and offers to pay the balance plus $20 interest if they will wait two months for it.

(l)   They visit their first client because he hasn't paid the $200 outstanding, but he is not available and a neighbour tells them that he has just gone bankrupt.

(m) They do no further business that month, and pay themselves $500 each as salary at the end of the month.

Update the spreadsheet and then draw up a profit and loss account for the month and a balance sheet as at the end of the month.

4 Accruals accounting

In this chapter we go into the detail of how to apply accruals accounting in practice. We will look at credit transactions and the timing of transactions for accounting purposes as well as the issue of how items of stock are transferred to the profit and loss account.

In the last chapter we looked at the balance sheet equation, how that works as the basis of the company's accounting database, and how the company's transactions are captured and recorded within that database. In short, we dealt with the basic approach to accounting measurement. In this chapter and the next one we are going to go into this in more detail, with a view to reaching the point where you can prepare basic financial statements, given a listing from the database and information about the surrounding circumstances. It is important that you should know the relationship between the database and the financial statements which are published using its data, and that you should feel comfortable with the contents of the balance sheet and profit and loss account.

Accruals basis of accounting

So far we have largely confined ourselves to looking at transactions in which articles were bought and sold for cash, but the real world of commercial trading includes many transactions where cash changes hands at a different moment from that where the item or service is provided; also, the classification of an item within a company's accounting system sometimes changes when the item is used up in the company's activities. To be useful, accounting needs to capture all the economic events that occur in a company, when they take place, and the cash movement is usually only a part of the picture. The profit and loss account gives a picture of a company's trading position over a period of time (for published accounts the relevant period is one year). In essence that is a simple enough concept, but examined in detail it poses questions as to which transactions of a company are properly taken in as being 'trading' and which transactions belong to which accounting period. In answering this question, accountants may well have to make allocations of expenses and revenues between different accounting periods, which brings in another subjective element in the preparation of financial statements.

To illustrate the point, let us imagine two cases: a company makes up its profit and loss account for the year to 31 December. In example (a) it takes delivery of five washing machines, cost $300 each, on 15 December, and pays the supplier on 31 January. The machines are sold for $400 each during the first week of January.

In example (b) the company obtains the washing machines on 15 December, pays in January, but sells the machines on credit on 20 December and receives payment in January.

Given that the months of December and January fall into different accounting periods, how should we deal with each set of transactions as far as the profit and loss account goes?

In example (a) the machines were acquired by the company in December, but paid for in January. Should they appear in the company's accounting statements in December or January, and in what way should they appear (in accounting terms, how should they be 'recognized')? Should they be recognized as an expense in the profit and loss account for the year ended in December?

In example (b) the company received the goods and made the sale in December, but it paid for the goods and received the money for the sale in January. If we tie the goods and the sale together and put them in the same profit and loss account, should they go in the December figures, or the January ones?

In order to resolve the dilemma we should go back to first principles. What is the purpose of the information given in a company's financial statements? The answer is to provide useful information for investors and creditors. If we put the expense in one profit and loss account and the revenue (the sale) in another, we are not actually recording the profit on the transaction within one profit and loss account, so the usefulness of both statements is impaired.

The IASC *Framework for the Preparation and Presentation of Financial Statements* says the following about accruals:

> *In order to meet their objectives, financial statements are prepared on the accrual basis of accounting. Under this basis, the effects of transactions and other events are recognised when they occur (and not as cash or its equivalent is received or paid) and they are recorded in the accounting periods to which they relate. Financial statements prepared on the accrual basis inform users not only of past transactions involving the payment and receipt of cash but also of obligations to pay cash in the future and of resources that represent cash to be received in the future. Hence, they provide the type of information about past transactions and other events that is most useful to users in making economic decisions.*

Using these principles we can resolve our two examples. First, the revenue and the expense relating to the same transaction should be recognized in the same accounting period, and that is the period when the transaction took place. When the washing machines were delivered the company was free to dispose of them in any way it wished up until the point where a customer agreed to buy them. The company possessed the washing machines from the time of delivery, so they should be recognized at the point of delivery, and a debt was owed to the supplier from that time, so that too should be recognized. However, the company had not disposed of the machines, so they would be recognized as part of its wealth, an asset, up to the point of sale. They should therefore appear in example (a) as an asset in the balance sheet at 31 December. In January the sale took place: the machines are no longer available to the company and change status from an asset to an expense at the moment of sale. Payment of the supplier subsequently can be seen as settlement of a balance sheet liability, just like the payment of any kind of debt.

In example (b) the customers agreed to buy the machines in December, but paid in January, so when did the transaction take place? The trading transaction took place at the moment when each customer agreed to buy the machine – legally the machine was theirs and the company selling the machine no longer had the right to dispose of it, and the customer had a legal obligation to pay the agreed purchase price. In example (b) the customers did not pay until January, but this did not affect the ownership rights of either party and in economic terms the deferral of the cash settlement is simply the selling company in effect making a loan for a period. The revenue from the sale relates to the moment the sale transaction took place, even though the cash receipt occurred at another time. In short, we can recognize a series of different states:

1. The company acquires the washing machines (an asset). It could exchange another asset (cash) for the machines but is allowed to defer the cash settlement which creates a debt to the supplier (establishes a creditor – a liability).
2. Some time later the company extinguishes the liability by payment of cash.
3. The company sells the washing machines, but again instead of taking a cash asset in exchange, it accepts a debt asset (the customer's promise to pay).
4. Later the customer settles the debt, cancelling the debtor in the company's balance sheet in exchange for an increase in cash assets.

Of the four different elements which can be seen above, only part 3 relates to the profit and loss account, all the others are changes in balance sheet components. In our example (b) no cash changes hands in either direction when the trading transaction takes place, and this is a central element of profit measurement through the accounting system – trading transactions are identified according to when they objectively take place, not according to when cash changes hands.

In many cases it is relatively easy to determine what is the point of delivery, but some cases require careful thought – for example, where goods are delivered (or services provided) over a relatively long time period. A ship may take several years to build – does the ship-building company only recognize revenue when the ship is actually handed over to the customer? A legal case may take many months going through the courts – does a solicitor only recognize the revenue in the accounting year when the case is settled?

In both examples it would be normal for the client to make payment in a series of instalments, but if the cash value of the instalments were taken to revenue, that would not be an objective assessment of what had been supplied. Usually such questions can be determined by making a professional valuation of the amount of work done within the single accounting period and using that as a base for allocating revenue, irrespective of cash payments.

Revenue recognition

Revenue is the money value of goods and services supplied, which is attributable to the current accounting period. The aggregate value for revenue in an accounting period is usually described as 'sales' or 'turnover'. Revenue is usually attributed to the accounting period in which goods are delivered to the customer or a service is rendered. In other words, revenue is recognized at the point of delivery of the goods or service.

There is another area of accounting recognition which is closely related, and this is the recognition within one accounting period of expenses which have not yet been invoiced and where supply is on a continuing basis, such as the supply of electricity and telephone. No physical delivery takes place, and unless invoicing to the company using these facilities coincides exactly with the company's accounting period there will be some adjustment required to ensure that this kind of expense is also properly allocated to the appropriate accounting period. It is worth mentioning here that there are transactions which are time based and not necessarily transaction based. Rent of premises is an obvious example where the cost is incurred irrespective of whether any physical use is made of the premises or not.

In this chapter we are focusing on matching transactions in order to recognize them in the appropriate time period. We shall now go on to review how this problem is handled within the accounting system. We can break this down into three related areas:

1. ordinary trade transactions on credit;
2. transactions where invoicing takes place periodically after the goods or services have been consumed;
3. recognition of changed status where an asset is sold and therefore becomes an expense.

Generally speaking, credit transactions are such an integral part of day-to-day trading activities that the data recording system is designed to track these transactions as soon as they occur. On the other hand, the other two types are frequently not built into the data collection system automatically, and involve the preparer of financial statements in adjusting the figures produced by the recording system.

Credit transactions

The purchase of goods for resale by a company, and the sale of goods by the company, frequently take place on credit, i.e. cash settlement follows after delivery, often with a delay of 30 to 60 days. Any trading company, as part of its management of cash resources, will try to obtain the maximum credit from suppliers of goods and give the minimum credit to customers. Of course the offer of generous credit terms is one of the weapons which can be used in marketing a company's products, and is a point of tension between financial management and marketing. Equally, the correct assessment of the creditworthiness of customers is vital.

This kind of trading generally takes place in an environment where suppliers and customers have a continuing relationship with each other and regularly trade, and is known as trading on 'open account'. That is, a supplier company knows its customer well, knows the customer's reliability as regards ultimate payment and is therefore willing to supply goods on a simple understanding that the customer will pay. No special agreement is necessary for credit to be given on any particular order; there is a continuing flow of orders, goods and payment.

In terms of accounting, we need to consider the two separate aspects of this: the purchase of goods on credit, and the sale of goods on credit.

When goods are purchased on credit, the company buying is gaining a new asset, but instead of exchanging the new stock asset for a cash asset, the company is acquiring a new liability as the other half of the exchange. In terms of the balance sheet equation the supplier of the goods is making a loan (albeit very short term) to the company:

$$\text{Assets} = \text{Liabilities} + \text{Equity}$$
$$+ \text{Stock } \$100 = + \text{Debt to supplier } \$100$$

Later on, when the company settles its debt to the supplier, it will cancel the short-term liability with an exchange for cash:

$$- \text{Cash } \$100 = - \text{Debt settlement } \$100$$

	1	2	Final
Assets			
Cash		−100	−100
Stock	+100		+100
Liabilities			
Suppliers	+100	−100	0

In the long run, the stock asset is being acquired in exchange for a cash asset, but in the short run there are two stages in the transaction: (1) the acquisition of the asset together with a debt to the supplier, and (2) the cancellation of the debt against a cash payment.

The stage 1 recognition of the stock and liability to the supplier means that the recording system will always be able to give an up-to-date picture of the amounts owed to suppliers, and the amounts acquired for stock, and will avoid the time delay in recognition which would occur under a system that only recognized cash transactions.

In terms of operating details, of course a company usually has many suppliers, and while for a picture of the company's financial state of affairs the only important number would be the total owed short term to suppliers (representing something which it will shortly be necessary to settle in cash), for internal management purposes the company also needs to know how much is owed to each individual supplier.

What is often done, therefore, is that the nominal ledger carries an account which aggregates all the amounts owed to suppliers, but the company keeps a separate ledger which duplicates the movements on the total supplier account but holds a separate account for each supplier. Suppliers who provide goods on credit are called 'creditors' and so this subsidiary ledger is often called the *creditors' ledger*, although it is also known in some companies as the *bought ledger* or *purchases ledger*. In the US this would be the *payables*. Again, although we describe this as a ledger, it is unlikely to be a book, but rather a computer file storing the details on disk and displaying management information on a screen or printing a hard-copy analysis of balances as required.

Definition of creditor

A creditor is an individual or another company to whom the firm owes money.

Examples of creditors:

- *Trade creditors*: Suppliers of raw materials, other stocks, equipment and services which are purchased in the course of business for resale, for which payment has not yet been made.
- *Other creditors*: Amounts owing to outsiders for various other reasons, such as interest payable; usually routine recurring debts for services and supplies ancillary to trading operations.

The EU formats for published balance sheets require that a distinction is made between amounts due for settlement within twelve months, and amounts due for settlement in more than twelve months. Trade creditors would nearly always be for settlement in substantially less than twelve months.

Sales on credit

The sale of goods on credit involves exactly the same type of transaction, but viewed from the opposite side. A company which sells on credit similarly needs to recognize the sale and the debt owed to it by its customer. The credit customer is known as a *debtor* for accounting purposes, because he or she owes a debt to the company.

Looking at the balance sheet equation, the company wants to recognize a sale (revenue which will increase the value of equity) and an asset (a debt which is a promise to pay cash to the company):

Assets   = Liabilities + Equity
+ Debtor $200   =   + Revenue $200

Subsequently the debtor will settle the cash owed to the company, and this becomes an exchange between one asset (the promise to pay) and cash:

– Debtor 200
+ Cash $200

	1	2	Final
Assets			
Cash		+200	+200
Debtors	+200	–200	0
Equity			
Profit and loss			
Sales	+200		+200

In the nominal ledger a company would keep an aggregate account of all debts owed by customers, but here again the operating convenience of managing debtors is best served by a further subsidiary ledger in which all debtors have an individual, personal account. This subsidiary record is called the *debtors' ledger* or *sales ledger* while in the US it would be known as the *receivables ledger*.

As with the recording of creditors, the system is tracking the daily transactions of the company and therefore reflecting properly the full current financial state of affairs. In other words, the significance of the accruals principle is that the accounts reflect the real changes that have affected the firm's assets, liabilities, revenue and expenses, even though the cash has not changed hands.

The cumulative effect of the entries in the accounts which have just been described is that at the accounting date, the nominal ledger shows the total amount owed to suppliers (with supporting detail in the creditor's ledger) and the amount receivable from customers.

The sales ledger function within the financial accounting unit of a company should use the data to monitor the amount of credit given to clients and the period of credit allowed. The data in the ledgers is useful not only in terms of constantly updating the picture of the company's profits and losses but also in managing credit effectively and reducing the risk of non-payment. The data in the creditors, payables or bought ledger similarly monitors overall liabilities and costs, but also permits of managing supplier accounts to take the maximum period of credit negotiated, making payments at due dates and checking supplier invoices against the delivery information. Both debtors ledger and creditors ledger should be exploited to manage the company's finances and to operate internal controls.

Stocks and profit measurement

The second part of the routine capturing of economic transactions within the system and matching revenue to costs is the treatment of stock. As we have seen, when a company buys goods to resell (or manufactures goods to resell, which we will also look at in this chapter) their value is treated as an asset by the company (i.e an item which will generate future positive cash flows for the company). But when the goods are actually sold, this cash flow is realized and the cost of the good has to be set against it – the stock has to be 'expensed'.

First we should note that in American English the term is inventory, and stock means shares in a company. Let us start just with an assumption that the business buys finished goods for resale, so that we only have one category of stock which is not processed in any way by the company.

The value of this stock has a key role to play in the measurement of profit. The cost of goods sold, or 'cost of sales', is the amount paid by the retailer to buy the goods which are deemed to have been sold in the current accounting period. The difference between the sales revenue and the cost of sales is known as gross profit, or gross margin, and is an important piece of data which can be used by management as a test of a company's efficiency, and represents the amount available to a company to meet its operating expenses. The gross margin of two businesses of the same size and selling the same goods should be comparable, and any difference is worth investigation.

The cost of sales is the amount paid by the company for its supplies of goods sold in the accounting period. When goods are bought for resale they become an asset – stock – which is subsequently expensed when the goods are actually sold. For profit measurement purposes a value has to be arrived at for the cost of the goods sold. Of course this might be done by expensing each item when the transaction takes place, and some systems operate that way. But in practical terms, this is often not worthwhile except where the company sells a very small number of items of high value – say, Rolls-Royce cars, Rolex watches etc. Usually the measurement may be made just as accurately in terms of the cost for the year (or for a month or a week) by simply calculating the value of goods available for resale during the year and then deducting those which are on hand at the end of the year:

Stock available at 1/1/X1	XXX
plus goods purchased during year	XXX
Goods available for resale in 20X1	XXX
less cost of stock on hand 31/12/X1	XXX
= Cost of goods sold during year	XXX

Within the data collection system, there are various ways of handling the stock and purchases of goods for resale (or for that matter, transfers into finished goods from the manufacturing process). The simplest way is to leave the opening stock account untouched, and accumulate acquisitions of finished goods in a 'purchases' account. Logically, purchases are made to replenish stocks of goods which have been sold, so in a broad sense, purchases could be expected to approximate to cost of goods sold over a period. At the point where one wants an accurate measure, one measures stock currently on hand and compares this with the opening stock value. Any difference is then adjusted against purchases. Supposing opening stock was $2,400, purchases during the period were $5,000 and stock at the end was $2,600, the adjustment would be to reduce purchases by $200, which is the increase in stock, and add that to the existing stock figure.

A more formal way of doing things is to move the opening stock into the cost of goods sold or similar account, and then remove the closing stock at the end of the period. The procedures are not really something you need to worry about. As with many things in accounting there are several different ways of doing it, and the company decides in the light of its information needs. For the purposes of exercises within this book, we will always use the method whereby the stock remains in a separate account and is adjusted at the end of the measurement period.

Taking a practical example, let us say that a company started the year with a stock of goods for resale which had cost $3,000. During the year it receives further deliveries: April $5,000, July $5,000 and November $6,000. The total value of goods available for sale in 20X1 was $19,000. Supposing that during the year-end stock-take it was recorded that the goods still on hand had an original purchase cost of $4,500, the cost of sales figure derived ($14,500) will appear in the profit and loss account. Supposing that the sales revenue in this case was $25,000, the profit and loss account would then show:

	$
Sales	25,000
Cost of sales	(14,500)
Gross profit	10,500

But note that the published profit and loss account might also be presented:

Materials purchased	16,000	Sales	25,000
Gross profit	10,500	Increase in stocks	1,500
	26,500		26,500

In terms of the company's accounting database, the adjustment would appear as follows:

	Closing balances	Stock adjustment	Income statement	Balance sheet
Assets				
Stock	3,000	+1,500		4,500
Financing				
Sales	25,000		25,000	
Purchases	−16,000	+1,500	−14,500	
Profit	10,500			

Calculation of stock value

You may be able to see at once that the question of the stock flow and valuation has critical importance in determining the profit of any particular accounting period, and has implications for other accounting periods. The closing stock at the end of the period is a component in determining the cost of sales (and therefore gross margin) for two periods: the one ending with that stock measurement, and the one beginning with that stock measurement.

This can probably best be seen with an example. Let us suppose that a company in its first two years of trading has the following figures:

	Year 1 $	Year 2 $
Sales	20,000	25,000
Purchases	17,000	21,000
Closing stock value		
	(a) 2,000	4,000
	(b) 3,000	

As you see, we have included two alternative stock figures at the end of year 1: figure (a), $2,000, is the one the owner has calculated, but the auditor thinks the owner has undervalued the stock and proposes figure (b), $3,000. The company was sold at the end of year 2, with a stock figure of $4,000 agreed by all parties. We have computed the gross profit for the two years, using the owner's and the auditor's stock figures as at the end of year 1:

Year 1

	Using stock (a) owner's view $	Stock (b) auditor's view $
Sales	20,000	20,000
Cost of sales		
Opening stock	0	0
Purchases	17,000	17,000
Goods available	17,000	17,000
Closing stock	(2,000)	(3,000)
Cost of sales	15,000	14,000
Gross margin	5,000	6,000
Gross margin to sales ratio	25%	30%

Year 2

Sales	25,000	25,000
Cost of sales		
Opening stock	2,000	3,000
Purchases	21,000	21,000
Goods available	23,000	24,000
Closing stock	(4,000)	(4,000)
Cost of sales	19,000	20,000
Gross margin	6,000	5,000
Gross margin to sales ratio	24%	20%

If you study the figures it will become apparent that where the closing stock at the end of year 1 had a higher value – column (b) – the gross profit was higher than (a), reflecting the impact of stock on the cost of sales measurement. But the closing stock is carried forward to become the opening stock in year 2, and since it was higher in (b) than (a), the cost of sales in year 2 for (b) is higher than for (a), so reversing the year 1 position. By looking at the gross margin percentages you can also see how the stock figure can distort the measurement of performance.

Of course, if you add the results for the two years together, you will find that the gross profit in aggregate is the same:

	(a) $	(b) $
Year 1	5,000	6,000
Year 2	6,000	5,000
2 year aggregate	11,000	11,000

So you can see that over the complete life cycle of the firm, the stock measure will have no importance; total profits will be the same. The importance of the stock measure is that it allocates cost between years, and therefore allocates profit between years. Companies trying to minimize profits (say for tax purposes) would be inclined to undervalue stock, while those trying to maximize profit would maximize stock valuation.

Your response to this may be that the whole question is irrelevant in that the value of the stock is surely something which can be empirically proved: you have ten items in stock and purchase invoices show that these ten cost $X each, so the closing stock value is $10X. In practice companies can rarely identify individual items of stock against the purchase price – nor for that matter would they necessarily find it worth the time and effort to identify individual purchases even if it were possible.

There is also the question of changing prices. In times of inflation, prices are generally changing, although rarely in step with one another, and in a global economy many items are sourced in different currencies. The prices of some items, particularly those reflecting rapid technological change or linked to prime commodities such as oil, coffee beans, wheat, etc., or priced in another currency, can fall dramatically or fluctuate quite widely in a short time. It follows that the prices a retailer will pay for items coming into stock will not normally be level or uniform during any one accounting period.

If identification of individual items is not possible, and prices are not stable, we are left with the major problem of how to ascribe a cost to stock on hand at the end of the year (or of any other accounting period).

The solution to this problem is that, since individual costs cannot normally be attached to individual items, the accounting measurement can be determined by using assumptions about stock movements, which need not necessarily coincide exactly with the actual stock movements, since we cannot be certain about the movement of individual items. Indeed, accounting principles such as prudence may call for valuation approaches which differ from physical stock flow patterns. Later in this session we will go on to look at the various methods available to ascribe an accounting cost to stock using various assumptions about stock utilization patterns.

Relevant costs

The allocation of purchase price to individual items is not the only problem, though. We must also consider whether the purchase price is in itself the appropriate reflection of the stock asset. There are two considerations here: on the one hand, prudence demands that we do not use a stock measure which overstates the value of the stock, and on the other hand, we should consider whether we have added any value to the goods since they were first purchased.

There is a risk of overstating stock values when prices fluctuate rapidly. For example, a British importer of a commodity, such as oil, may have ordered 1m tonnes at $28.00, while the £/$ exchange rate was £1 = $1.20, giving rise to a historical cost of £2.34m. Assuming that the oil was held in stock, but that the £/$ rate moved to £1 = $1.50, although the price of oil in dollars might remain fixed, the market value of the lm tonnes in sterling would drop from £2.34m to £1.87m. Is it then reasonable to continue to value the stock at £2.34m? Accounting principles usually require that if an asset is held for resale and its historical cost exceeds the market value (this is usually called the 'net realizable value' – that is, what the company could obtain by selling the stock at the market price, less any selling costs), the value should be 'written down' (i.e. reduced) to reflect the unrealized loss.

The other side of the valuation question, additions to value, is perhaps rather more difficult to pin down. It may be that in most cases a retailer, for example, buys goods wholesale, puts them on display and sells them, without in any way changing them. But if the retailer is involved in any costs which improve the product or change it in some way (e.g. a PC hardware supplier buys processors, screens, keyboards and CD readers from separate suppliers and sells them together as a workstation), it could be argued that these costs (repackaging) are part of the stock asset since they represent an aspect of the cost in bringing the goods to the condition where they can be sold to the customer.

The problem may perhaps be more clearly seen in relation to a second-hand car dealer. Supposing the dealer buys a car in bad condition after a crash but then repairs it, resprays it and generally restores it to a better condition. The item which is finally put on display and sold is not the same item which was bought in the first place. Should its stock value be the purchase price alone, or should it reflect the purchase price and the costs of renovating it, or indeed should it be valued at what it would cost the dealer to buy a car in renovated condition?

If the stock value was only the purchase price this would ignore the extra costs associated with bringing the car to a saleable condition, so arguably, it would not match that cost and the subsequent profit on sale, which is what accounting tries to do.

But what about carrying the car at a value based on what it would have cost to buy it already renovated? There certainly appears to be a case for it, since one can argue that it is possible to perceive two stages in the dealer's profit-creating: stage 1 is buying a car and working on it to increase its wholesale value, while stage 2 is simply selling the car. There is a case for recognizing the value gained in stage 1 at a theoretical level, but this brings us back to the problem of prudence: the gain has not been realized, i.e. it is purely notional since the car has not been sold. The dealer has increased his or her profit potential, but until the car is sold, no accounting profit has been made.

The principle should now be clear: all the costs associated with creating a particular asset should be expensed at the same time as the asset is consumed (sold to the customer), in order to match revenues with expenses. Until the item is sold the costs should accumulate as part of the value of the asset, subject to the rule of being carried at the lower of cost or net realizable value.

Accounting techniques

Having reviewed the problems underlying the accounting measurement of stock values, we can now look at the practices employed. In this area we can identify three different categories:

1. continuous inventory, where individual items are identified for accounting purposes;
2. measurement methods that rely on assumptions about stock movements (but do not increase stock value by adding in any associated costs);

3. methods used where the stock value of goods for resale includes costs other than the initial purchase price.

Continuous inventory

Although in most industries it is impractical to attach to individual goods the cost of acquiring them, there are some cases where either the nature of the business or the technology used to control stock permits of this 'actual' valuation.

If a business deals in a small volume of high-value items which are not homogeneous, as, for example, does a dealer in fine art, it is perfectly possible to keep records of the cost of each individual item of merchandise, so no assumptions need to be made about stock movements. Each item can have its acquisition cost recorded and this can be expensed individually when the item is sold, leaving a closing stock value which relates quite specifically to the items still in stock.

Computer technology has also made possible the treatment of individual stock items at their actual purchase price because the ability of a computer to deal with an enormous volume of data means that there is a facility for keeping this information available. However, such techniques are unlikely to be used simply so that stock can be on an actual basis – generally it is part of the management information system to monitor levels of stock (for reordering and checking how fast individual items are moving) and to keep a check on buying prices to be sure that selling prices achieve the required gross profit margin on an item-by-item basis.

In short, what is called a 'continuous inventory' system has considerable management benefits in a sophisticated retail business. One advantage may be the ability to calculate an actual cost of sales, though the cost of the system is justified not by that, but by the management controls and profit maximization which it provides.

Accounting assumptions

In this area we are taking the cost of each individual item as given, and then using methods based on assumptions about stock movements to allocate those costs between the cost of sales expense and the stock asset carried forward to the next year.

These methods would be applicable to any retailing business and to the retailing side of a manufacturing business. For example, going back to our used car dealer, once cars had been refurbished they would come into stock at a figure which included initial costs plus refurbishing costs. These systems deal with the subsequent transfer of those costs to expense at the time of sale, and are therefore equally applicable whether the company is buying finished goods in from outside and simply reselling them, or whether it is adding value in some way by processing before selling. These systems come into play once the good is ready for resale and enters the retailing system.

There are three generally recognized systems for accounting for stock within a historical cost framework: LIFO, FIFO and weighted average.

1. LIFO (Last In First Out) assumes that the first item of stock to be sold will be the last item delivered into the stores. It allocates an accounting value to the cost of sales which uses the most recent purchase of goods into the stores.
2. FIFO (First In First Out) assumes that stock will be rotated in an orderly manner consistent with good housekeeping: newly delivered items will go to the back of the shelf and the oldest items will be the first sold.

3. Weighted average, on the other hand, ascribes a cost to sold units based on the average cost of all the items of that type which were in stock at the time of sale. A new average is computed each time a sale takes place.

Common-sense physical stock control tends to follow FIFO principles: stock would be rotated so that the oldest stock is sold first. But there may be good reasons why, for accounting purposes, we should make the opposite assumption.

In periods of rising prices (and if we disregard temporary fluctuations and goods where technological change has affected their manufacturing cost, the trend for the past hundred years has been for prices to rise), LIFO will provide the lowest stock value and the lowest profit (making it popular for tax purposes in some countries). FIFO, however, provides a higher stock value and consequently a higher profit measurement. Weighted average provides a compromise solution to stock valuation problems in so far as it always produces a final value between FIFO and LIFO. In the UK the vast majority of companies use FIFO for stock valuation. Practice in other countries is more mixed. Weighted average is popular in mainland Europe, whereas a significant number of US companies use LIFO.

Company policy in this area is much influenced by their tax environment and their profit objectives. A low value ending stock will reduce current year profits and carry them forward as a kind of hidden reserve in the form of undervalued stocks. If the tax regime permits such practices, a private company will certainly adopt a low stock value strategy (in the UK, LIFO is not allowed for tax purposes, but in Switzerland, companies are allowed to reduce the accounting value of their stock by one-third every year as a tax incentive). Where artificially low values are not allowed, private companies will tend to 'lose' stock, while public companies may prefer anyway to record a higher current profit.

Note that the principle of consistency does not allow a company to switch stock valuation methods from one year to another.

Later, when comparing one company's performance with another, you should check stock valuation methods used to see that they are equivalent. Note also that US companies, if they use LIFO, are required to state the FIFO value of their stocks in the notes to the accounts.

Worked example to compare LIFO/FIFO and average methods

A detailed knowledge of each basis is not necessarily useful for non-accounting management, but in order to see how each system works in practice, there follows a very simple set of stock transactions. You can follow these through, if you wish, to see how they can acquire a different accounting value according to each of the three methods.

Imagine a student who spends his summer selling cold drinks on the beach in the South of France. He buys his stock from a wholesaler and sells individual cans on the beach. During the summer his stock turnover works out like this:

	Buys	*Sells*
June	100 crates @ $1.00	90 crates
July	150 crates @ $1.20	120 crates
August	150 crates @ $1.30	160 crates
Total	400 (cost $475)	370

At the end of August, therefore, he has on hand thirty crates of drinks and in order to arrive at an accounting measure of profit he needs to work out a cost of sales for the 370 crates sold, and a stock value for the remaining thirty crates.

Notice that:

1. We are not concerned with the selling price of his goods. We are trying to measure the cost of those goods, which is entirely independent of what he received when they were sold. Of course we need to know in due course what the sales revenue was, in order to deduct cost of sales and arrive at a profit figure.
2. The wholesale price is rising throughout the period. If the buying price were stable, then the cost of sales would be the same under all three methods. It is only under conditions of changing prices that there is a problem about allocating cost in this context.

LIFO

The LIFO model charges out withdrawals from stock at the value of the most recent invoice, subject to the constraint of quantities. If the stock withdrawal is for 100 units and the last invoice was for 120, that price is used; but if the last delivery was 80, then the excess of 20 will be costed at the price of the next to last delivery and so on.

Use of the LIFO system has made the following allocations:

	$
Cost of sales ($90 + $144 + $207)	441.00
Closing stock	34.00
Total goods purchased	475.00

Notice that the original stock at the end of June is still part of the accounting value of stock, and this is a particular feature of LIFO. Unless a business actually runs out of stock, the accounting measure of stock is likely to be at a very old rate (imagine a company which is still selling the same goods after fifty years), while the cost of sales will be a recent purchase cost.

	Cost of goods in	*Cost of goods sold*	*LIFO stock*
June			
	100 × $1.00	90 × $1.00=$90.00	10 × $1.00=$10.00
July			
	150 × $1.20	120 × $1.20=$144.00	10 × $1.00=$10.00
			30 × $1.20=$36.00
			Total=$46.00
August			
	150 × $1.30	150 × $1.30=$195.00	10 × $1.00=$10.00
		10 × $1.20= $12.00	20 × $1.20=$24.00
		Total=$207.00	Total=$34.00

Note that in July the delivery was in excess of the withdrawal, so the July price was used for the withdrawal, while in August the withdrawal was greater than the delivery, so was costed at a mixture of the August delivery plus the balance from the July delivery remaining in the stock valuation.

FIFO

The FIFO model assumes that all transfers out of stock are made from the oldest stock in store at that time. Using our cold drink figures as for LIFO, this would give us the allocations between cost of sales and stock which are shown below:

	Cost of goods in	Cost of goods out	FIFO stock
June			
	100 × $1.00	90 × $1.00=$90.00	10 × $1.00=$10.00
July			
	150 × $1.20	10 × $1.00= $10.00	40 × $1.20=$48.00
		110 × $1.20=$132.00	
		Total=$142.00	
August			
	150 × $1.30	40 × $1.20= $48.00	30 × $1.30=$39.00
		120 × $1.30=$156.00	
		Total=$204.00	

The system has allocated the cost of the deliveries as follows:

	$
Cost of sales ($90+$142+$204)	436.00
Stock at end of period	39.00
Total purchases	475.00

Notice that in this case the closing stock value is at the most recent price. Where prices are rising this means that FIFO will give the highest closing stock figure – and therefore the lowest cost of sales. But if prices are falling the opposite will hold good.

Weighted average

The weighted average method adjusts the average price of all units in stock each time there is a new purchase. For example, if the existing stock is ten units with an average cost of $7.00 and then five more units are delivered at a cost of $8.00 each, any subsequent withdrawal will be costed at:

$$(10 \times \$7 + 5 \times \$8)/15 = \$7.33 \text{ per unit}$$

The allocations made by the weighted average using our original example are:

	Cost of goods in	Cost of goods out	WA stock
June			
	100 × $1.00	90 × $1.00=$90.00	10 × $1.00=$10.00
July			
	150 × $1.20	150 × $1.20+	
		10 × $1.00=$190	
		120/160 × $190=$142.50	40/160 × $190=$47.50
August			
	150 × $1.30	150 ×$1.30+	
		$47.50=$242.50	
		160/190 × $242.50	30/190 × $242.50
		=$204.20	=$38.30

The allocation of the purchases under this method works out as follows:

	$
Cost of sales ($90 + $142.50 + $204.20)	436.70
Closing stock	38.30
Total purchases	475.00

The main disadvantage of this method is that it can be quite cumbersome in use, given that the average has to be recalculated every time there is a new delivery of merchandise.

Impact on gross profit

The next stage in considering the use of different stock valuation systems is to see what impact the choice of method has on the state of the financial affairs of the company.

If we say that the sales revenue achieved by our student selling coke was $740, his results would look like this:

	LIFO	FIFO	Weighted average
	$	$	$
Sales	740.00	740.00	740.00
Cost of sales	(441.00)	(436.00)	(436.70)
Gross profit	299.00	304.00	303.30
Balance sheet: value of stock	34.00	39.00	38.30

The choice of stock measurement system provides a choice of profit measures. In our particular example the difference between each of the three is not great, but then the quantities involved are not substantial. In a major company the stock on hand could run to several million pounds, therefore a method which has a result 10 per cent different could result in quite a different view of the company's performance.

Manufacturing accounts

We would regard it as beyond the scope of this book to examine in great detail how a manufacturing business (or any business which processes goods before resale) accounts for and allocates costs between expenses and the asset value of the finished goods (this is a complex and relatively controversial question normally dealt with in the context of cost and managerial accounting). However, a general picture is certainly germane to your understanding of financial accounting.

As we have discussed, the matching principle calls for revenues and expenses which relate to the same transaction to be recognized in the profit and loss account for the same period. It follows that all the costs of manufacturing a product should therefore be expensed at the moment when the product is sold. Typically a manufacturing concern buys raw materials, processes them and then sells them. The actual amount of time taken for the production cycle to be completed will vary from one industry to another, but may last many months between the initial delivery of raw materials and the finished goods moving into the warehouse.

Until the goods enter the warehouse, all the costs associated with producing them are accumulated and treated as an asset. However, the problems arise in defining exactly what are the costs associated with producing the finished good.

We can easily distinguish between two broad categories of cost: direct cost and overhead. Direct costs are those costs which arise directly from the manufacture of the product – for example, the raw materials, the cost of the workers who actually produce the good, packaging, etc. These can be seen quite clearly to form part of the asset.

Where we run into problems is in the area of overheads where the cost cannot be so easily allocated. Typical overheads might be:

- Supervisory production staff;
- Cost of machines used in production;
- Cost of energy used in production;
- Cost of factory building (rent, maintenance, rates, etc.);
- Cost of product design team;
- Cost of accounting department;
- Cost of general management.

As you go down the list, the costs become more remote from the production of the finished good, and it is a considerable problem as to where exactly the line is drawn between costs which should be allocated to the finished product and costs which should be immediately expensed as part of the general operating expenses.

The answer differs from one company to another, and indeed this is another factor which is influenced by national characteristics and the tax environment. Where tax measurement is linked closely to the company accounts, there is an incentive to carry the minimum of costs in the accounting value of manufactured goods, and pass as many costs as possible immediately into expense, to defer tax. As a rule of thumb, expenses such as those of operating the factory (where they can be separated) might be allocated to the asset, while general business operating expenses such as office staff would not be treated as part of the asset. However, some companies may well treat only direct costs such as direct labour and raw materials as part of the asset and expense the rest immediately. One side-effect of this is that where two companies in the same industry make different allocations, their financial statements will not be directly comparable: what is an operating expense in one, may be treated as an asset in the other and expensed in the next period.

By way of a simple example, let us suppose that a small factory produces ashtrays. It buys plates of stainless steel which are stamped out by a press into the shape of an ashtray. The factory is operated by four people; three are directly employed producing the ashtrays, while the fourth manages the business and handles sales. The monthly payroll is $2,800, of which $1,000 goes to the manager. The factory is rented and costs $1,000 a month; the building includes the offices in which the manager works, and these occupy one-tenth of the floor space. During the month of August the electricity bill is $100 and the raw materials consumed were worth $1,210. We might allocate the costs as follows:

	Total costs $	*Production costs* $	*Operating costs* $
Payroll	2,800	1,800	1,000
Rent	1,000	900	100
Electricity	100	90	10
Raw materials	1,210	1,210	—
Totals	5,110	4,000	1,110

You can see that even in so simple an example the allocations are problematical – does the manager not supervise production in any way? Is it reasonable to allocate the electricity bill on the basis of floor area when the machines probably use proportionately more than the office?

The main point though is that $4,000 would be treated as costs incurred in producing the finished goods. If the production in the month was 2000 ashtrays, these would appear in the balance sheet at a stock value of $2 each ($4,000 divided by 2000 units) and would pass into the retail part of the business (the equivalent of 'purchases') as being delivered at $2 each. You can see that, if the rent, for example, were treated as a period operating cost, and not allocated to the product, the average product cost would decrease to about $1.50: it follows that for internal management purposes, it is vital to understand fully how costs are allocated within the company's system; ignorance could lead to wrong decisions, such as how great is the unit profit margin.

The $1,110 would be expensed immediately as operating expenses. The ashtrays, however, would be expensed only when they were sold – and at a value which depended upon whether LIFO, FIFO or weighted average was in use.

It is also worth mentioning at this point that a manufacturing business will have a number of different components to its stock. Aside from the stock of finished goods, it will also have stocks of raw materials, and probably a value for 'work in progress' (sometimes 'work in process'). The latter simply acknowledges that, where the production cycle takes some time, there will at any given balance sheet date be products which are only part completed.

And ...

It would be useful just to consider a concept which may help to provide underpinning for the detailed techniques: working capital and the working capital cycle.

Working capital

We have seen that the use of accruals in accounting leads to the existence within the balance sheet of a number of short-term assets and liabilities which are linked to the trading cycle, and because they are part of a cycle, linked to each other, even if the balance sheet presentation splits the liabilities from the assets. Conventional thinking in this area talks about the concept of 'working capital' and the working capital cycle (Figure 4.1). This models the trading activity of the company as being:

- Purchase of goods for resale gives rise to creditors and stocks.
- Stocks are sold to clients, which reduces stock and creates debtors.
- Debtors pay their invoices, which reduces debtors and increases cash.
- Cash is used to pay creditors, and a residual cash balance is left, representing the profit (assuming a profit has been made!).

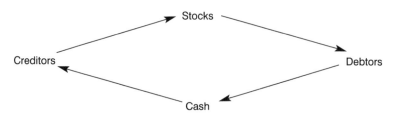

Figure 4.1   The working capital cycle

This is a useful management model for showing the interrelationships within the operating cycle, and some Anglo-Saxon balance sheets present current assets and current liabilities together, to emphasize that they are economically linked. However, it does not in all cases explain the cash balance in a company, which is essentially a residual which includes short-term elements of financing and investment.

You should see that, because accounting tries to capture data when there is an economic event, and not just a cash transaction, the operating cycle involves a series of changes in working capital before a particular cycle is complete and the operation has been completed and a net inflow or outflow of cash has occurred. If a company stopped operating, this part of its balance sheet would disappear, since it is only concerned with short-term trading events, and equally, when we wish to explain why, over a year, the profit does not equal net cash flow, changes in working capital are a significant part of the answer.

Summary

In this chapter we have dealt with that part of the company's accounting which captures sales and expense 'events' as they happen and keeps track of amounts due to suppliers and amounts owed by customers. Regular trading also involves constant changes in the stocks of purchased or manufactured goods which are held for resale. We have seen that mostly companies do not transfer the costs for sold goods into the income statement on a transaction-by-transaction basis, but rather calculate the cost of goods sold by adding up the value of all goods available for sale, and calculating the value of goods still unsold, so that the difference between these two is the accounting value of goods sold. The trading cycle (goods being obtained on credit, put into stock, being sold on credit giving rise to debtors and then finally turning into cash) links together these economic events in the accounting system and is known as the working capital cycle.

Questions

1. Allocate revenue between different accounting periods in the following cases:

   (a) Carolyn works as a freelance journalist. In November 20X1 she wrote an article for a magazine; the article appeared in the February 20X2 issue and she was paid in March 20X2. She draws up her accounts to 31 December.

   (b) Merseyside Shipbuilding Inc. receives an order to build a small cargo ship. The work starts on 1 July 20X2. At 31 December 20X2 the ship is 10 per cent complete, at 31 December 20X3 it is 80 per cent complete and the ship finally leaves the yard on 30 June 20X4. During this period Merseyside Shipbuilding received the following payments from the client: 31 July 20X2 $500,000; 1 January 20X3 $500,000; 30 June 20X3 $500,000; 31 December 20X3 $500,000; 30 June 20X4 $750,000; 1 January 20X5 $1,250,000 (final instalment).

   (c) Wirral Electrical sells electric appliances wholesale. In November 20X1 it sold twenty fan heaters at $15 each to a retailer (Meols Stores) and in December a further thirty at $15 each to the same customer. In February 20X2 Meols Stores pays its outstanding account, subject to deduction of $30 for two defective heaters which it returned at the same time. In April 20X2 Meols Stores sends back a further heater, demanding a refund because it does not work. How would Wirral deal with this situation in its accounts?

2. Wirral Electrical had the following balance sheet as at 31 December 20X1:

	$
Assets	
Stock	400
Debtors	2,500
Cash	1,500
	4,400
Liabilities and equity	
Creditors	3,200
Equity	1,200

During 20X2 the following business was done:

	$
Cash sales	8,500
Credit sales	14,000
Receipts from debtors	13,250
Payments to creditors	17,500
Purchases on credit	18,400
Overheads paid cash	3,000

You are asked to:

(a) **Enter the opening balance sheet and subsequent transactions on a spreadsheet (or any other working paper).**

(b) **Prepare a profit and loss account and balance sheet as at 31 December 20X2 (closing stock was $600).**

3. The owner of Mansfield Supply Co. Ltd is considering a change of accounting policy as regards closing stock valuation. For the first three years of the business the company has used FIFO but the owner is now considering a change to weighted average. Condensed financial statements are given below.

You are asked to provide alternative statements based on the alternative stock valuations. The relevant year-end stock valuations according to the new method would be: 31 December 20X1 $7,400, 31 December 20X2 $9,800, 31 December 20X3 $6,900.

Profit and loss account for year ended:

	31 Dec. 20X1		31 Dec. 20X2		31 Dec. 20X3	
	$	$	$	$	$	$
Sales		120000		150000		110000
Opening stock	—		6300		8100	
Purchases	68000		82900		63400	
Closing stock	6300		8100		6700	
Cost of sales		61700		81100		64800
Gross profit		58300		68900		45200
Dist./Admin. exp		59100		64800		44800
Net profit/(loss)		(800)		4100		400

Balance sheet as at:

	31 Dec. 20X1	*31 Dec. 20X2*	*31 Dec. 20X3*
	$	$	$
Fixed assets			
(net)	36000	32000	28000
Stock	6300	8100	6700
Cash	2700	10900	13300
	47000	51000	48000
Capital			
Shares	40000	40000	40000
Reserves		(800)	3300
Profit/(loss) for year	(800)	4100	400
	39200	43300	43700
Creditors	5800	7700	4300
Total	47000	51000	48000

4. Complete the missing figures:

	A	B	C	D	E
Opening stock	...	236	647	9,375	5,296
Closing stock	12,200	110	...	8,760	5,820
Purchases	110,500	937	5,122	76,420	...
Cost of sales	108,950	...	4,928	...	33,996

5. The following transactions took place at a wholesale wine merchants during the month of August:

1	Opening stock 72 crates @ $20
2	Purchase 20 crates @ $21
4	Sale 40 crates @ $30
5	Purchase 60 crates @ $23
9	Sale 60 crates @ $30
12	Sale 35 crates @ $30
13	Purchase 40 crates @ $24
17	Sale 10 crates @ $32
20	Purchase 50 crates @ $25
22	Sale 30 crates @ $32
23	Sale 30 crates @ $32
24	Purchase 45 crates @ $26
28	Sale 40 crates @ $32

You are asked to:

(a) **Compute the closing stock according to FIFO, LIFO and weighted average assumptions.**

(b) **Compute gross profit under each assumption.**

5 Fixed assets and depreciation

In this chapter we are going to look at how the costs of manufacturing plant, computers and other equipment which are used up by the business are passed through the profit and loss account and disappear from the balance sheet as part of the matching process.

Introduction

We have earlier used the model of the company as an empty shell where finance is put in, the finance is used to buy productive capacity and then profits are made (hopefully) by using this capacity. However, the productive capacity (i.e. long-term assets such as machinery or buildings) are used up over time in a company's operations. Accordingly that use must be recognized as an expense in the profit and loss account, and adjustments made to the balance sheet value of the assets. The profit measure each year would be an over-estimate, if no attempt were made to *match* the using up of the productive capacity with the revenues that are derived from its use.

Just as the stock of finished goods is consumed and expensed in the course of a company's trading operations, many other assets are also consumed – although they are frequently consumed at such a slow pace that it may not at first be evident that they should be considered as an expense. Indeed, in the nineteenth century, early companies such as the railways took the view that their fixed assets had such a long potential life that only repairs required to maintain them at the appropriate level should be expensed – no reduction in accounting value from the original cost was provided.

However, most long-lived assets are eventually 'consumed'. For example, a simple retail operation might take place in a shop on the main street of a town. If the business owns the premises outright, you might ask whether the premises are in any way consumed during business operations. Well, the shop front will deteriorate in condition (wood or aluminium has a finite life) but perhaps more important, the business may well depend on an attractive, modern presentation to attract customers and therefore it is necessary to modernize the shop front every five years or so. In either case, there is some limitation on the life of a long-term asset and it will ultimately have to be replaced. If the asset is replaced by a new one, it follows logically that the old asset has been consumed, and this expense should be recognized.

For some long-term assets the consumption may be clearer: a business that uses vans for distributing its product, or cars for its sales force to visit the customers, has assets whose life is limited. Say a van is bought for $20,000, is used in the business for two years and then sold for $5,000, it is quite clear that in those two years the business has consumed $15,000-worth of van. For the accountant there is a problem: there is an expense of $15,000 covering two years which (a) must be recognized in the profit and loss account as such; (b) reflects a diminution of asset value which should therefore be reflected in the balance sheet value of the asset; (c) needs to be matched with the operations to comply with the matching principle and therefore should be allocated across two years of operations.

Looked at from another point of view, every asset is an unexpired expense, and at every accounting date a company must review to what extent each individual asset has been consumed during the financial year. The expense must be 'recognized' (brought into the accounts) and offset against revenue for a more accurate measure of net income, and the revised value of the asset shown in the balance sheet. In principle all assets can be regarded as a bundle of goods or services which are held by the company for subsequent use in the business. As the goods or services are used, some expense must be recognized and the unexpired expenses carried forward (this is in fact an important point about asset values under historical cost accounting: they are simply expenses of future periods; they do not represent any independent valuation of the asset's 'worth' in any external sense).

IASC Framework

The Framework says that an asset should recognized if (a) it is probable that a future economic benefit associated with the element will flow to the enterprise, and (b) the item has a cost or value that can be measured reliably.

Applied to a van, this means that, provided that the van is useful in the company's operations, and its purchase value is certain, it should be treated as an asset. As the van is used, the amount of future economic benefits is decreasing.

We can divide the accounting issues to be considered into two parts:

1. How do we determine the appropriate value of an asset at the point of acquisition?
2. How do we then systematically recognize the using up or expensing of the asset period by period? (The deduction of the expense from the opening value will provide a revised balance sheet value at the end of each period.)

Asset valuation

At first sight there might not seem to be any difficulty about the initial valuation of an asset. When a company buys a van, for example, a price is agreed, paid and that surely is the cost of the asset, and the value at which it will initially enter the accounting system. In essence that argument has much to support it, but if we look a little closer, we will see that there is a need to define more carefully what the asset has cost – or rather what aspect of the cost is an asset, and what an expense.

Supposing the van purchase was invoiced to the company (as is usually the case) at an 'on the road' price of $20,000, the invoice would then be made up of a number of items, as shown below:

Van supply	$
Basic vehicle	19,700
Special gear box	700
Petrol	20
Annual vehicle tax	<u>150</u>
	20,570
less Discount	(<u>570</u>)
Net payable	20,000

Should the van enter the books at the invoice price of $20,000? To answer that we have to consider whether all the items paid for on the invoice are really assets, i.e. does everything included within the $20,000 purchase price have a life longer than the end of the current accounting period? In this case, there are two items, the petrol and the annual tax, which are ordinary running expenses which will be consumed within the current accounting year, so we should immediately treat those as an expense for operating the van. The discount may also be a problem. Clearly in this case it has been given to arrive at a round sum price, so arguably the expensed element, petrol and tax, should be reduced by the discount. Against that, it is unlikely that the dealer intended to offer discounts on petrol or tax, and there is a strong argument for applying the discount to the asset value alone. In this case the costs would be allocated as shown below:

Van asset	$
Basic	19,700
Gear box	700
less Discount	(<u>570</u>)
Fixed asset:	19,830
Operating expenses	
Petrol	20
Annual tax	<u>150</u>
Total invoiced	20,000

Let us consider one further complication: suppose that the company then employs a sign-writer to paint some advertising on the side of the van, and this costs a further $500. Should that be treated as an expense, or part of the cost of the asset? Is there any difference in nature between what the sign-writer contributed to the final product and what the vehicle manufacturer contributed? The answer has to be 'no', since both are costs associated with providing the van in the form required by the company. The final asset value of the van in the company's books would therefore be $20,330: $19,830 being the cost from the dealer and $500 being other costs associated with reaching the desired final asset.

Would it make any difference to the asset value if the sign-writing on the van had been done by the company's own staff? Suppose the $500 consisted of $100 for paint and $400 staff wages, would that influence the asset value? Logically the source of the cost should have no bearing, and that is the case here. If a company uses some of its own resources in creating an asset, the cost of those resources becomes part of the cost of the asset. This is the same principle as that applied in manufacturing accounts (see Chapter 4) – just as wage and other costs were allocated to the value of the stock of manufactured goods, so here the cost of increasing the economic benefits from the van is added to its accounting value.

We can therefore go some way to defining what we understand by the cost of the asset. It consists of all the costs associated with creating the asset in the form required by the company.

This principle applies in general to the measurement of all assets in the framework of historical cost accounting. The total asset value recorded can include not only costs paid to a supplier, but also extra items which have all contributed to the bringing into service of the asset. For example, a manufacturing company might well buy some machine tools which are installed in its factory by its own maintenance staff. In that case the asset value at the point where they come into service will include the amount (exclusive of any expenses to do with operations) paid to the supplier, cost of delivery on site, cost of installation including maintenance staff wages, and so on.

The basic test in allocating cost between asset value and expense is, was the cost a part of bringing the asset into service? If so, it would be allocated to asset value. (A small corollary to that is that in some jurisdictions, e.g. France, services such as agents' fees, costs of testing and similar items are not added to the accounting value of the asset to which they relate, but are treated as a separate balance sheet item, a 'deferred charge'. This is then depreciated over five years rather than the full life of the related asset, which means that the tax benefit is gained earlier. You do not need to apply this, and deferred charges are not typically of significant value in a balance sheet, but you may come across them in making cross-border comparisons.)

Normally, then, the initial value of an asset will be its cost, but this is subject to a limitation as in the case of stock valuation. This valuation is subject to the constraint that these costs should not exceed the future economic benefits which will derive from using the asset. Prudence requires that asset values should not be overstated in the balance sheet. For assets which are held for use in the business (as opposed to being held for resale), the rule is that they should be held at the lower of cost or 'recoverable amount'. Recoverable in this sense is normally taken to mean through use in the business. To use our van example, the fact that the van had been painted with advertising on the side would immediately reduce its resale value, but the company was not intending to resell it. The intention was to keep the van and use it in the business for deliveries etc. – so its cost will be recovered through being operated as part of the business.

Nonetheless, fixed assets are subject to special write-downs when there has been some 'permanent impairment' of their value. This might occur if, for example, a company built a factory for manufacturing microchips, only to find that demand falls away – the cost of the factory is unlikely to be recovered through manufacturing the chips and its value should be reduced.

Expensing assets

Companies acquire assets in order to generate profits by their use. Such operating assets are consumed by the business over a period of time: machines wear out. The cost of these assets must therefore be expensed in order to match with the revenues produced by using them.

Although that may seem potentially quite a complex operation, in fact systems have been evolved which deal with it pragmatically. In the first place it should be made clear that the problem is again one of allocation. That is, accountants are not concerned primarily with assessing the reducing value of the asset in external terms, rather they are concerned with allocating the original cost of the asset over the period of its use ('depreciating the asset').

Depreciation accounting

5. The depreciable amount of a depreciable asset should be allocated on a systematic basis to each accounting period during the useful life of the asset.

7. The useful life of a depreciable asset should be estimated after considering the following factors:

   (a) expected physical wear and tear
   (b) obsolescence
   (c) legal or other limits on the use of the asset

12. The depreciation method selected should be applied consistently from period to period unless altered circumstances justify a change. In an accounting period in which the method is changed, the effect should be quantified and disclosed and the reason for the change should be stated.

14. The valuation bases used for determining the amounts at which depreciable assets are stated should be included with the disclosure of other accounting policies.

15. The following should be disclosed for each major class of depreciable asset:

    (a) the depreciation methods used
    (b) the useful lives or the depreciation rates used
    (c) total depreciation allocated for the period
    (d) the gross amount of depreciable assets and the related accumulated depreciation

Source: IAS 4 Depreciation Accounting (extract)

You should note that accounting doctrine distinguishes between two different kinds of reduction in the accounting values of assets: there is (1) systematic expensing of the cost of an asset over the period which benefits from its use – depreciation or amortization – which takes place routinely every year, and (2) special write-downs where, usually at balance sheet date, all assets should be considered for 'impairment' and their depreciated accounting value compared with their recoverable value. Any excess must be removed, but this is an unusual event.

The important elements are that the asset has a value at the point where it comes into the company, and when the company has finished with the asset, it may also have a resale or scrap value at that time. The difference between the acquisition cost and the disposal revenue (depreciable amount) is the expense which has to be recognized and allocated in some reasonable way across the financial years when the asset remains in use. This is another significant estimate in the accounts where we can only say for certain what costs really were when an asset is sold, sometimes many years after it entered service.

This allocation of cost has significant effects on measured profitability which in turn may impact upon taxation. In some jurisdictions (Netherlands, UK, USA) depreciation for tax purposes is calculated separately from that for financial reporting purposes. However, in most mainland European countries the rate of depreciation charged in the accounts is heavily influenced by tax considerations. In France, for example, the tax authorities will look at what is charged in the annual statements as the upper limit of what can be charged for tax purposes. We will discuss below the theoretical basis of depreciation, but you should be aware that there is a strong link with taxation in many countries, and therefore accountants will be likely to look at the agreed tax rates rather than apply accounting standards. Put another way, the accounting standards are sufficiently flexible for it to be possible to comply with both tax and accounting rules, but the possibility of deferring tax by using high depreciation rates will cause a company to be perhaps more prudent in its estimates than might otherwise be the case … .

Reverting to our example of a van, bought for $20,000 and sold for $5,000 two years later, the expense is $15,000 (difference between entry and exit values) and the decision to be made is how to allocate that expense over the two years to match the use of the van with the revenues generated by its use. (It is always a temptation to think that depreciating an asset has something to do with approximating the balance sheet value to a declining second-hand value. This is not the case: depreciating is a cost allocation process, which equally is why assets in the balance sheet should be thought of largely as unexpired costs rather than values – even if some of them have substantial resale potential.)

Of course, the accountant cannot know precisely how many years an asset will remain in use, nor its precise scrap value, at the time when a decision has to be made on allocating the expense. These therefore have to be estimated, and corrections made (sometimes years later) if the estimates prove to be wrong. (Remember that the process of measuring the annual profit is in any event one of estimation – a question of trying to work out what proportion of the firm's lifetime profit was earned in that twelve-month period.)

There are several methods used to calculate depreciation on a systematic basis to match the expensing of the asset with its use. Broadly these fall into one of two kinds: those which allocate over time, and those which try to match depreciation to use.

With the time-based approach, having arrived at the acquisition value of the asset, an estimate is made both of the likely working life of the asset within the company and of its expected scrap or salvage value at the end of that working life. The difference between the original asset cost and the expected scrap value is called the 'depreciable amount' of the asset – that is, the total expense to be allocated over the working life. One of the methods we shall now consider will then be selected to allocate the depreciable amount over the working life of the asset. We shall look first at these methods, and then at the way in which depreciation is reported in the financial statements.

Straight-line depreciation

This method is the one most favoured by companies, probably because it is the simplest and easiest to use. The straight-line method, as its name implies, assumes that the use of the asset is uniform throughout its working life, and therefore allocates the expense accordingly.

The annual expense (annual depreciation) is found simply:

$$\frac{\text{Depreciable amount}}{\text{Estimated working life}} = \text{Annual depreciation}$$

For example, supposing a company buys desks and other office furniture for $5,000, and estimates that they will be used for ten years and have no scrap value. The annual depreciation would be charged as follows:

Depreciable amount: $5,000 *less* 0 = $5,000
Working life: ten years

Annual charge $\dfrac{5,000}{10}$ = $500

This method is most appropriate to assets whose consumption takes place in a uniform manner. Examples of this would be assets such as a shop front, a building, a lease premium, furniture, and so on.

Reducing balance

A method which allocates a high proportion of expense in the early life of the asset is reducing balance. This uses a method which gives a geometric reduction in the charge in succeeding years. A basic difference is that the annual charge is calculated by applying a percentage not to the depreciable amount but to the asset value after deduction of all previous years' depreciation. The net value of the asset after deduction of the depreciation might be called the balance of the asset, which reduces year by year, hence reducing balance. (The net value after depreciation is also known as 'net book value' or 'carrying value'.)
There is a mathematical formula for calculating the depreciation rate to be used:

$$rate = \{1 - n\sqrt{\text{salvage value/cost}}\}*100$$

This rate is then applied each year to the balance of the asset at the beginning of the year in order to arrive at the annual depreciation expense.

To take a concrete example, suppose that an asset was acquired for $1,050 and was expected to have a five-year working life and a scrap value of $50; the annual rate would be 44.6 per cent.

This is applied to the asset's net value each year as follows:

	Net book value start of year $		Depreciation expense $	Net book value end of year $
1	1050	*44.6%	= 468	(1050 – 468 =) 582
2	582	*44.6%	= 260	(582 – 260 =) 322
3	322	*44.6%	= 144	(322 – 144 =) 178
4	178	*44.6%	= 79	(178 – 79 =) 99
5	99	*44.6%	= 49	(99 – 49 =) 50

Reducing balance allocates a high proportion of expense to the early years of the asset's life. It is therefore suitable for assets whose future service life is subject to uncertainty, such as computer hardware or software, or which have a high maintenance cost in the latter part of their lives. At a practical level, reducing balance is not used very widely by companies, and normally where it is used, the annual rate is approximated (in the above example a company would probably accept 45 per cent as the rate). Very often, reducing balance is used when the tax authorities allow it (governments like to collect taxes, but they also sometimes use tax to influence behaviour, and high initial depreciation encourages companies to invest – and therefore keep up with technology and create employment in the industries which make equipment).

Tangible assets

Tangible assets serving business operations which are used for more than one year are recorded at acquisition or manufacturing costs reduced by scheduled straight-line depreciation. Manufacturing costs include all costs directly or indirectly attributable to the manufacturing process. Borrowing costs are not capitalised. The tangible assets' useful lives correspond to the expected useful lives in the Group. Exclusively tax-based depreciation is not recognised.

New aircraft and spare engines are depreciated over 12 years to a residual value of 15 per cent.

Buildings are assigned a useful life of between 20 and 45 years. Buildings and leasehold improvements are depreciated according to the term of the lease or a lower useful life. In general depreciation rates are between ten and twenty per cent a year. The useful life of technical plant and equipment is up to ten years. Office and plant equipment is depreciated under normal conditions over three to ten years. Reconstruction commitments resulting from leasehold improvements are recognised on a pro rata basis over their useful lives through setting up accruals.

Source: Lufthansa, Annual Report 1998, Notes to the consolidated financial statements

---

Tax depreciation

As we have noted, tax rules can have a potentially distorting effect on the application of depreciation rules and consequently on comparisons between companies. Take the following example where the profit after all expenses but before depreciation is $20,000 and the tax rate is 25 per cent. A company buys a vehicle for $30,000; the tax rules say that this may be depreciated at 40 per cent reducing balance without regard to residual value, and the company estimates it will use the vehicle for four years, after when it can be sold for an estimated $10,000. The two approaches would give the following results:

	Profit before depreciation	*Annual depreciation*	*Profit after depreciation*	*Tax at 25%*
Tax method				
Year 1	20,000	(12,000)	8,000	2,000
Year 2	20,000	(5,400)	14,600	3,650
Year 3	20,000	(3,780)	16,220	4,055
Year 4	20,000	1,180	21,180	5,295
Totals	80,000	(20,000)	60,000	15,000
Straight line/economic				
Year 1	20,000	(5,000)	15,000	3,750
Year 2	20,000	(5,000)	15,000	3,750
Year 3	20,000	(5,000)	15,000	3,750
Year 4	20,000	(5,000)	15,000	3,750
Totals	80,000	(20,000)	60,000	15,000

This illustrates fairly well what tax planning is about – both sequences give the same four-year total deductions, but the tax method reduces early profits and pushes tax payments towards later in the life of the asset, so the company is getting the maximum benefit in financing the asset. Of course, from a management perspective, the tax is distorting the quality of the information, turning a stable situation (same before-depreciation profit each year) into the appearance of a company which is becoming more profitable year on year (after-depreciation profit gets bigger over the four years).

This said, the distortion is mitigated in a large company because this will have a portfolio of assets, some of which are changed each year. A company with four vehicles, one of which is replaced each year, will have the same total annual depreciation ($20,000 every year) whichever method is used. Another point is that while in some jurisdictions accelerated methods of depreciation are available to help companies, they must be used for the shareholder accounts. However, as we shall see later in the book, if these companies are part of a group, the group accounts can be prepared using normal economic methods such as straight line.

Special tax method

It may be useful to know that in some countries, notably France and Germany, the tax authorities use a depreciation method which is a combination of reducing balance and straight-line methods. The problem with reducing balance is that it cannot, by definition, depreciate an asset to zero, and the method if applied indefinitely leaves a very long tail of small annual charges. The tax authorities get around this by permitting a combination method where the company uses declining balance in the early years and then switches to straight line once this gives a higher annual charge, and this is applied without regard to any salvage value.

Year	Opening book value	Rate	Annual charge	Closing book value	Remaining life
1	50,000	40%RB	20,000	30,000	4 years
2	30,000	40%RB	12,000	18,000	3 years
3	18,000	40%RB	7,200	10,800	2 years
4	10,800	50%SL	5,400	5,400	1 year
5	5,400	50%SL	5,400	—	0

The depreciation calculation switches from reducing balance (RB) to straight line (SL) in year 4 in this case. This is because at that point the reducing balance calculation would give a lower annual charge ($10,800 *0.4 = 4,320). Applying straight line to the asset value as it stands at that point ($10,800) gives two years at $5,400 and enables the asset to be depreciated to zero, whereas the strict application of reducing balance would leave the asset with a value of $3,888 at the end of the fifth year.

There are other time-based methods, but these are the two which are classically used. As far as usage-based methods are concerned, there are potentially many. For example, it would be relatively simple to allocate depreciation on a van according to the number of kilometres travelled in the year. In practice such methods are rarely used, except by companies which extract minerals, particularly oil companies.

Depletion basis

Mineral resource companies usually expense the mineral asset as it is extracted for sale – this is called the depletion basis. Supposing a company acquires a quarry for extracting ore, and the acquisition cost was $5m. The unexpired expense represented by this asset would be the unmined ore available on the site, and it is relatively simple to allocate the acquisition cost on the basis of the amount of ore extracted. If the engineers estimated that the quarry contained 10m tonnes of ore, the cost of the quarry could be divided over the resource:

$$\frac{\$5\text{m acquisition cost}}{10\text{m tonnes ore in quarry}} = \text{Depreciation } \$0.50 \text{ per tonne}$$

As the ore was extracted, the quarry asset could be expensed in direct relation to the ore. So if extraction was as follows:

Year	Tonnes extracted
1	500,000
2	1,200,000
3	1,400,000
	etc.

the annual charge for depreciation would be:

Year	Annual depreciation
1	(500,000 × $0.50) $250,000
2	(1,200,000 × $0.50) $600,000
3	(1,400,000 × $0.50) $700,000 etc.

Clearly the accuracy of the method depends upon the accuracy of the estimate of the ore in the quarry, and this method is only suitable for assets where such estimates of the resource are possible and the utilization of the resource can be monitored in that way. However, it is a method of allocating expense which most closely follows the economic use of the asset, rather than working on an assumed utilization pattern.

Hidden reserves

Depreciation is also one of the ways in which companies which wish to follow highly 'prudent' accounting may reduce their profitability. This is done simply by charging excess depreciation against assets and profit. The consequence is that the company appears to have fewer assets than are actually in use, and these are one form of hidden reserve. In fact accelerated depreciation for tax purposes (offered by governments as an incentive to companies to invest) has the effect of writing off assets while they are still in use, but some companies (rarely if ever those listed on stock exchanges!) go further than that.

Bosch

Straight line as well as accelerated depreciation methods were applied. Items of minor value were (fully) depreciated during the year of acquisition. In addition we applied all special depreciation allowances according to tax regulations in all host countries.

Source: Extract from Bosch annual report, Principles of classification and evaluation

---

Accounting for depreciation

Every year part of the asset cost is expensed in the profit and loss account and the balance sheet shows a reduced net value for the asset. In record-keeping terms, though, the net value of the asset is preserved through two accounts: opening cost, and accumulated depreciation. As depreciation is expensed the asset account is not reduced directly. Rather a separate, linked account is opened to accumulate the value written off. In the published balance sheet a company must disclose both the original cost of an asset and the cumulative amount written off (frequently this detail is found in the notes rather than directly in the balance sheet, but that does not change the principle). This disclosure is facilitated if the information is kept on two separate data files in the records – in a large company it would be impossible to give the information without taking that kind of precaution.

General Electric

Notes to Consolidated Financial Statements (extract)

15. Property, Plant and Equipment
(including equipment leased to others)

December 31 (in millions)	1998	1997
Original cost		
GE		
Land and improvements	$459	$459
Buildings, structures and related equipment	6,579	6,375
Machinery and equipment	19,491	18,376
Leasehold costs and manufacturing plant		
under construction	1,757	1,621
Other	24	24
	28,310	26,855
GECS		
Buildings and equipment	4,828	3,987
Equipment leased to others:		
Vehicles	9,825	9,144
Aircraft	9,321	7,686
Railroad rolling stock	2,804	2,367
Marine shipping containers	2,565	2,774
Other	3,447	2,844
	32,790	28,802
	61,100	55,657
Accumulated depreciation		
and amortization		
GE	16,615	15,737
GECS		
Buildings and equipment	1,733	1,478
Equipment leased to others	7,021	6,126
	25,370	23,341

Source: General Electric Annual report 1998
www.ge.com/annual 98

If we take an asset which cost $15,000, had an expected life of five years, and nil scrap value, it would be depreciated at a rate of $3,000 a year on the straight line basis. The table below shows how the book value of the asset would appear over the years.

Year	Annual charge $	Gross cost $	Accumulated depreciation $	Net book value $
20X1	3,000	15,000	3,000	12,000
20X2	3,000	15,000	6,000	9,000
20X3	3,000	15,000	9,000	6,000
20X4	3,000	15,000	12,000	3,000
20X5	3,000	15,000	15,000	nil

For 20X1, the depreciation charge would be accounted for as follows:

Profit and loss account	– 3,000 (reduce equity)
Accumulated depreciation	–3,000 (reduce assets)

The net book value of the fixed asset would be the sum of the fixed asset account and the accumulated depreciation account relating to that asset at any given point.

Asset	15,000
Accumulated depreciation	–3,000
Net book value at end 20X1	12,000

It follows from this that the accounting records are likely to have two accounts involving depreciation in any one year: the profit and loss account expense through which the appropriate part of the asset value is charged against profits in the year; and the reduction of the asset which is accumulated in a separate data file from the asset and accumulates over the life of the asset the total amount by which it has been charged against profits at any given moment.

The accumulated depreciation is simply the reduction of the asset value, but it is held in a separate account in order to facilitate disclosure. It always represents amounts which have already been expensed. Most corporate disclosure rules require that the business shows both the original cost of the assets and the accumulated depreciation.

In some sophisticated accounting systems the regular depreciation expense is recognized on a month-by-month basis and is written into a monthly accounting program within a computerized system, so that it takes place automatically. However, in general terms it is an adjustment to the financial records which must be made at every balance sheet date to recognize the consumption of some of the unexpired expenses which the company's assets represent.

Note that the management accounts of a company should normally make a deduction for depreciation in arriving at monthly profit and loss figures for operating units. A unit which makes a 'profit' before depreciation, but not enough to absorb the depreciation, is still making some contribution to the company's overheads, but in the long term is obviously not making sufficient money to repay its investment, let alone add to the value of the company. At the same time, the basis on which the depreciation charge is calculated should be checked because, as we have seen, this may not accurately represent the economic consumption of the assets concerned, which therefore distorts the performance measure.

We have dealt with depreciation as simply a question of absorbing the costs of the company's productive capacity as it is used up. This is generally how depreciation is regarded these days, but you may come across alternative notions which are not necessarily incompatible.

Worked example

The figures below represent the data in the company's accounting database as at 31 December 20X1. As you can see, the company has the following fixed assets: land $120,000 (not depreciated, considered to have an infinite life), buildings $80,000 (policy is to depreciate on a straight line basis over 40 years – i.e. 2.5 per cent per annum) and plant $45,000 (being depreciated at 25 per cent reducing balance – note that the figure consists of several components bought at different times). We have to update the accounting database for the annual depreciation charges, prior to issuing the annual financial statements. We need to depreciate the buildings and plant:

$$\text{Buildings } \$80,000 * 0.025 = \$2,000$$

Plant ($45,000–18000) * 0.25 = $6,750 (we deduct the accumulated depreciation which has been charged in previous years to find the net book value and then apply the reducing balance rate)
   Total charge for 20X1 = $8,750

	Database	Adjustment	Income	Balance sheet
Assets				
Land	120,000			120,000
Buildings	80,000			80,000
Accumulated				
depreciation	–14,000	–2,000		–16,000
Plant	45,000			45,000
Accumulated				
depreciation	–18,000	–6,750		–24,750
Stock	19,500			19,500
Receivables	17,250			17,250
Cash at bank	8,340			8,340
Totals	258,090	–8,750		257,340
Financing				
Share Capital	80,000			80,000
Reserves	62,100			62,100
Profit for the year				16,040
Debt	75,000			75,000
Accounts payable	16,200			16,200
Income statement				
Sales	200,000		200,000	
Cost of sales	–82,310		–82,310	
Personnel	–61,200		–61,200	
Other expenses	–26,700		–26,700	
Interest	–5,000		–5,000	
Depreciation charge		–8,750	–8,750	
Totals	258,090	–8,750	16,040	257,340

(Notice that the income statement data has been thrown into a separate column to identify it separately from the balance sheet, but of course the net profit of $16,040 also appears in the balance sheet.)

For example, in the past some accountants considered depreciation rather as a means of building up a replacement fund to buy new equipment when the old is worn out. This leads to the idea that instead of reducing the cost of the asset year by year in the balance sheet, you create a provision in the financing side which will be used to buy the new asset. The snags with this are that (a) the user has no way of knowing how old the assets are because in the asset side of the balance sheet they are all shown at original cost, no matter how old they are, and there is no direct link with the replacement provisions in the financing side of thebalance sheet; (b) would the company necessarily want to replace a particular asset at the end of its life – business changes rapidly? (c) would the same asset still be available? (d) how do you know what it would cost? (this argument also leads to the argument that one should use replacement cost as the basis of depreciation).

Another argument is that depreciation is the repayment, either to shareholders or to lenders of the money used to buy the equipment. Of course, the depreciation charge does not involve any cash movement – it is purely a paper adjustment of values within the accounting database. However, it should be realized that if no depreciation were charged in calculating profit, and all the profit were paid out in tax and dividend, the original capital would have been lost, so depreciation, by restricting profit, reduces tax and dividends and preserves the original capital.

This question of not involving a cash movement is also important in recognizing the difference between a company's profits for the year and its cash flow – the cash flow will be systematically higher than the profit by the amount of the depreciation charge.

Summary

In this chapter we have looked at the question – central to profit measurement – of the treatment of the costs of using up the company's productive capacity. We have seen that where an asset has a determinable life within the company, the cost of using up the asset must be allocated over this life, and impacts upon the estimate of profit for each accounting period. We have seen that there are several conventional bases for measuring depreciation and these do not necessarily reflect their economic consumption when there are tax considerations involved. We have noted that the depreciation charge reduces profit but does not cause any cash flow, thereby introducing another systematic difference between profit and cash on a period-to-period basis.

APPENDIX TO CHAPTER 5

Specific asset valuation problems

We did not want to get involved within the general presentation of assets and depreciation with a discussion of particular assets. However, we now present a number of different kinds of assets and discuss their particular attributes for accounting purposes.

IASC Framework defines an asset:

> An asset is a resource controlled by the enterprise as a result of past events and from which future economic benefits are expected to flow to the enterprise.

IAS38 Intangible Assets

8. Enterprises frequently expend resources, or incur liabilities, on the acquisition, development, maintenance or enhancement of intangible resources such as scientific or technical knowledge, design and implementation of new processes or systems, licences, intellectual property, market knowledge and trademarks (including brand names and publishing titles). Common examples of items encompassed by these broad headings are computer software, patents, copyrights, motion picture films, customer lists, mortgage servicing rights, fishing licences, import quotas, franchises, customer or supplier relationships, customer loyalty, market share and marketing rights.

19. An intangible asset should be recognised if, and only if:

    (a) it is probable that the future economic benefits that are attributable to the asset will flow to the enterprise; and
    (b) the cost of the asset can be measured reliably.

20. An enterprise should assess the probability of future economic benefits using reasonable and supportable assumptions that represent management's best estimate of the set of economic conditions that will exist over the useful life of the asset.

39. It is sometimes difficult to assess whether an internally generated intangible asset qualifies for recognition. It is often difficult to:

    (a) identify whether, and the point of time when, there is an identifiable asset that will generate future economic benefits; and
    (b) determine the cost of the asset reliably. In some cases the cost of generating an intangible asset internally cannopt be distinguished from the cost of maintaining or enhancing the enterprise's internally generated goodwill or of running day to day operations.

40. To assess whether an internally generated intangible asset meets the criteria for recognition, an enterprise classifies the generation of the asset into:

    (a) a research phase; and
    (b) a development phase.

41. If an enterprise cannot distinguish the research phase from the development phase of an internal project to create an intangible asset, the enterprise treats the expenditure on that project as if it were incurred in the research phase only.

Source: IAS 38

As we discussed in the early part of the section, the value which a company will use for its fixed assets will incorporate the full cost of bringing the assets into service. We have not examined the implications of this in respect of major categories of assets and we shall therefore now review some of the more frequently encountered types of asset and the accounting practices normally followed. The EC Fourth Directive calls for fixed assets to be split between intangible assets, tangible assets and investments, with slightly different valuation rules for each.

Intangible fixed assets

So far discussion of assets has been confined to physical operating assets such as buildings or machinery, but companies also have other assets which are not physical in nature; these are called 'intangible assets'. Typical intangible assets would be research and development, brand names, patents. The standard approach to asset value applies to these assets as well, although current practice imposes some limitations on assets such as research and development. A major problem which arises with intangible assets is that of uncertainty surrounding the future economic benefit which arises from expenses of this nature. For example, if a company spends money training its staff, the object is to improve future operations and hopefully profitability. However, the improvement is not certain, and the staff may leave at some future point, taking their improved efficiency with them. Similarly, advertising is done to generate future sales, but the long-term effects are generally impossible to estimate.

Research and development

In some sense research and development expenditure is the archetypal intangible asset and raises a number of basic issues. Where a company has invested in researching new products, it does not seem unreasonable that the cost of creating a new product should be considered as an asset, provided that the new product will lead to a commercial exploitation. This, however, leads to two problems: defining exactly what costs are associated with creating the new product, and then determining over what period the asset should be expensed. Very often it is relatively late in the research process that one can be reasonably certain that an asset (in the sense of something which will bring a future economic benefit) has been created.

In defining cost there is the problem of the treatment of the costs of unsuccessful research. For example, supposing a chemist sets out to create a new headache tablet and takes four years, during which he tries five alternative bases, of which only the last is wholly satisfactory. Does the research asset include the costs only of the research into the alternative which was ultimately accepted, or should one consider that the process of defining the unsuccessful alternatives is part of finding the usable alternative, and therefore all the costs should be treated as a research asset?

In the US the difficulty of finding a suitable definition, plus the operation of prudence, have led to a situation where all research and development costs must be expensed as they are incurred. In Europe generally the treatment is more flexible: general research must be expensed immediately, but research involved in refining and developing a specific product may be treated as an asset and expensed over its economic life (although many companies expense all research and development expenditure immediately anyway, not least because it qualifies immediately as a deduction for tax purposes).

The other problem is estimating the useful life of research and development. As with patents, there is a strong economic argument for spreading this over the whole expected commercial exploitation of the project. But again there is the problem of uncertainty – can one reasonably expect that a new headache tablet, for example, might be expected to be exploited for as long as twenty years? The estimation of the useful life of the asset should be made on a prudent basis.

Intangible assets are increasingly important to companies and are a continuing source of accounting problems. It is very difficult to attach a historical cost to some intangibles, such as brands names, which are built up slowly over years. Even if one can attach a cost and therefore have an accounting asset, there is still the question of amortization.

IAS 38 Intangible Assets

42. No intangible asset arising from research (or from the research phase of an internal project) should be recognised. Expenditure on research (or on the research phase of an internbal project) should be recognised as an expense when it is incurred.

45. An intangible asset arising from development (or from the development phase of an internal project) should be recognised if, and only if, an enterprise can demonstrate all of the following:

   (a) the technical feasibility of completing the intangible asset so that it will be available for use or sale;
   (b) its intention to complete the intangible asset and use or sell it;
   (c) its ability to use or sell the intangible asset;
   (d) **how the intangible asset will generate probable future economic benefits.** Among other things, the enterprise should demonstrate the existence of a market for the output of the intangible asset or the intangible asset itself or, if it is to be used internally, the usefulness of the intangible asset;
   (e) the availability of adequate technical, financial and other resources to complete the development and to use or sell the intangible asset; and
   (f) its ability to measure the expenditure attributable to the intangible asset during its development reliably.

59. Expenditure on an intangible item that was initially recognised as an expense by a reporting enterprise in previous annual financial statements or interim financial reports should not be recognised as part of the cost of an intangible asset at a later date.

Source: IAS 38

Brand names

In many bulk product areas where there are several competing products with very similar characteristics (coffee, chocolate, cars, washing machines etc.) it has become increasingly understood by management that what is important to the success of a business is not so much its manufacturing capacity (or not exclusively its manufacturing capacity) but also its ability to sell the products. Very often this is associated with the creation and maintenance of brand names. Ownership of a brand name may be described as a right to a future economic benefit (and therefore potentially an accounting asset), but having that brand name appear in the balance sheet is extremely problematical.

Where a company buys a brand name from another company, there is no problem – a clear historical cost value emerges from the transaction. But where a company creates a brand name – very similar to creating a new product – there are the problems of how early in the expenditure programme does it become reasonable to categorize the costs as being an asset? when can one be certain that there is indeed an asset?

IAS 38

51. Internally generated brands, mastheads, publishing titles, customer lists and items similar in substance should not be recognised as intangible assets.

The problem has so far arisen in Europe mostly in the context of take-over activity. A further issue that has arisen is the question of amortization of brand names. Many large companies which carry brand names argue that the regular advertising and promotion budget maintains the value of the brand, and depreciation is therefore unnecessary and represents a double charge.

Intellectual capital

Intellectual capital is a relatively new and enigmatic concept, relating primarily to the intangible, highly mutable assets of the firm or as some have put it, the "brain power" of the organization. This brain power accounts for an increasing proportion of the capital in traditional industries and forms the backbone of the rapidly growing technology and knowledge-intensive sectors in the global economy.

Microsoft is used as the example of the hidden value of these intangible assets of the firm. In 1996 Microsoft's market value was 11.2 times its tangible asset value. This "missing" value to a large degree represents the market's estimation of Microsoft's stock of intellectual capital that is not captured in its financial statements.

This is not the exception but rather the rule in financial reporting and illustrates one of the major limitations of the current financial reporting model. The Canadian Institute of Chartered Accountants concludes that accounting for intellectual capital will require developing accounting measures that can differentiate between firms in which intellectual capital is appreciating versus firms in which it is depreciating, and measures that will show the long run return in investment in people skills, information bases and the technological capabilities of organizations.

Source: Extract from "Buried treasure" by Ramona Dzinkowski, *World Accounting Report* May 1999

Patents

Patents are in effect a legal protection of an invention which prevents anyone using the invention without permission. As such they are sometimes costly to establish, but once established they do have a future economic use to the company (either from making or using the product or from licensing others to use it) provided that there is a demand for the particular invention.

Assuming that a patent does represent a future economic benefit to the company, it should be recognized at cost and then the cost expensed over the expected useful life of the asset in the normal way. The exact depreciation pattern to be used is a matter for debate, but unless exploitation can be foreseen with a high degree of certainty, patents are a good candidate for methods which load depreciation into the early years.

As with brands, where a company buys a patent, its historical cost value is clear, but where it invents the subject of the patent, then the same problems of defining costs and being certain of the existence of future economic benefits come into play.

Purchased goodwill

Sometimes companies expand by 'buying' customers from other suppliers, and when this happens a company is said to be buying 'goodwill'. For example, a solicitor who was planning to retire could sell the goodwill of his or her practice to another solicitor. His or her clients would presumably still need a solicitor, and although they cannot be forced to move to the alternative selected, he or she can write to them recommending a specific alternative.

The person recommended would have paid a fee for this to happen, and would have an excellent chance of retaining the customers. Unigate plc, the dairy products company, is famous for having purchased milk rounds as an intangible asset in its balance sheet.

The figure paid by an entity which acquires customers in this way is treated as an asset, and must be expensed in the usual way. Views differ as to the appropriate length of the period and the tendency is towards a short economic life on the basis that once the customers have tried the alternative service it is the quality of the alternative which will determine whether they remain customers or not.

This kind of goodwill is not frequently encountered in company accounts. There is a second type of goodwill (goodwill arising on consolidation) which is a product of accounting for groups of companies and will be discussed in that context.

Tangible fixed assets

Historically these have been the major assets of companies. A detailed analysis of these assets, divided into major classes and showing original cost (or valuation) and accumulated depreciation, has to be shown and is usually given in the notes to the accounts.

Land and buildings

In general terms a company would recognize such an asset at a value which was based on the acquisition cost and any other ancillary costs. A simple case would be where a company buys a ready-built factory, and may only have ancillary costs for professional fees such as for a surveyor and the solicitor who drew up the contract. Both the acquisition price and the fees would be capitalized in the value of the asset – the fees represent an integral part of the cost of bringing the asset into use.

A more complicated case might be where a company buys a plot of land on which there is a derelict building, demolishes the building, clears the site and builds a new factory. The value of the factory in the company's accounting records would include all those costs, as well as perhaps architect's fees and so on.

The aggregation of these elements provides a base cost, but the accounting problems and depreciation approach will depend on the legal means whereby the land is held. A company may either acquire a lease – a licence to use the land for a specific number of years – or it may own the land outright. Under a lease the problem is that the company's right to use the land will cease after a specified period, but the implications of that depend on the length of the period. If the lease is for a relatively short period, say five years, the asset must be expensed over that period. However, leases are also issued for much longer periods, occasionally as long as 999 years, in which case the cessation of the company's right to use the land is so remote as not to be worth considering. Leased property is usually depreciated over the life of the lease, with a maximum depreciation period for buildings of around 50 years.

Land which is owned outright provides a different problem because of the trend for land prices to rise. This means that in the classic approach to depreciation, the depreciable amount (acquisition cost less salvage value) may actually be negative. Supposing you acquired a piece of land for a project limited to ten years and that the land cost $500,000, it could be that with the rise in land prices expected over the ten years the salvage value would be (say) $600,000, giving a negative depreciable amount of $100,000.

Land is not therefore usually depreciated, even when values have been falling (companies argue this is a temporary, not permanent, diminution in value). This remains an exception and IAS 4 notes (para 6) that 'It is considered that depreciation should be charged in each accounting period on the basis of the depreciable amount irrespective of an increase in the value of the asset.'

That also still leaves the question of the buildings which may stand on the land. The traditional approach would be to arrive at separate values for the land and buildings (perhaps by asking a professional valuer to give estimates of each and then applying the proportion to the historical cost) and then depreciate the buildings separately from the land – usually over fifty years on a straight-line basis.

Here again some companies argue that there seems little justification for depreciating buildings whose value may also rise, but which in any event sit on land whose value is rising in the long term. Consequently, although it is professionally recommended to depreciate buildings, not all companies necessarily do that, unless the law requires it. It is a point analysts should check when looking at a new company's accounting policies.

An issue which has not really presented itself very strongly yet is the question of creating provisions for the eventual re-instatement of land to its natural state. This has surfaced in respect of the decommissioning costs of nuclear power stations. It can be argued that any company which builds a factory should make provisions for the ultimate removal of the factory when its useful life has ended. This is not yet the case, but if it were, this would probably call for another regular charge, alongside depreciation, to match the decommissioning costs to the asset's revenue-earning period. Companies are becoming increasingly aware of the potential for future charges to repair ecological damage. Many oil companies now provide for decommissioning costs in relation to the extraction of crude oil.

Plant and equipment

Here again the acquisition cost of the plant may well be only a part of the total costs of bringing the plant into service. Ancillary costs to be capitalized might include elements such as site preparation, engineers' time in assembling and testing the plant on site, cost of transport to the site, etc. Sometimes a company's own workforce may be involved in the preparation of the asset. The fact that the company's workforce is involved does not change the basic concept – their wages, etc. should be treated as part of the installation cost.

Leased assets

Sometimes a company acquires plant and equipment, or other assets, on a lease agreement rather than buying them outright. The increasing use of this method of financing has highlighted a particular accounting problem. If a company acquires an asset under a lease agreement and in effect has the use of the asset throughout its working life, should that asset be recognized in the balance sheet? Should the obligation under the lease to make payments to the lessor be recognized as a liability?

If, for example, a company borrows $100,000 to buy some plant worth $100,000, both the plant asset and the debt liability would appear in the balance sheet. When a company hires equipment on a lease for substantially the whole of its useful life, the company is in effect acquiring the asset's economic value while incurring a liability to pay for it in instalments. The instalments would include both an element of interest and an element of repayment of the value of the asset. Is this situation different in principle from that where the company borrows the money and buys the asset in two separate transactions?

The US, UK and IASC all have standards requiring that where a company acquires substantially all the risks and rewards of ownership of an asset under a lease, then that asset should be recognized in the balance sheet as well as the liability to the lessor (e.g. IAS 17).

It is not particularly useful in the context of an accounting course to analyse in detail the methods which are used for arriving at a precise value of the asset, and splitting the total amounts payable under the lease into repayment of the loan and interest charges. In principle the asset is valued at a 'fair' value (its purchase price if bought on the open market) and this value is recognized as an asset. A balancing liability for the same amount is recognized as an obligation to the lessor. The amount payable over the length of the lease will normally be more than this, since it includes an interest element. The interest element is allocated over the length of the lease, ideally in relation to the outstanding value of the lease liability.

Take a simplified example where a company leases a machine for five years at a rate of $10,000 a year. If the company had bought the machine on the open market it would have cost $35,000. Accordingly the machine will appear in the balance sheet at $35,000 and there will also be a balancing lease liability of $35,000. This means that the difference between the 'fair' value assumed and the total of the lease payments ($10,000 $\times$ 5 years = $50,000) is $15,000 and this represents the implied interest charge on the transaction.

The $15,000 needs to be allocated over the life of the asset in proportion to the amount of the loan outstanding, and this can be done accurately with a computer program or there are simplified approximations to work out the effective rate of interest being charged. If we simplify in this case and say that the implied rate of interest is 10 per cent, then the first annual payment of $10,000 would be split for accounting purposes as $3,500 interest charge ($35,000 lease liability $\times$ 10%) and $6,500 as repayment of the lease liability, leaving $28,500 outstanding at the start of the second year.

In the second year the interest charge is 10% $\times$ $28,500 = $2,850 and the balance of the annual payment, $7,150, is used to further repay the lease liability. This continues until the lease liability is extinguished.

The asset is depreciated in the same way as assets which are owned once a value has been arrived at.

Cap Gemini Group

Notes to the consolidated financial statements (extract)

g) Capital leases

A capital lease is a lease that transfers substantially all the risks and rewards incident to ownership of an asset. When a fixed asset is held under a capital lease, its value is restated as an asset and the present value at the beginning of the lease term of future minimum lease payments during the lease term is recorded as an obligation. The asset is depreciated over its useful life as per the Group's policy and future minimum lease payments are amortised over the lease term.

Source: Cap Gemini Group,
Financial Report 1998

Investments

This is the third category of long-term asset. Companies may make investments both on a short-term and a long-term basis. Short-term investments are often made in liquid securities when a company has a temporary excess of cash. These are sometimes called *treasury investments*, and would appear as a current asset, often as part of cash at bank.

Where a company makes an investment for strategic purposes, which it intends to hold for some length of time, this will appear in the fixed asset category. Companies may invest in other companies for a number of reasons – to secure a relationship with a major customer or supplier; to participate in a new development but spread the risk with other interested parties; as a forerunner to a takeover. Where a company has a substantial stake in another (less than 50 per cent but large enough, for example, to be given a seat on the board) this is called an investment in an *associated company* (the technique for accounting for associated companies is dealt with in Chapter 14). Where companies set up joint ventures (for example, oil companies sometimes jointly own pipelines) these are often shown as an investment in an associate.

As with other assets, such investments are valued at the full cost of acquisition, subject to any permanent impairment of value. The company must disclose the market value of the asset at balance sheet date in the notes to the accounts. This is straightforward if the security is listed on a stock exchange, otherwise the directors have to give their own valuation.

Questions

1. Profit forecasts

   A company is considering investing in a project with a five-year life. The project involves paying $75,000 for a licence to manufacture a new product and equipping a production line at a cost of $300,000. The product is expected to have a life of five years only, and at the expiry of that time the production line will be sold and should yield a salvage value of $50,000. In order to launch the product the company plans a three-month advertising campaign which will cost $100,000.

   Assuming that in each year the expected sales are $1,000,000 and expenses other than those detailed above are $800,000, draw up two alternative series of profit and loss accounts for the project using (a) straight-line, and (b) reducing balance depreciation of 30 per cent per annum, for the plant, while treating the other expenses consistently in each set.

   If, for policy reasons, the company wished to maximize profits in the first two years of operation, what accounting choices could be made (within the terms of generally accepted accounting principles) to achieve this?

2. A company had the following situation in its accounting database at 31 December 20X1:

Assets	
Land	150,000
Buildings	50,000
Accumulated depreciation	–4,000
Plant and equipment	46,800
Accumulated depreciation	–19,300
Vehicles	52,500
Accumulated depreciation	–27,300
Stock at 1 January	9,400
Receivables	17,300
Cash	24,600

Financing	
Share capital	100,000
Reserves	189,300
Trade payables	5,400
Sales	247,200
Purchases	–69,600
Salaries	–131,000
Other expenses	–41,300

You are asked to draw up an income statement and balance sheet after making the following adjustments:

(a) Provide depreciation on the following assets: buildings, 2 per cent straight line, plant and equipment 15 per cent straight line, vehicles 40 per cent reducing balance.

(b) Closing stock at 31 December was 10,650.

3. A company decides to replace one of its production lines with new machinery. All the costs associated with the exercise are grouped together by the accountant in the same account, pending later analysis. The items appearing in the account after three months are:

	$
Removal of old machinery	2,800
Installation of new power lines	350
Resurfacing factory floor	825
Purchase of new machines	62,100
Transport of machines to factory	3,200
Hire of crane to position new machines	450
Servicing after first month's production	375
Replacement of conveyor damaged in production	580
Engineer's fee to check installation	250

In addition to the above items, the payroll records show that the company's maintenance crew spent 300 hours on installing the machines. The usual charge-out for labour is $5.75 per hour.

Which of the above items should be part of the asset value of the new plant?

6 Refining the database and making distributions

In this chapter we are going to look at another area where the accountant intervenes in the accounting database to refine the information, usually as part of the process of preparing the annual accounts and with a view to giving a more precise profit estimate and balance sheet. We are going to look at accruals and prepayments, as well as provisions, both for loss of value in assets and to anticipate future expenses.

The routine accounting system works very well for things like invoices to clients and recording deliveries from suppliers. However, there are transactions that fall slightly outside this convenient framework and need to be brought into it, or aligned with it when making accurate profit measurements. For example, we consume electricity and gas, and use telephones, and are invoiced afterwards; generally company lawyers or auditors do not send in monthly bills, but rather invoice us at the end of delivering a series of services which frequently do not correspond to our accounting year. In these areas the accountant has to intervene and form a judgment as to what expenses have not been brought into the database but should be incorporated into the profit estimate.

Accrued expenses and prepayments

Accrued expenses (sometimes called just 'accruals') and prepayments are the near cousins of creditors and debtors. These are items where the economic transaction takes place at a different time from the cash transaction, but where the volume or frequency of the transactions does not warrant a continuing record in the basic accounting system, or the invoice arrives sometime after the consumption has taken place – or sometime in advance of this. We have a timing difference between notification of the item and the economic event, so the accountant must make adjustments when preparing the annual financial statements. (Note that a highly sophisticated database which is used for preparing monthly internal accounts may well make monthly adjustments for accruals, or use standard charges or some other device to bring these time-based items regularly into the database. For our purposes, the first need is simply to be aware of this type of transaction, and then later we will need to take these into account when preparing annual statements.)

Typical transactions in this area would be invoices for items such as telephone, gas or electricity, where the bill is received after the service or product has been used. For example, supposing a business prepares accounts to 31 December each year but receives in February a gas bill for the months of November, December and January. The proportion of the bill which relates to November and December is an expense of the financial year ended on 31 December. Such an expense is called an 'accrued expense' and calls for an adjustment to be made in the financial statements for the year to 31 December to recognize the outstanding charge.

Supposing in this case the invoice referred to was for $1,200. In the absence of any specific information about how much related to each month, the accountant will make a straightforward allocation on a time basis: the invoice covers three months, two of those are in the previous financial period, so the accrued expense is:

$$2/3 \times \$1,200 = \$800$$

This adjustment would be inserted in the recording system in order to allocate the expense across the appropriate years. The $800 expense would be deducted from the profit, while the corresponding liability would be put in a temporary account and appear in the balance sheet as a short-term liability. In the following accounting year, when the $1,200 bill was paid, only $400 would be treated as an expense, while $800 would extinguish the year-end liability:

	Year end	Following year
Assets		
Cash		−1200
Totals	0	−1200
Financing		
Liabilities		
Accrued expenses	800	−800
Equity		
Profit year 1	−800	
Profit year 2		−400
Totals	0	−1200

The operation of the accrual account ensures that the actual payment of the bill automatically expenses the correct portion into the new year operating expenses as well as cancelling the accrual.

Not all accruals fall across two accounting periods; there would, for example, be a major accrual each year for the audit fee, which is conventionally treated as an expense of the year being audited (on a matching basis) although the work is carried out in large part in the following year.

A further point to note is that not all accruals are for known amounts. That is, when the accountant is drawing up the financial statements he or she may not have received an invoice such as the gas bill examined above. Part of the exercise in drawing up the annual statements (sometimes called the 'year-end exercise') involves checking expense accounts to see whether all charges for the year have been received. If they have not, the precise details of the charge may not have arrived and the accountant will be obliged to estimate – based on previous year charges, or current trends as appropriate (just one of the many instances where the data in the annual accounts is not a matter of indisputable fact).

Prepayments

Prepayments are the opposite of accruals – they are payments made in one financial year which relate to a future financial year. Some items, often rent and insurance for example (also prepaid mobile phone cards!), are paid in advance. As such they are an asset at the time of payment and only become an expense as time elapses and the service or good is used up.

Typically the accounting system would not record such items as assets since in practical terms they start to be used up immediately. Usually such transactions are accounted for as expenses when first entering the accounting records, and as a further part of the year-end exercise the accountant would examine such expense categories to check that the whole of the asset had indeed expired and was properly an expense. Frequently there would be an unexpired portion, since rental periods, for example, rarely coincide exactly with a company's financial year, and in order to match the transaction to the correct financial periods, the expense needs to be diminished and an asset recognized at balance sheet date, representing the unexpired portion of the expense.

If we take an insurance premium as an example, suppose an annual premium is paid on 1 April and the company's financial year runs to 31 December. Nine-twelfths of the premium should be expensed in the year of payment and three-twelfths recognized as an asset at 31 December – to be expensed in the following year.

Assuming that the premium was $2,400 and that it was initially treated as an expense, three-twelfths ($600) should be recognized as an asset at the year end:

	Original payment	Year-end adjustment	Next year
Assets			
Cash	−2400		
Prepaid expenses		+600	−600
Totals	−2400	+600	−600
Equity			
Profit for the first year	−2400	+600	
Profit for the following year			−600
Totals	−2400	+600	−600

The use of the temporary prepaid expenses account allows the part of the expense which relates to the following year to be carried forward to the expenses for that year.

Provisions

Provisions can appear, at first sight, to be rather a fluid subject. Essentially a provision is a deduction from profit which is made either to reflect an anticipated loss of value of an asset, or a potential future outflow of resources to meet an expense. The key issues are that the provision is generally an estimate, and that, like an accrued expense, it involves making a deduction from current year profits which will be carried forward in the balance sheet. Students tend immediately to think that provisions must give company accountants a splendid opportunity to manipulate profits, which is true but of course tax authorities are well aware of this and strictly control what provisions if any are accepted in calculating the taxable profit.

> **IAS 37 Provisions, contingent liabilities and contingent assets (extract)**
>
> **14.** A provision should be recognised when:
>
> (a) an enterprise has a present obligation (legal or constructive) as a result of a past event;
> (b) it is probable that an outflow of resources embodying economic benefits will be required to settle the obligation; and
> (c) a reliable estimate can be made of the amount of the obligation.

A provision is an amount charged against the profit and loss account and carried forward in the balance sheet in anticipation of a future expense whose timing and amount are uncertain, but which derive in some way from current circumstances (i.e. the event generating the potential cost has already taken place). The provision can always be released back to the profit and loss account at some future time if it proves not to be needed. Generally a provision is made where some current event may have future consequences which will create an expense for the company. Prudence and matching both require that this possibility is recognized, but typically neither the exact amount nor the moment when it will crystallize is known, so a provision is created for an estimated amount.

Common examples of this kind of situation are where a company agrees to pay a pension in the future to employees, where an airline offers airmiles as incentives which can in the future be converted to free tickets, where a company decides to restructure or close down an operation. Usually a company which manufactures goods will have a provision for warranty claims.

Pensions are often a special case, and we will come back to those later in the book in more detail, but you can see that where, for example, the company gives long service awards, the right to the award is gained by (say) ten years of service, and is therefore being earned during the ten years and is strictly a cost of those ten years, but it is difficult to predict how many employees will qualify for these at any given time. This is a classic provision – the company is contractually committed to pay such awards, but does not know how many people will eventually claim them, nor when, so it is a case for a provision.

From an accounting perspective, the provision is created by reducing profits and increasing liabilities:

Equity	*Create provision*
Profit for the year	–15,000
Liabilities	
Provisions	+15,000

Note that the provision for expenses is accounted for in the balance sheet as part of liabilities (although generally separated clearly from debt) and is normally considered part of the long-term financing of the company.

Generally speaking, the extent of the use of provisions is one of the areas where Anglo-Saxon practice is noticeably different from practice in continental Europe, and as usual this is driven by tax considerations. Many European tax authorities are more sympathetic to provisions than their anglophone counterparts, which leads to a greater use of them, since they reduce profit. The IASC definition of a provision (see above) requires there to be a firm commitment to make a payment, whereas in many other regimes a provision is justified if there is simply a possibility of making a payment.

> **Potential legal liability**
>
> The Board of Trinity Mirror plc today announces that it has discovered irregularities in the reporting of the circulation numbers to the Audit Bureau of Circulations in certain of its Birmingham titles.
>
> ... The problem has been confined to the reporting of circulation numbers only, and does not impact reported turnover or profits for these titles. In addition, independent research undertaken by Research Surveys of Great Britain show that between 1996 and 1999 there was a relatively stable readership figure for the total readership research area for the Birmingham Evening Mail and the Sunday Mercury. The Group believes that readership numbers are the most relevant measure for the majority of advertising clients of the three titles, and these continue to demonstrate the strength and value of these titles.
>
> ... In view of the fact that readership figures have remained relatively stable, it is extremely difficult for the Group to quantify the extent of any potential liability facing the Group. On the basis of information currently available, the group believes that any such liability would, at a maximum, be in the order of £20 million and is likely to be significantly less.
>
> Extracted from company press release of 4 November 1999

Asset impairment

The term provision is also used in a related context where the company decides to reduce the carrying value of an asset because of a perceived or expected drop in value. For example, the company has bought shares in another company and the market value of these shares has dropped below the historical cost. This is a provision for asset impairment. Like an ordinary provision, when it is created, this is done by making a deduction from the income statement, but where the opposite entry for a provision for expenses goes into the financing side of the balance sheet as a liability, the asset impairment provision is a deduction from the asset value, and is handled just like depreciation.

IAS 36 *Impairment of assets* says that a company 'should assess at each balance sheet date whether there is any indication that an asset may be impaired'. The company should estimate the 'recoverable amount' and reduce the carrying value accordingly.

Bad debts and doubtful debts

Probably the most commonly occurring asset impairment provision is that relating to non-collection of company debts: a company's suppliers will naturally expect to be paid in full, but on the other hand the company may not expect to collect all the debts owing to it. At first sight that might seem a little odd, but there are various reasons why this may be:

1. A customer may be a bad risk: it is difficult to assess creditworthiness, so mistakes are made and credit given to those who cannot pay, or again, a company with a good credit record may suddenly hit bad times.
2. A customer might be disputing the amount of the invoice you sent: perhaps s/he thinks the price charged was higher than that agreed, or the quantity greater than that delivered.
3. A customer may have refused to accept some of the goods because they were faulty, or may be planning to send some faulty goods back but this has not yet been picked up by the accounting system.

There are many reasons why the debtors' balance at any given point is unlikely to be collected in full. If the full accounting value was used in the balance sheet, it would therefore overstate the value of the asset and of the profit for the period.

There are two separate aspects of assessing a 'prudent' value for outstanding debtors. First, there is the case of specific debts which on the evidence available are not likely ever to be paid, and second, there is a more general assessment of the collectability of all debts.

In the first case it is a routine part of credit management to inspect all outstanding debts and particularly those which have been outstanding a long time. What exact length of time is appropriate depends upon the normal terms of credit in a particular industry – in most cases if a debtor has not paid within sixty days of the issue of the invoice (or perhaps by the end of the month following the month of issue), the credit manager will regard the debt as overdue, and in need of follow-up. After ninety days the debt is a source of concern, and normally a credit manager would be in touch directly with the debtor at that point to discover why payment has not been made. After six months the credit manager and the accountant should consider the debt together with whatever information the credit manager has gleaned from the customer (or indeed the sales force) to decide whether the debt is likely to be settled. It may be that the client is going into liquidation or disputes the bill and refuses to pay and a decision has to be taken about recoverability. If it is decided that the amount is not recoverable, then the debt becomes categorized as a bad debt and should be removed from the debtors' total.

The debt, although it derives originally from a sale, is considered to be an expense. After all, the original sale took place; it is the payment of the debt which has not happened. Accordingly there is a simple transfer to credit the debtor account (and therefore cancel the amount outstanding) and debit the profit and loss account. This evaluation of individual debts should take place routinely throughout the year, but in any event it will also be a part of the exercise undertaken in preparing financial statements to ensure that no bad debts are included in the debtor total.

The second consideration is that of taking a prudent view of the likely value to be received from the current debtor balance at the accounting date when statements are being prepared. As we noted, there are many reasons why the total of debtors may not be ultimately converted to cash, but most of the problems on individual debts only come to light after the debt has aged a little. Consequently as the bulk of the debtors outstanding at any one moment will be current, there is no way of knowing which will cause problems.

The prudent response to this is to set aside a 'provision for doubtful debts'. This is an amount expensed in the profit and loss account but simply held as a credit balance in the nominal ledger against the day when any of the debts outstanding at balance sheet date is classified as bad.

The object of making this general provision for doubtful debts is to show a prudent value of total debtors. Exactly how much should be set aside in the provision is a matter for consideration in the context of the business of each company. In general terms a company might be guided by:

1. industry practice generally;
2. average percentage of actual bad debts experienced by the company in previous years;
3. an estimate consisting of a high proportion of debts outstanding more than (say) three months plus a low proportion of current debts.

The precise amount will be a matter of the opinion of the accountant preparing the statements and the auditor.

It may be helpful to look at the impact of such a provision in the context of a profit and loss account and balance sheet. Let us say that Wholesale Merchants Ltd has total debtors in its nominal ledger of $115,000 and that in preparing the annual financial statements the accountant has decided that $1,000 of debts should be treated as definitely bad, while a further $1,300 should be set aside as a provision for doubtful debts.

The impact of this will be to create an expense of $2,300 and reduce the published balance sheet value of debtors by the same amount. Within the company's records, the transactions would be:

	Write off bad debt	*Create provision*
Assets		
Debtors	−1,000	
Provision		−1,300
Equity		
Profit for the year	−1,000	−1,300

The book value of the debtors goes down by $1,000 directly, and in the published balance sheet the debtors figure would also be reduced by the provision, although in the nominal ledger the provision will be held in a separate account, and in practical terms all the 'live' debtor acounts will continue to be followed up with monthly statements etc.

Normally a company will set aside a provision each year, and in the next set of statements will simply add to or subtract from the existing provision to reach the required figure. For example, a company with an unutilized balance on the provision of $500 brought forward from the previous year would determine the required provision for the current statement, let us say $750, and then expense the difference ($250) needed to bring the provision up to the required amount.

It is important to realize that the provision for doubtful debts is an adjustment made in order that the published accounts show a reasonably prudent view. Notice that none of the individual accounts of the customers is credited. They still record the full amount due. The provision will be used during the following year, as the bad debts materialize. This ensures that the bad debts do not affect the expenses (and hence the profit) of the year in which they prove to be bad, but rather the year in which the business was done.

Hidden reserves

Clearly provisions provide great scope for reducing profits under a prudent accounting regime, even though they are not necessarily considered to be an 'allowable' (i.e. accepted by the tax authorities) expense for calculating the tax base.

Bosch Group Balance Sheet (extract)

	million DM
Equity	7,859.3
Tax exempt reserves	130.3
Provisions	11,564.0
Liabilities	4,872.9
Deferred income	25.6
Total	24,452.1

Analysis of provisions

Accrued pension and similar obligations	4,597.8
Accrued taxes	279.1
Other*	6,687.1
	11,564.0

* Note: this provides for obligations in the areas of sales, personnel and fringe benefits, obligations from subsidiaries as well as miscellaneous other risks. For deferred maintenance, we also included provisions for expenditure which will be incurred from four to twelve months after the close of the fiscal year.

Source: Bosch Annual Report

Such provisions can be used to even out profits – shareholders expect profits to grow each year – and provisions which have been created with a view to concealing profits or storing them for the future (the SEC talks about 'cookie jar' provisions) could be considered to constitute 'hidden reserves'. By way of illustration, suppose that in 20X1 a company reported profits of $100m; the position might be:

	20X1	*20X2*	*20X3*
	$m	*$m*	*$m*
Reported profit	100		
Market expectations		120	140

In 20X2 the draft accounts show profits of $150m but the company does not expect to be able to sustain that level of profitability, which was caused by unusual trading conditions. If it reports that profit, the situation would be:

Reported profit	100	150	
Market expectations			225

So it makes a provision:

Draft profit		150	
Provision		(30)	
Reported profit	100	120	
Market expectations			140

The following year is particularly bad:

Draft profit			110
Release provision			30
Reported profit	100	120	140

Pressure on immediate profitability in the international field means that such provisions are used less often than they used to be, but it is normal practice for companies to try to even out profit flows a little by matching windfall profits with extra costs, and frequently pursued by German, Austrian and Swiss companies (known as 'income smoothing'). The SEC has recently been complaining about US companies doing this also. Apart from anything else there is a closer correlation between profit and dividend and shareholders look first at the dividend, not the profit, but also check the dividend as a percentage of profit.

The term 'reserve' has a specific connotation in technical accounting jargon – it is an amount set aside from profit after tax, and will appear in the balance sheet as a component of owners' equity. Hidden reserves (also secret reserves, silent reserves) are rather different. These are deductions from measured profit, which do not appear separately in the profit and loss account when charged, and are not visible in the balance sheet. Historically, such reserves might be created by:

- writing down assets excessively;
- creating provisions for fictitious risks;
- increasing liabilities.

The pressures for increased transparency of accounting mean that in many jurisdictions such activity is now illegal, and where it is legal (as in Switzerland) some disclosures have to be made when reserves are released. Clearly, while such reserves may be defended on the grounds of prudence, they provide endless opportunities for disguising the true state of a company's profits and can cause creditors and investors to provide finance where they might not otherwise do so.

Capital structure

Broadly, companies are financed externally either with equity or debt. Equity participates fully in the risks and rewards of ownership – has no guaranteed return, but no upper limit either. Companies have limited liability so the equity-holder's downside risk is limited to the amount of his or her investment. The equity is only ever repaid to the individual investor in the event of liquidation. Ordinarily an investor realizes the investment by selling to someone else, although in restricted circumstances companies can buy back their own shares. (Exact regulation varies quite substantially from one jurisdiction to another.)

Debt is usually advanced to the company for a fixed period, earns a fixed return (although the interest rate may float in line with market rates) and must be repaid at the end of the period. The debt may be for a short, medium or long term, may be in foreign currency and can derive from a variety of sources. Many large companies obtain debt by issuing bonds or debentures which are bought and sold on the international financial markets.

This traditional distinction broke down somewhat during the 1980s as a result of financial engineering – banks have competed with each other for corporate clients by devising ever more complicated debt instruments which incorporate many characteristics of equity.

The decision as to what proportion of debt and equity to use in a company is a major issue. In principle a company which uses a high proportion of debt (a highly geared company) has the possibility of enhancing the return to shareholders at the cost of making the return more volatile, more risky to the shareholder (to be discussed). The ratio of debt to equity is one of the key aspects reviewed by the markets, and some companies put a lot of effort into massaging this ratio.

Generally companies have a target debt/equity ratio around which they operate, but which they do not usually achieve in practice. Issuing new equity can be expensive (professional fees, underwriting etc.) and therefore companies tend to use internally generated funds and debt to finance new projects in the first instance and then every few years issue new equity to move back closer to their target gearing.

Components of equity

The main type of share is the ordinary shares. The ordinary shareholders are the ultimate owners of the company and all other forms of finance rank ahead of these for payment. Their interest in the company is called equity – what is left after all other calls have been met.

Equity in a balance sheet consists of ordinary shares and reserves. Reserves are either capital or revenue in nature. Capital reserves may not be distributed to shareholders (except on liquidation); revenue reserves are usually derived from the company's profit-making activities and may be paid over to shareholders by way of dividend. The archetypal revenue reserve is accumulated or retained profits.

Ordinary shares have a *face* or *par* or *nominal value*. When companies are created, legal documents are drawn up which specify the upper limit on the number of shares which can be issued. Companies are not obliged to issue all these, and their effective voting share capital is the *issued share capital*. Note that sometimes companies have different classes of ordinary shares – 'A' shares, 'B' shares etc. – often this is to give different voting rights to different groups of shareholders, a practice not entirely popular with the market.

Ordinary shares are rarely issued at par value and the difference between issue price and par value is also part of equity. It is called *share premium* and is a capital reserve. Costs of issuing shares are offset against share premium.

Preference shares

These shares attract a fixed return (hence '7% preference shares') and holders do not routinely have voting rights so have the characteristic of debt; on the other hand the preference dividend may not be paid if there are no profits and does not qualify as a deduction before tax. Usually if no dividend is paid preference shareholders are enfranchised. Typically preference shares are cumulative – if the dividend is not paid, the right to receive it accumulates against future profits. Dividends cannot be paid to ordinary shareholders ahead of preference shareholders. It is a matter of opinion as to whether preference shares should be treated as debt or equity for the purposes of calculating gearing.

Convertibles

Convertible securities – either preference shares or debt which can be converted at some point in the future into ordinary shares – are another form of debt which was particularly popular at the end of the 20th century. The merit of these is that the initial fixed return status means that there is little risk to the lender, while the possibility of converting to equity in the longer term means that if the company does well the holder can convert to equity and participate in the growth. For the issuer it means a finer issue price and if converted, a relatively cheap way to issue equity. For the analyst there is a problem as to whether convertible debt should be treated as debt or equity for analytical purposes.

In recent years companies have issued all sorts of complex financial instruments which combine both elements of debt and elements of equity.

The earliest instruments were probably convertible debentures or preference shares, where companies might argue that they should be considered to be part of the equity component rather than debt. Variants on this might be debt (sometimes called mezzanine debt) which ranked behind other debt for repayment and received a return based on profitability of the company.

More recent developments are capital bonds and perpetual loan notes. If a loan is never to be repaid, it can be argued that it is more like equity than debt.

Summary

In this chapter we have dealt largely with matters affecting the financing side of the balance sheet. In the first instance we have discussed year-end adjustments and the recognition of expenses which have not been invoiced, and indeed in the case of provisions where we do not know when or sometimes even how much is to be paid. We have also visited briefly the equity side of financing, looking at how this is made up.

Questions

The following balances were extracted from the accounting records of Arlington SA as at 31 December 20X1:

100,000 ordinary shares	100,000
10% preference shares	50,000
12% debenture	50,000
Premises	130,000
Motor vehicles (gross cost $48,000)	36,000
Purchases	219,700
Administration expenses	73,200
Distribution costs	102,600
Sales	476,900
Debtors	39,250
Creditors	23,600
Stock at 1 January 20X1	21,250
Bank balance (asset)	70,420
Investments at cost	45,800
Reserves	48,220
Debenture interest	3,000
Preference dividend	2,500
Ordinary dividend	5,000

You are required to draw up a profit and loss account and balance sheet for the company as at 31 December 20X1, after taking into account the following

adjustments (note that expenses have been analysed by function, not by type, in this example):

(a) The closing stock (31 December 20X1) was valued at $19,300.

(b) Preference and ordinary dividends were paid halfway through the year, as well as debenture interest, but an accrual should be made for the balance of the debenture interest for the year. The company proposes a final dividend of $7,500 on ordinary shares.

(c) The audit fee has been agreed at $5,000.

(d) Insurance (included in administrative expenses) has been paid in advance and $950 relates to 20X2.

(e) There are accrued expenses of $480 for telephone (included in admin.) and $620 for light and heat (distribution).

(f) The debtor balance includes $1,200 of bad debts which should be written off.

(g) Depreciation of 25 per cent on a straight-line basis should be charged on the motor vehicles (which are vans used in distribution).

(h) The market value of the investments at 31 December 20X1 was $44,100.

(i) It is estimated that the tax charge for 20X1 will be $20,000.

(*Comment*: this question is presented in an unhelpful way! You should reorganize the information from the database onto a spreadsheet in a way with which you are comfortable and then deal with the adjustments. You will not have come across one or two adjustments, and should just suggest a way of dealing with them based on what you know so far.)

7 Making financial statements

In this chapter we are going to reach the end of our journey to the first major objective, which is the ability to put together a simple profit and loss account and balance sheet. The techniques we have been using are not those used directly by accountants, but the object is to understand the principles, in order better to be able to use financial statements as managers. This chapter will serve to bring together and review the different allocations and adjustments we have discussed so far, and should confirm the techniques learned.

Constructing financial statements

The basic technique for the preparation of a profit and loss account and balance sheet consists of taking the aggregate transaction data from the accounting records as at the end of the financial year, quantifying the adjustments necessary to convert the data to reflect generally accepted accounting principles, then putting the base data and the adjustments together in the approved statement format.

There is no prescribed way of carrying out this exercise, but most accountants prepare working papers on the basis of what is called an 'extended trial balance'. This is not exactly the method we shall use, but is presented here for information.

The base data with which the accountant starts is the trial balance as at the end of the year – that is, the listing of all the balances on all the nominal ledger accounts at the end of the year. The accountant must then refine this data by adjusting for unrecorded bills, depreciation, bad debts etc. This may seem a potentially limitless exercise involving a major investigative activity, but in fact the accountant always starts of with the previous year's adjustments and then checks to see what has changed subsequently, so that the 'year-end exercise' is built up incrementally as the business develops.

The adjustments which are calculated at this stage are put into working papers in the first instance and a draft set of statements prepared. These will form the basis of discussion with management and auditors, since usually they will involve taking a position about open transactions and other uncertainties (and will also impact on issues like taxation and profit-related bonuses).

The traditional extended trial balance working paper consists of four sets of debit and credit columns which will be added across to give the final picture. You will recall that, formally speaking, the accounting database is constructed with two columns for each account (see Chapter 2) although we have not replicated that presentation since our object is to understand how the figures work rather than run an accounting function.

Ledger + *balances*	*Adjustments =*	*Profit and* *loss*	*Balance* *sheet*
Dr / Cr	Dr / Cr	Dr / Cr	Dr / Cr
$ $	$ $	$ $	$ $

Mathematically, the ledger balances and adjustments are added together horizontally. Each adjusted balance will have its place in either the profit and loss account or balance sheet and the adjusted total is entered in the appropriate column. The total debits and credits in the first column will equal each other, as will those in the adjustments column, but the profit and loss account and balance sheet columns must be added together to get balancing totals.

For our purposes we shall continue to work with single column spreadsheets, and we will add across to the right as we put in adjustments and so on.

The adjustments consist typically of all the elements we have looked at in the preceding sessions and which are necessary to provide accounts which fully comply with generally accepted accounting principles. Specifically this involves the following:

1. *Calculation of cost of sales*: Insertion of closing stocks to arrive at the measurement of the cost of the goods sold during the period.
2. *Adjustment for accruals/prepayments*: Bringing into the accounts details of expenses relating to the period but unrecorded and unpaid at balance sheet date; carrying forward the unexpired expense for payments made which relate to future periods. (The information for this in a practical situation comes from examining individual ledger accounts to check the periods covered by payments, and examining payments after the balance sheet date.)
3. *Charging annual depreciation*: Debiting the operating expenses and crediting accumulated depreciation to reflect the expensing of assets consumed during the year.

The easiest way to see what happens in practice is if we now take an example, and work through the adjustments individually.

Worked example

The trial balance of Mornington Crescent Emporium SA as at 31 December 20X1 was as follows:

Mornington Crescent Emporium SA
Trial balance as at 31 December 20X1

	$
Assets	
Land	30,000
Equipment	15,000
Accumulated depreciation	−4,500
Stock at 1 Jan. X1	13,250
Debtors	23,000
Bank	18,560
	95,310
Financing	
Share capital	50,000
Retained profits	10,500
Creditors	16,850
Sales	193,000
Purchases	−145,000
Salaries and wages	−15,325
Rent	−10,000
Insurance	−2,500
Legal and professional exps	−1,250
Telephone	−345
Light and heat	−620
	95,310

In reviewing the accounting transactions both before and after the balance sheet date, the following information comes to light:

1. The value of the stock of goods for resale at 31 December 20X1 was $14,150.
2. Rent is payable quarterly in advance and rent for the three months January–March 20X2 was paid in December 20X1.
3. An insurance premium of $1,000 was paid in September 20X1, covering the period October 20X1 to March 20X2 inclusive.
4. A telephone account of $120 was received in February 20X2 and related to the three months ended 31 January 20X2.
5. An electricity account (the most recent one paid) for the three months up to the end of November 20X1 for $150 was paid in December 20X1.
6. The accounts must be audited, and the estimated cost of this is $2,000.

The accountant normally provides depreciation on a straight-line basis for the equipment owned by the company (note there is already accumulated depreciation in the trial balance) on the basis that it will have a nil salvage value and a useful life of ten years.

The above details represent the accountant's blueprint for action. S/he will set out the trial balance information on the extended trial balance worksheet we have described, and will then set out to incorporate the adjustments which are required on the worksheet, in order to calculate a draft set of statements.

We will not go through the formalities of the extended trial balance as such but will use a spreadsheet. While managers are unlikely to have to prepare a set of accounts themselves, they need to understand the mechanics of the process, since they may well be involved in making decisions about year-end adjustments, and in any event need to know what are the areas of certainty and uncertainty which are concerned with the profit measurement process. Generally, some hands-on practice at drawing up statements fixes the basics more clearly in the mind!

Adjustments

(a) Stock of goods

The trial balance already contains a 'stock' figure – the opening stock at the beginning of the year. The value of the stock at the end of the year (independently established either by the company or by outside stock takers) is $14,150. Stock levels have increased by $900 and this must be reflected in the final balance sheet. As we have discussed previously, this also fixes the cost of sales, and we can adjust the trial balance as follows:

Stock of goods for resale	+900 (+ assets)
Purchases (becomes 'cost of sales')	−900 (+ equity)

(b) Rent prepayment

The information outside the trial balance shows that the $10,000 expenses recorded in the rent account include a payment for the first three months of 20X2. The rent account must therefore be adjusted to show the 20X1 expense only and recognize that at the balance sheet date there is an asset, the unexpired rent expense for three months. From the information given the rent account balance represents fifteen months' rent, so the unexpired element must be three-fifteenths, or $2,000. Therefore the expense account is reduced by $2,000 and a new asset must appear:

Rent expense	−2,000 (+equity)
Prepayments	+2,000 (+ assets)

(c) Insurance prepayment

The accountant also knows that the last insurance paid ($1,000) referred to a six-month period of which only half was in 20X1, so here again he or she has to recognize an unexpired expense. The last payment related half to 20X1 and half to 20X2, so $500 (1/2 × $1,000) should be recognized as an asset. Again the expense account is reduced, and prepayments increased:

Insurance expense	−500 (+equity)
Prepayments	+500 (+assets)

(d) Telephone accrual

The telephone account paid in 20X2 included elements which related to 20X1, and are therefore expenses for 20X1. They must be incorporated in the profit and loss account and recognized as current liabilities. The proportion of the bill relating to 20X1 was two-thirds – the months of November and December, so two-thirds of the bill should be accrued ($80). Telephone expenses for 20X1 are reduced and another new balance sheet account opened up, this time accrued expenses:

Telephone expense	+80 (−equity)
Accrued expenses	+80 (+liabilities)

(e) Electricity accrual

The electricity account also needs adjusting for accrued expenses, but the basis of calculation this time is different. The accountant has discovered from the ledger that the electricity account only includes charges up to the end of November, but no invoice for December charges has yet come in. Notwithstanding, he or she has to make an accrual, and must base the calculation on something else. Sometimes this is done by taking the previous year's figure and making an allowance for inflation, sometimes by taking a proportion of the most recently paid bill. In this case the most recent bill was for three months, so using that as a basis an accrual of one-third of the earlier bill (l/3 × $150 = $50) is made. You may think this is a rather crude approximation, which it is, but the amount in relation to overall expenses is not material so a more precise approach is not necessary. As before, the light and heat expense account is reduced and accrued expenses increased:

Light and heat	+50 (–equity)
Accrued expenses	+50 (+liabilities)

(f) Accrued audit expense

The cost of the annual audit (although the actual work may in part take place after the balance sheet date) is considered to be part of the operating expenses for 20X1 and this accrued expense should also be recognized. The figure in this case is $2,000 and a new expense line is created for it. The adjustment is:

Legal and professional	+2,000 (–equity)
Accrued expenses	+2,000 (+liabilities)

(g) Depreciation

The company's equipment appears in the balance sheet at $15,000 original cost and must be depreciated over ten years on a straight-line basis. The annual expense will therefore be:

$$\frac{15,000}{10} = 1,500$$

This is entered by creating a new expense line for the annual charge to operating expenses, and crediting the other side of the transaction to the accumulated depreciation account to reflect the reduced value of the asset:

Depreciation expense	+1,500 (–equity)
Accumulated depreciation	+1,500 (–assets)

The classic problem with the adjustments is to have non-balancing adjustments, with the effect that although one starts from a database where assets equal liabilities and equity, this equilibrium is destroyed by the adjustments. Of course, computerized worksheets build in control of this nature to avoid the problem. MBA students in an exam context have less luck, generally.

Worksheet

	Trial balance	Adjustments	Income statement	Balance sheet
Premises	30,000			30,000
Equipment	15,000			15,000
Accummulated depreciation	−4,500	(g)−1,500		−6,000
Stock at 1 Jan X1	13,250	(a)+900		14,150
Debtors	23,000			23,000
Bank	18,560			18,560
Prepayments		(b)+2,000		2,500
		(c)+500		
Totals	**95,310**	**+1,900**		**97,210**
Share capital	50,000			50,000
Retained profits	10,500			10,500
Profit for year				(h) 17,730
Creditors	16,850			16,850
Sales	193,000		193,000	
Purchases	−145,000	(a)+900	−144,100	
Salaries and wages	−15,325		−15,325	
Rent	−10,000	(b)+2,000	−8,000	
Insurance	−2,500	(c)+500	−2,000	
Legal & prof	−1,250	(f)−2,000	−3,250	
Telephone	−345	(d)−80	−425	
Light & heat	−620	(e)−50	−670	
Accruals		(d)+80		2,130
		(e)+50		
		(f)+2,000		
Depreciation		(g)−1,500	−1,500	
Profit			(h) −17,730	
Totals	**95,310**	**+1,900**		**97,210**

Since we are splitting out on the work sheet a separate column for the income statement, the balance sheet sections will not balance internally – the profit is missing from the equity section. In order to correct this and 'prove' the balance sheet, we need to calculate the profit figure and enter it into the balance sheet (entry (h)).

You have now completed working papers for the profit and loss account and balance sheet as they would appear in the company's books, and all that remains is to set them out in an acceptable format for publication.

Mornington Crescent Emporium SA
Profit and loss account for the year ended 31 December 20X1
(format for use internally)

	$	$
Sales		193,000
Cost of sales		(144,100)
		48,900
Expenses		
Salaries and wages	15,325	
Rent	8,000	
Insurance	2,000	
Light and heat	670	
Depreciation	1,500	
Legal and professional	1,250	
Telephone	425	
Audit	2,000	(31,170)
Net income		17,730

Profit and loss account for the year ended 31 December 20X1 (published format)

	$	$
Sales		193,000
Cost of sales		(144,100)
		48,900
Expenses		
Personnel costs	15,325	
Other operating costs	14,345	
Depreciation	1,500	(31,170)
Net profit before tax and interest		17,730

Mornington Crescent Emporium SA
Balance sheet as at 31 December 20X1

	$	$
Fixed assets		
Tangible:		
Freehold land and building		30,000
Equipment cost	15,000	
Depreciation	(6,000)	9,000
		39,000
Current assets		
Stock	14,150	
Debtors	23,000	
Prepayments	2,500	
Bank	18,560	58,210
		97,210
Shareholders' funds		
Share capital		50,000
Reserves	10,500	
	17,730	28,230
		78,230
Trade creditors		16,850
Accrued expenses		2,130
		97,210

Accounting adjustments

In preparing annual accounts we have so far dealt only with the operating result. We now need to add to that adjustments for interest payments and taxation, and consider the dividend.

Interest is usually paid in arrears (sometimes monthly, or quarterly or every six months – customs differ between countries and types of borrowing) and will often need to be considered when calculating year-end accruals.

Taxation also varies from country to country. Tax on company profits may be levied at a national level only or at both national and regional level. It is rarely found at local municipality level. In some countries it is paid after the accounting year, once annual profits have been determined; in many countries, companies make payments on account based on their own estimate of the profit for a quarter year or half year. At the year end there will normally be an amount to be accrued.

The deduction of interest and taxation normally figures separately in the profit and loss account:

Net income before tax and interest	XXXXX
Interest payable	(XXXX)
Net Income before taxation	XXXXX
Provision for taxation	(XXXX)
Net income available to shareholders	XXXX

There remains after that the question of dividends to shareholders. Large listed companies will usually pay a dividend every six months and this will be charged directly against accumulated profits in shareholders' equity (companies listed on the New York Stock Exchange have to produce figures every quarter and some pay a dividend every quarter as well). The amount of the final, year-end dividend has to be approved by the shareholders in a general meeting, which takes place when the accounts have been finalized, as they too are approved at that meeting.

In some countries this final dividend is also shown within the profit and loss account as a deduction from profit and in the balance sheet as a liability, but treatment varies from country to country. More often the dividend is shown simply as a deduction from reserves once it has been paid.

Worked example

In order to demonstrate how the adjustments would look, let us return to the financial statements we prepared in the last session and rework them on the basis of a different capital structure. We can also include a provision for bad debts and one for taxation.

The share capital in the original example was $50,000. Let us now substitute a different structure:

	$
Ordinary shares	40,000
5% debenture	10,000
Total sources	$50,000

The company would need to make the following adjustment:

Debenture interest $500   (5%*$10,000)

The total debtors outstanding was $23,000. If the company wanted to make a provision of 1 per cent, this would involve a charge of $230 against profits and a reduction of the asset, in this case, by the same amount:

Create provision	−230 (reduce equity)
Debtors	−230 (reduce assets)

Assuming that the tax provision was at a rate of 30 per cent, the company would also need to set aside $5,100 as a provision (original profit was $17,730; deduction of $230 bad debt provision and $500 debenture interest would leave $17,000, of which 30 per cent is $5,100).

Assuming that you are using the same working papers as before, the adjustments are entered into the adjustment column and then extended across horizontally into the profit and loss account and balance sheet. One occasional source of confusion is that in making the tax adjustment, for example, the debit and the credit will both appear under 'provision for taxation', one being a profit and loss account entry, and the other a balance sheet entry.

Tax provision (income)	−5,100 (reduce equity)
Tax provision (balance sheet)	+5,100 (increase liabilities)

The adjusted financial statements are shown on the following page:

Mornington Crescent Emporium SA
Profit and loss account for the year ended 31 December 20X1

	$	$
Sales		193,000
Cost of sales		(144,100)
		48,900
Salaries and wages	15,325	
Other operating expenses	14,345	
Depreciation	1,500	
Provision for bad debts	230	(31,400)
Net income before interest and tax		17,500
Interest payable		(500)
Net income before tax		17,000
Provision for taxation		(5,100)
Net income attributable to shareholders		11,900

Mornington Crescent Emporium SA
Balance sheet as at 31 December 20X1

	$	$
Fixed assets		
Tangible assets:		
Freehold land and buildings		30,000
Equipment cost	15,000	
Depreciation	(6,000)	9,000
		39,000
Current assets		
Stock	14,150	
Debtors	23,000	
less provision	(230)	
Prepayments	2,500	
Bank	18,560	57,980
Total assets		96,980
Shareholders' funds		
Ordinary shares		40,000
Reserves	10,500	
	11,900	22,400
		62,400
Debenture		10,000
Trade creditors		16,850
Accruals		2,630
Taxation		5,100
Total liabilities and equity		96,980

Uses of financial statements

This is by way of recapitulation of some of the issues which we considered at the start of the course. It is a major problem of financial reporting that a single set of numbers is expected potentially to satisfy all manner of diverse objectives:

- measure how much dividend might be paid;
- provide reassurance of a company's financial strength to creditors;
- provide a basis for measuring future growth for stock market analysis;
- measure management performance in a principal/agent context;
- provide the basis of taxation of the company;
- give employees an idea of the company's strength.

It will be clear to you that (a) some of these objectives are contradictory, and (b) accounting leaves open some choices which can affect how the company looks.

It needs also to be understood that the large, listed company which has operations in many parts of the world sees its annual report as a public relations document for trumpeting the group's strength and viability.

A private, family-controlled, company may see its accounts as something secret, to be disclosed to as few people as possible, and where profit is minimized in order to keep taxation low and to retain as much cash as possible in the company.

Questions

1. You are asked to prepare the annual financial statements for Reno Wholesalers Inc. for the year ended 30 June 20X4. The trial balance extracted from the company's books at 30 June 20X4 is shown below.

	$
Assets	
Land	5,000
Buildings	10,000
Depreciation – premises	−1,000
Equipment	10,000
Depreciation – equipment	−2,000
Investments	6,200
Stock at 1 July 20X3	18,650
Debtors	12,600
Bank	11,750
Financing	
Share capital	20,000
Reserves	2,700
Creditors	21,700
Sales	278,000
Purchases	−185,300
Rent	−15,000
Salaries	−47,500
Light and heat	−3,400

You also have the following information:

- The value of stock on hand at 30 June 20X4 was $17,300.
- Depreciation on the premises is over twenty years and the equipment over ten years.
- The debtor total includes two debts, one for $900 and one for $200, which are thought to be irrecoverable and should be written off. The company wishes to make a provision for doubtful debts of 2 per cent.
- An electricity bill of $900 was paid in August 20X4, relating to the three months ended 31 July.
- The investments had a market value of $10,500 at 30 June 20X4.

2. The trial balance of Arénières Inc. at 31 December 20X4 was:

	$
Land	82,100
Buildings	120,000
Accumulated depreciation	−36,000
Equipment	89,500
Accumulated depreciation	−53,700
Bank account	83,200
Trade debtors	91,300
Stock at 1 Jan.	214,300
Share capital	100,000
Reserves	185,600
7% debenture	50,000
Trade creditors	184,800
Sales	942,700
Purchases	−398,100
Salaries	−343,600
Other expenses	−102,200
Interest	−3,500
Interim dividend	−25,000

(a) The closing stock at 31 December was $216,300.

(b) No depreciation has been provided for 20X4. The company assumes zero residual values and uses the following straight-line rates: buildings 2 per cent and equipment 20 per cent.

(c) The audit fee for 20X4 is expected to be $20,000.

(d) The company estimates that it had phone costs of $1,200 and energy costs of $1,350 outstanding at the year end.

(e) Included in other costs is a business insurance policy which cost $3,000 and which runs for the year from 1 April 20X4.

(f) The company decides, on the recommendation of its auditors, that it would be prudent to create a provision of $10,000 against a claim for damages resulting from faulty merchandise and one of $15,000 for corporate income tax.

Please draw up an income statement and balance sheet.

3. The trial balance of Ansermet Inc. at 31 December 20X6 was:

Land	155,000
Buildings	560,000
Accumulated depreciation	−112,000
Plant	1,890,200
Accumulated depreciation	−1,039,610
Share capital	750,000
Share premium	220,000
Reserves	254,790
Debt	600,000
Stock	619,300
Debtors	414,700
Bank	208,100
Creditors	336,800
Sales	2,740,500
Purchases	−1,247,000
Personnel costs	−691,300
Other costs	−268,100

(a) The closing stock was valued at $584,600.
(b) The audit fee is estimated to be $50,000.
(c) The company paid outstanding December travel expenses for various staff in January: total value $2,750.
(d) No interest had been paid at 31 December on the long-term debt, which was contracted at 7 per cent.
(e) Depreciation should be provided at a rate of 2 per cent straight line for the buildings (assuming no residual value) and 30 per cent reducing balance for the plant.
(f) The company is facing litigation from an employee who has left and considers it prudent to make a provision against legal costs of $20,000.
(g) The tax advisers suggest that the company will have to pay about $60,000 tax on the 20X6 profit.

Please draw up an income statement and balance sheet.

Part Three

An introduction to financial statement analysis

8 A framework for interpretation

The object in this part of the book is to start to develop some ideas about what financial statement analysis is for and how it is done. Up until now we have been looking at the nuts and bolts of constructing financial statements, essentially so that you understand the fairly strict framework within which accounting data is produced. Now we move on to ask why analysts look at financial statements (this chapter) and then we start to use some of the traditional tools (next chapter).

Introduction

In this chapter we look at the fundamental questions an analyst is asking and review some of the management models which guide companies and against which we measure their performance. This section of the book is intended to deepen your understanding of financial statements in terms of interpreting the data disclosed in them, rather than, as previously, in terms of understanding the rules of measurement.

In interpreting financial statements it is necessary to make assessments of how a company has behaved in relation to how it might have been expected to behave. In order to have a framework of expectations it follows that one must have theories about how companies should behave, and it is that area which we will discuss in this chapter. You will, of course, have your own views about how companies should behave, and other courses within the programme will also have provided many other insights. The reason for raising the issue of company behaviour is that you cannot make assessments of a company's performance without some idea of how you expect it to perform. Inevitably the treatment here will address first principles: the objective is to provide a basic set of ground rules against which to judge company behaviour, rather than any detailed discussion of the theoretical background. You should extend this yourself. You need to bring to financial analysis a mixture of accounting, finance and strategy.

Financial analysis mainly concerns itself with two areas: evaluation of the financial structure and policy of a company, and evaluation of the management's performance. A potential lender to the company will be assessing slightly different aspects from those assessed by a potential investor, or perhaps the same aspects but with a different weighting.

The first question to evaluate is that of financial risk. The more borrowing a company already has, the more risky it is to lend more. As we discussed earlier, the level of borrowing also impacts upon the variability of profit. A potential investor will need to assess the degree of financial risk in order to decide whether the profit prospects of the company are sufficiently attractive. Business is about taking risks, so investors (and lenders) do not shun 'risky' investments, but they do expect a higher potential return as compensation for a higher degree of risk. For the investor, therefore, there is a link between financial structure (= risk) and management performance (= future potential profits). The return which an investor wants should be sufficient to (a) compensate for inflation; (b) equal the return available from no-risk investments; (c) provide compensation for the risk. This can be represented graphically (Figure 8.1).

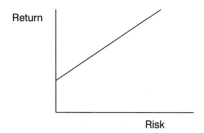

Figure 8.1   The risk/return relationship

This risk/return relationship holds good for both investors and lenders, and is behind the analytical approach which looks at financial structure and management performance: the first to assess risk, the second as a basis for forecasting future returns, so that the financial decision can be made. We will now take a look at considerations in financial structure (including dividend policy and working capital management) and management performance.

Financial structure

It is worth revisiting the balance sheet of a company to re-examine it from a point of view of analysis. You remember that the company is simply a legal vehicle into which investors have put money. This in turn has been used to buy productive capacity which is used to generate profits (Figure 8.2).

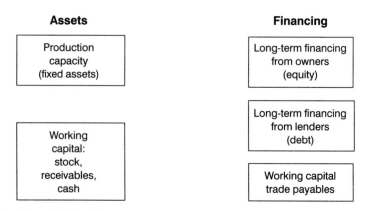

Figure 8.2   Financial structure

The balance sheet is structured in such a way as to show how the company has dealt with a number of strategic issues, and enables the analyst to see clearly the long-term financing structure, the different components of working capital and their relationship to each other.

The issues in relation to basic structure are firstly that of the proportion of debt to equity (often known as gearing), and then within debt, the term structure, or maturity mix (when does the debt fall due for repayment?). Other questions which arise are the security ranking of different debt sources, and, in the case of a multinational, the currency make-up.

As regards the basic gearing of a company, there is no satisfactory guide as to what is a 'good' debt/equity mix. Of course, in general terms higher debt will both increase the return and increase the risk of a company. What one tends to find is that there are industry patterns which reflect other aspects of risk. For example, high technology companies have a high operational risk and tend to have little financial gearing as a result.

Size and ownership are also factors in debt structure. Family-held or director-controlled businesses typically try to avoid issuing equity to outsiders because of the loss of management control that this might bring, so they tend to prefer to borrow. Small and medium-sized companies therefore often have higher gearing than their larger competitors.

Gearing has the additional benefit that, under tax law, interest is deductible as an expense in arriving at taxable profit, while the return to the shareholder is after tax. Therefore, given a tax rate of 30 per cent, the real net cost of a 10 per cent interest rate is 7 per cent when compared with the return to equity.

There are no real guidelines as to the appropriate ratio between debt and equity in any industry. Gearing varies enormously from one industry to another and in assessing the gearing in any one company the safest approach is a comparison with the gearing in similar companies. An examination of the balance sheet of a company will reveal its gearing, and comparison of several balance sheets over a period of time will reveal the trend of that particular company.

Most companies work to a notional debt/equity target ratio. But when raising new finance, they do not automatically split the financing requirement between equity and debt. Normally they borrow for specific needs and then every few years have a major share issue to restore the debt/equity ratio.

Sources of finance

Share issue

When an existing company wants to raise more equity capital it will usually ask its existing shareholders to subscribe more (companies listed on a stock exchange are generally obliged to offer new shares to existing shareholders first). This is done by means of what is called a 'rights issue'. If, for example, a company has 1m shares already issued, the current price on the stock exchange is $3.00 per share and the company wants to raise approximately $1.25m in new finance, it could give existing shareholders the right to buy one new share for every two held, and at a price of $2.50 a share.

The reduction (discount) between the market price and the price of the new share would reflect an expectation that the future profits would have to be split between more people, albeit in the longer term the extra profits created by the expansion of the company would compensate for this. The shareholder may then either buy the shares or sell his or her right to them on the stock exchange.

Normally a company would have the share issue 'underwritten', that is, specialist institutions would guarantee to the company to buy all unsold shares at a predetermined price. The underwriter receives a large fee for accepting this risk, and this is one reason why share issues are not undertaken frequently. Any share issue has to be accompanied by detailed statements ('prospectus') about the company's past performance and future expectations. This involves the use of experts to check and confirm the information and is another reason for the high cost of raising equity.

An alternative to a rights issue is to issue shares on a different capital market. This has the advantage of opening up new sources and not obliging the company to sell the new shares at a discount, as well as potentially bringing in finance denominated in a foreign currency. This is not a common tactic and most stock exchanges require that existing shareholders are at least given the right to participate in any future issue of shares, but is likely to become more so amongst large companies as the market becomes ever more global and companies want to have the many strategic advantages of being listed on several stock exchanges.

Loans

Loan finance can be obtained in a number of ways, either through institutions or directly through the public markets. Typically, many small and medium-sized companies arrange long-term loans from their commercial banks, or from merchant banks, in a single direct transaction. However, very large companies can also arrange 'syndicated loans' where the finance is provided by a group of banks or other lending institutions. Syndicated loans are commonly arranged by governments or state agencies for financing development or budget deficits, but they are also sometimes provided for special transactions by commercial companies such as the purchase by an airline of a new fleet of aircraft.

The rate of interest chargeable on such loans is usually a 'floating rate' which goes up and down in accordance with a market interest rate indicator. Central banks fix a minimum lending rate and loans are usually expressed as X per cent over minimum lending rate – in Europe the European Central Bank's interest rate is considered to set the basis for commercial borrowing and lending rates. Although actual rates offered to a customer are fixed individually by the banks, there is usually no difference in rate between banks.

Bonds

Companies also raise large blocks of finance by issuing debt directly to the capital market, known as bonds. Frequently such bonds are issued at a fixed interest rate. Bonds, like shares, can be taken up in small quantities by individuals: so bond debt could be raised from a large number of sources. Medium-sized family companies in Europe are often quite active in raising finance on the bond market since that offers public financing and a stock exchange listing but without dilution of control, since only debt is listed and not equity.

Leasing

Another possible source of finance is leasing. Here the company in effect rents an asset with finance often supplied by the supplier of the asset. This has the advantage of avoiding the need to raise finance separately when buying new assets. As discussed in Chapter 5, the accounting requirements now ensure that liabilities under leases appear in the balance sheet in the same way as other sorts of finance.

Other methods

Other aspects of debt management are 'maturity mix', currency and interest rates. The maturity mix is the scheduling of repayment of debt – has the company borrowed in such a way that all its borrowings will fall due at the same time? It may be expensive to carry out a massive refinancing in one exercise and it is usual to spread out the maturity dates of debt.

This also impacts upon interest rates – raising long-term debt at fixed interest rates means locking the company into a high interest charge for a long period if such a manoeuvre takes place when the market rates of interest are high. Borrowing on floating rate agreements can be expensive if made when the market is low but then it subsequently rises. The ideal is to borrow long-term on fixed rates when the market rates are low, and to borrow on floating rates when the market is high.

Hedging

The possibility of raising finance other than in sterling, either on the Eurobond market or on foreign national markets, brings in a further element of financial strategy. This is the question of hedging foreign investments. The existence of the euro may well reduce the amount of borrowing done in foreign currencies by European companies, but the currency mix can be an important issue and is something normally to be disclosed by companies.

Run a risk or plant a hedge?

Every time there is a currency 'shock' the spotlight inevitably falls on the management of foreign currency exposures – a complex art due to the many subtle interactions of trading and international capital flows between different economies. Mastering this art begins with exploration of the origins of currency exposure and the risks which flow from it. It is usual to group these risks into three main types depending upon whether the exposure is transactional translational or economic.

Source: Extract from article by Martin Scicluna, Deloitte & Touche, *Accounting & Business*, May 1998

When a French company buys a US subsidiary, if it provides the cash from its home resources, it has debt raised in French francs and an investment denominated in US dollars. There is therefore a transactional exchange exposure: the exchange rate between French francs and the US dollar fluctuates regularly. A company investing in a foreign currency risks two things: (a) that the investment will of itself yield a suitable return, and (b) that the exchange rate will not vary so widely as to make the loan finance more costly over a period of time.

To illustrate the problem with our USA/France example; suppose a French company buys for US$100m a small US company which subsequently achieves annual profits of a steady $15m – an acceptable return of 15 per cent. The purchase is financed by a domestic loan and at the time of purchase the exchange rate was $1.00 = FF5.00. The French company would therefore have borrowed FF500m and let us say that the interest rate was 10 per cent. To illustrate the exchange risk, if we ignore the commercial risk of the investment itself and assume profits remain steady at $15m, the French franc outturn of the investment will also depend on the exchange rate. Table 8.1 shows the situation at the time of the initial investment, and the impact of rate changes in both directions.

Table 8.1 Impact of rate changes

US profit $	Rate $1 =	French profit FF	Interest FF	Net result FF
15.0m	FF5.00	75m	50m	25m
15.0m	FF3.00	45m	50m	(5m)
15.0m	FF7.00	105m	50m	55m

As you can see, the result in terms of the French parent's receipts can vary widely as a result of the exchange exposure. The exposure, of course, extends to the value of the investment as well: if the exchange rate went to $1 = FF3.00, the French franc equivalent of the original investment drops from FF500m to FF350m, giving an additional balance sheet 'loss' of FF150m.

This kind of problem was a major contributor to the South-East Asian financial crisis of the late 1990s. A number of indigenous companies borrowed heavily in US dollars to finance expansion in the area. When their exchanges rates started to slide, this meant that the local currency value of their debt increased enormously, as also did the relative cost of interest. At a stroke the companies became both loss making and with rapidly worsening debt/equity ratios.

A decision has to be made as to whether a company wishes to accept both the commercial risk and the exchange risk, and usually the answer will be negative. The exchange risk can be minimized by raising the finance in the country where the investment is made. So in our example above, if the French parent company had borrowed $100m on the US capital market, both the investment and the associated loan and interest would be denominated in the same currency, thereby cancelling one risk with another. The company would have hedged its investment, and the exposure would be limited to the difference between the US revenue and US interest payment.

A look at the debt analysis provided in the annual financial statements and the investment analysis will give some indication of the extent to which any particular company hedges its foreign investments with foreign borrowing – although precise details of the investment in subsidiaries are rarely provided as such.

Dividend policy

If it is assumed that the major preoccupation of the managers of a company is to maximize the gain for their shareholders, a major question will be how, in practice, this is best achieved. A shareholder gains from the investment in two ways: (a) through the receipt of dividends, and (b) through the increase in the stock market price of the shares (and note in passing that although the creation of profit should help in both these aims, it is not the creation of profit in itself which is the objective).

Following on from the identification of these two gains, there arises the question of what importance to give each aim in relation to the other. Is the shareholder indifferent as to whether the gain comes from dividend or market appreciation, or does he or she prefer dividend at the expense of growth in price or vice versa?

One school of thought is that the dividend is unimportant – if a company retains the bulk of its profits in order to finance new profit-making opportunities, the market price of the shares should rise in anticipation of the higher levels of profit to be earned in the future (remember, as we have discussed before, that the market price of shares is determined by expectations of future performance). The shareholder benefits by an increase in market price. If the shareholder needs cash flow from the investment, then he or she can independently convert the market gain into cash flow by selling some of the shares.

However, other theorists say that shareholders give a priority to receiving an assured cash flow from dividends. They hold the shares not for long-term price appreciation, but for short-term, continuing cash flows. Therefore if the company does not pay a dividend, these shareholders are disenchanted, sell the shares, and their price falls because expectations of future dividend cash flows are low. Management is therefore failing in both aspects of maximizing shareholder wealth.

In practice, some companies apparently see a need to pay a continuing cash flow to shareholders irrespective of profit, while others are influenced in determining the amount of a dividend by the current profit. In looking at published financial statements, a comparison of net income after tax with the dividend payments will show whether the dividend is determined independently of the profit level.

Some theorists point out that in all probability it is incorrect to assume that all shareholders are looking for the same type of return – some may want dividends, others prefer price appreciation. Consequently there could be no discernible pattern in shareholder preferences and those who want high dividends will invest in companies that offer high dividends, while those who want price appreciation will invest in the companies which offer that possibility. This is called the 'clientele effect' – companies acquire the clientele which prefers their particular approach to the question.

There is no overall best practice in this area against which to evaluate individual companies, but the question of dividend policy is an integral element of financial management because of its potential effect on shareholder wealth (the main objective of management) and subsequently because of the effect on the company's cash flows and its financing. A company with high dividends will have that much less cash available from internal operations – but depending upon which theory you prefer, may find it easier to issue new shares. In any event, internally generated cash flows are an important part of a company's financing and dividend payments a major use of that finance.

Working capital management

Financial management in this area consists, on the one hand, of keeping to a minimum the cash tied up in working capital, while, on the other hand, preserving sufficient cash or readily convertible current assets to meet payment needs. We have already reviewed working capital movements and their impact on cash flows in Chapter 4. The working capital cycle consists of the following elements:

1. Raw material stock – creditors – cash paid
2. Work in progress
3. Finished goods
4. Debtors
5. Cash received.

In general terms, cash flows are benefited by withholding payment to creditors for as long as possible, while keeping stocks at the various stages of production and debtors to a minimum. However, restriction of cash outflows is not the only objective of management, and there are interactions between the commercial success of a company and these working capital elements:

1. *Stocks of raw materials.* The unit cost of raw materials may be reduced by bulk buying, and maintenance of stock at very low levels risks the possibility of production being halted by a late delivery of an essential item.
2. *Stocks of finished goods.* High stocks of finished goods allow sales always to be satisfied quickly – a sudden increase in sales can be supplied instantly. Sales may be lost because of delays in supply to the customer.
3. *Debtors.* Every company, in the interests of cash management, wishes to buy on credit, and have as long a credit period as possible. Customers therefore will take into account the credit available from each supplier when deciding between competing supplies of uniform products.
4. *Creditors.* When buying supplies it may be that the supplier who offers the best unit price, or the best value for money in terms of product quality, is also the supplier who offers the least credit (since they have a competitive edge).

It follows that each company has to determine its working capital management in the light of the trade-offs between the ideal financial management policy and the ideal commercial policy. What exactly these trade-offs amount to will depend on the circumstances of each company and the nature of the industry within which it operates. 'Just in time' stock management, developed in particular by Japanese manufacturers, says that tight management control of stock levels should eliminate production stoppages or failure to supply customers, while keeping stocks at a minimal level and reducing capital requirements. Suppliers are expected to maintain stocks and deliver to the customer 'just in time'.

It is impossible to suggest any general guidelines as to what is appropriate. In evaluating the working capital policy of any particular company it is essential to compare its policy with that of other companies in the same field, or industry norms. The only overall guidelines are that companies should, on the one hand, keep their working capital levels at a minimum consistent with commercial policy, while, on the other hand, ensuring that they are generating sufficient short-term cash flows (from stock and debtors) to meet their requirements for settling amounts due to creditors and other payments (i.e. that they are sufficiently 'liquid').

Liquidity is the other aspect of working capital management and as a concept it is easy to grasp – simple domestic management proceeds smoothly as long as cash is available to meet bills as they fall due for payment. Liquidity as applied in a particular company is a rather more difficult matter to grasp because of the extreme variability of circumstances for each company.

In essence each company needs to plan its cash outflows and its cash inflows and try to time them so that they coincide with each other. If inflows are large but at infrequent intervals (for example, in large-scale civil engineering contracts), the company is likely to need to maintain high stocks of cash or overdraft facilities, whereas if inflows are regular (for example, in food retailing), cash balances may be kept low and surplus funds invested in the short-term money market.

We can sum up the factors which affect working capital management as follows:

1. *Length of production cycle.* If it takes a long time to move from delivery of raw materials to completion of the finished product, stocks of raw materials and work in progress will be high.
2. *Variability of demand/flexibility of production.* If demand levels fluctuate, high stocks of finished goods may be required, except where the production cycle is short and volume of production can be changed rapidly.
3. *Scale of credit sales.* In some industries all sales are on credit, in others virtually none. The length of credit demanded will also vary. A high proportion of credit sales and long credit periods will mean a high volume of debtors.
4. *Frequency of sale transactions.* A company which sells a high volume of units, each having a relatively low unit price, will tend to have a regular cash inflow. One selling a small number of high-value objects will have an irregular cash inflow. Cash levels will be low where there are regular inflows, but higher where inflows are irregular.
5. *Frequency of payments.* Where outflows are high and infrequent, cash levels may be kept low between outflows, but this pattern is relatively rare since basic running expenses such as wages and overheads form a fairly large and regular component of outflows.

By way of example, one would expect a company in the heavy capital goods industry, say one which manufactured turbines to order, to have a long production cycle and infrequent cash inflows. It could therefore be expected to have a high level of stocks, debtors and cash, and therefore a high proportion of current assets to current liabilities.

At the other extreme a retail organization such as a hypermarket would experience frequent, high-volume sale transactions and no credit sales (although the trend towards retailers issuing in-store credit cards is changing that pattern slightly). Its stocks, debtors and cash balances would therefore be very low. The relationship between current assets and current liabilities would be in a completely different proportion.

Generally, however, this relationship should be stable. As sales increase or decrease, the absolute value of stocks, debtors and creditors should normally fluctuate in proportion to sales, but remain constant in their relationship towards each other. Any marked shift in this relationship means that something has changed in the way the company is managed. One would also expect the relationship between the elements of working capital to be broadly comparable as between companies which work in the same business sector.

In the next chapter we shall be looking at financial statement analysis, and one of the measures used for evaluating balance sheets is the proportion of current assets to current liabilities (known as the 'current ratio'). You will realize from the discussion of working capital that the nature of the current ratio can be expected to vary from one industry to another and care should be exercised in evaluating it!

Performance measurement

While the financial statements provide considerable information about financing, they do not really do the same for a wider appreciation of performance. Of course, one major measure of performance is profitability, and the statements will give that in a number of different forms, but there are other areas not mentioned. By way of example, a particular UK company published its business objectives in the annual report and these were:

1. Maximize use of existing assets (rather than diversify).
2. Increase market share.
3. Build on strong personnel traditions.

Only the first objective can be related to the financial statements as such, although the company includes data in its annual report about the other aspects. Evaluation of performance involves many considerations other than those which are visible from the annual accounts. However, our concern here is the information available in the published statements.

In its financial objectives the same company stated that its target return is 25 per cent on the assets used, and this of course can be evaluated from the statements themselves. The financial objectives are also expressed as a 5 per cent increase in real terms in earnings per share, and this too can be evaluated by reference to the financial statements.

But notice certain characteristics of the targets for evaluating performance: the absolute profit measure, for example, is not mentioned – the important measures are profit in relation to assets, and net earnings in relation to the individual share (after adjusting for inflation). You cannot judge performance in an absolute sense, but only in relation to another aspect of the company's structure. So a target of (say) profit before tax of $200m is meaningless, whereas a target of 25 per cent return on assets can be compared usefully with other companies.

Currently, improving shareholder value is the fashionable target for company management to aim for. We will come back to the subject later and look at what this means, but it can be taken to be not only making current profits but ensuring that future profits are better as well. The target of increasing market share cited above is one example of a strategy which should yield current profits but future profits as well. For example, increased marketing expenditure is probably necessary to boost market share, causing a short-term decline in profitability, but once that share has been achieved, it can probably be maintained with less marketing, and the higher volume of business should reduce average unit costs, thereby increasing profit both by increasing sales and by reducing average costs.

Summary

Corporate finance and its management is a very wide subject, and in this chapter we have made a very short examination of some of the major areas. Within such confines it is impossible to be other than superficial, but at the same time a total ignorance of corporate finance issues makes analysis and interpretation of financial statements a less productive exercise.

We have examined the structuring of company finance between debt and equity: this will influence both the volume and variability of the return to the shareholders. Equity is normally raised through the home stock exchange, although flotation on foreign exchanges is both possible and increasingly popular. Usually equity on the home market will be raised by first offering new shares to existing holders. However, issuing shares is an expensive exercise and is not, therefore, done at short intervals.

Debt finance may be obtained from a variety of sources, both individual lenders and capital market issues. The possibility of raising debt on foreign markets allows companies making foreign investments to hedge their investment – to limit their exposure to exchange rate fluctuations.

A major policy decision for companies is their approach to dividend payments to shareholders. Theorists are not agreed as to the best policy and some companies try to maintain a steady flow to shareholders irrespective of profit performance, while others gear their dividend to profits. The effect on share price of the dividend policy is not certain, and it is possible that different shareholders have different preferences, and buy shares in those companies whose policy most nearly satisfies their preference.

Working capital management is an important aspect of finance, but the composition and best policy towards working capital will be influenced by commercial considerations and the actual circumstances of the individual company within an industry. Some industries require very high levels of current assets, while others need very little. Policy therefore has to be evaluated in relation to the individual company.

Performance measurement has implications wider than purely assessing profit, although profitability is clearly an important measure. Profitability can most easily be stated by expressing it in relation to another aspect of the company's structure, such as assets employed in the business.

Questions

1. Why does an analyst need to take a view about the riskiness of a company as well as its profitability?
2. Distinguish between debt and equity and explain the importance of this ratio in financial statement analysis.
3. What is the working capital cycle, and what are the likely conflicts in managing this from a financial point of view as opposed to a sales or production point of view?

9 Financial statement analysis I

This is the first chapter to address the tools for conventional financial statement analysis. It introduces ratios, the classical working tool, and explains how the ratio facilitates comparisons, and what key ratios are particularly useful in gaining a quick insight into company performance.

Introduction

Although this chapter is entitled 'Financial statement analysis', to an extent that is misleading because of course the whole book is about financial statement analysis. The preceding chapters which dealt with the preparation of financial statements are intended to give insights into the measurement framework within which financial statements are prepared and the limitations of that framework. The chapters which follow will look at more variables in statement preparation and how these impact upon interpretation of financial information.

Given that framework, we are now going to look at some technical elements used in the process of evaluating the financial statements of individual companies in order to arrive at conclusions about the company. We are going to examine financial statements through the eyes of accounts-users and, in particular, look at the tools which are used to aid analysis and provide useful information about the company.

The purpose of analysis

We have identified a wide range of potential users of financial statements, but for the purpose of analysis we are going to focus primarily on the needs of equity investors (or potential investors) and to a lesser degree those of suppliers of credit. Such users will each be interested in different aspects of the company and will also have differing levels of technical expertise available to them to interpret what they see. This is an underlying problem in the preparation of such statements – they should contain information to enable sophisticated users to make good investment decisions, while at the same time not obscuring the broad picture with so much detail that the less sophisticated user cannot understand them. However, financial statements are increasingly complex and is doubtful whether they are at all meaningful to those with no special training. Many companies include a section in the report (usually entitled 'Highlights from the year' or something similar) which gives a synopsis for the user who is not equipped to undertake a detailed analysis of the figures.

Value of accounts

(The annual report) provides an essential service whose key features must be preserved. That essential service is of relatively increased importance in the case of smaller listed companies. The main features may be summarised as:

- acting as a significant landmark in the cycle of business information;
- prompting questions and indicating trends;
- providing a basis for decision-makers to create their own model of the company;
- giving reassurance because the financial statements are subject to regulation and to audit and there is awareness that auditors at least cast an eye over the non-statutory sections of the annual report; and
- providing progressively greater detail, such as segmental information, for those who wish to probe the various aspects of the business.

Source: ICAS: *Corporate communications: views of institutional investors and lenders* (Research Committee, Institute of Chartered Accountants of Scotland, 1999)

The tools of analysis which we are going to examine in this chapter are those used by the sophisticated user, and we should consider their objectives in making the analysis to see the relevance of the tools to that purpose. Stockbrokers and investment analysts examine financial statements in order to advise on investments in the shares – or bonds – of commercial companies. The investment might be made by a private individual or an institutional investor such as a pension fund, insurance company or unit trust. The trend in most markets is away from individual investors and towards institutional investors. Many people prefer to make their investments by way of a collective investment vehicle such as a mutual fund or a policy with a life assurance company, so stock exchange investment is increasingly professionalized. However, the Internet could change all that. Already in the US there is a developing use of on-line brokers by individuals. Some people apparently like to get up early in the morning, check what the financial reports on the television and radio are saying, and then buy and sell shares. They then go to work, and when they get home in the evening check out the Net to see how their investment plays have worked out.

As we discussed in Chapter 8, users are primarily interested in answering two questions:

1. How well did the company perform?
2. How strong financially is the company?

Their purpose in posing these questions, however, will differ, as will the relative importance of the one question to the other. Investment analysts are mainly interested in assessing future performance of the company. They are therefore only interested in the financial statements as a predictor of the future. The information about what the company did last year has no value of itself; its only relevance is as to whether it will do better or worse next year, and whether the expected return is adequate for the expected level of risk.

Typically such analysts are specialists in a particular industry and their investment advice is based on an assessment of the likely performance of the industry in the future, combined with an appreciation of which company within the industry is most likely to perform well within the anticipated economic environment. The performance of any individual company will be affected by the economic environment within which it operates: it is affected by general levels of economic activity, changes in exchange rates, commodity prices, introduction of new technology, inflation levels, etc.

Management cannot control these external forces which will affect all companies within a particular industry in the same way. But the best management will be able to minimize the impact of negative external forces and maximize the impact of positive external forces. Financial statement analysis provides one method of assessing how well managements perform from one company to another in the same industry.

The emphasis for the lender making a credit decision is likely to be different. Lenders do not participate in success in that the return they receive is not geared to profit. In addition, payment of interest will take place irrespective of the level of profit, so the lenders' concern in future performance is merely that there should be sufficient cash flow for the company to stay in business and pay the interest ('interest cover').

The greater concern for lenders is the financial strength of the business. The lenders' main risk is that the company should fail and be unable to repay the loan ('default risk'). Future performance will of course have an impact on this, but the stability of the company's finances is the first concern, and then the marketability of the company's assets. The debt/equity gearing will therefore be a key issue, as will the relationship of the company's assets to its liabilities and the external value of the assets. (For example, if it costs $100m to open a microchip factory, this asset is useful while there's a profitable market for microchips, but if the company failed following a slump in demand for microchips, a lender would find it difficult to raise $100m on the factory.)

If we look at the nature of the questions themselves, it can be seen that each is the sum of a number of different questions. Management performance might be measured according to growth in assets; profit generated in relation to assets used or success in reducing tax liability; or extent of cash inflows, etc. The relevance of each detailed question will vary from one company to another, since no two companies are exactly the same and no two industries require the same proportion of fixed assets to current, current assets to liabilities, debt to equity, etc.

What may be a useful and relevant measure of success in one industry may be totally irrelevant in another industry. For example, the ratio of sales to assets may be useful when comparing one retail company to another since it says something about the efficiency with which their premises are employed. But such a ratio would be meaningless in relation to an advertising agency, where perhaps a better measure of efficiency would be sales in relation to staff numbers or staff cost. This point should be borne in mind when considering the application of the analytical tools.

Traditional analysis

Financial statement analysis has been carried out ever since financial statements existed, but the methods of analysis have become more sophisticated over the years, and in particular the development of computers has permitted the use of complex statistical analysis and the development of financial models. In this chapter we shall look at the longer-established methods and review recent developments later in the book.

The basis of traditional analysis is comparison. An absolute number has little information value: to say that Nestlé made $995m last year means very little. If we say

Nestlé made $995 but a similar company (say Danone) made only $750m then the information begins to fit into a framework and have more use. But an important point in analysis is the relevance of the comparison. To say Nestlé made $995m but Air France lost $500m tells us nothing about either company, merely what we already know, that their operations and objectives are quite different.

The framework for comparison may be either the company's own performance in other years, or the performance of another company in the same industry, or an industry average. Comparison over a period of years is known as a 'time series analysis' (or 'intertemporal comparison') while that with a different entity or an industry average is called a 'cross-sectional analysis' (or 'interfirm comparison').

Time series analysis

At a simple level, time series analysis would compare the figures for one year with those of the preceding year. But this is not very sound from a statistical point of view because such a short period may not reveal trends or may have been distorted by individual events. Analysts therefore, and particularly when making predictions, use at least a five-year base, and often prefer a ten-year base. Companies usually provide a five- or ten-year summary of principal figures within their annual report.

Such a long time base will raise questions about the impact of inflation – even a 5 per cent inflation rate will lead to a 40 per cent loss of value in the measuring unit over ten years. The impact of inflation on the numbers must therefore be considered in time series analysis. If it is thought to be significant, a simple remedy is to convert the measurement unit to a common value by use of the retail price index – although where property revaluations have taken place during the series, care should be taken in the interpretation.

Cross-sectional analysis

Cross-sectional analysis involves making a comparison with other companies in the same industry for the same year. Potentially this may yield insights if the companies have very similar products, since differences will be the result of different management strategies in the face of the same problems.

Useful comparisons can still be made even if the companies are not exactly similar in their product line, but in evaluating the figures produced it is necessary to make allowances for the differences between the companies. This can become particularly difficult in relation to comparisons with companies which have diversified activities. For example, if one was doing an analysis of listed international media companies, one would find Walt Disney, News Corporation and Pearson. However, while Walt Disney and News Corporation (Twentieth Century Fox) both make films, and all three have significant television activities (but Disney owns the ABC network in the US), only Pearson and News Corporation publish newspapers. They also both publish books, but Pearson has a wide educational range (e.g. Prentice Hall) where News Corporation is mainly a producer of bulk fiction (Harper Collins). Walt Disney, of course, has theme parks, while News Corporation is part owner of an airline (Ansett) and Pearson until recently had a stake in a bank, Lazards.

Useful comparisons can still be made, but the interpretation must take account of the differences between the companies. A general point to remember is that analysis rarely offers very exact comparisons: you can often only say 'X is worse than (better than) Y as regards such and such an attribute', not 'X performed 22.58 per cent worse (better) than Y'.

The other possibility in cross-sectional analysis is the use of industry averages. Many industries have trade associations which collect and publish such data, and some specialist financial data companies also compile this type of information for sale. These can provide some useful comparisons, but here again interpretation must be cautious because the 'average' may be distorted by a number of factors. Because many companies have peripheral activities or more than one product, they may be included in an industry average for their main product, but their accounts will include the results of the other operations, leading to some distortion. Again the definition of the industry grouping may be so wide as to make comparison useless.

Sometimes the grouping is dominated by one or two large companies, as would be the case with media companies in Germany, dominated by Bertelsmann, so it may be that the national 'industry average' reflects heavily the structure of one or two companies.

Tools of analysis

A simple approach to analysis would be to compare one component of the balance sheet with the same component of the other balance sheet. However, in cross-sectional analysis this would not be very helpful if the two companies being compared were of different size. The size problem is overcome by the use of financial ratios.

Ratios are a very simple device whereby instead of comparing absolute amounts from financial statements, one uses a ratio to express the relationship between two elements of the financial data, and compares that relationship with the same relationship in the other company. That is more easily understood in relation to an example.

Suppose we wished to compare the profit performance of two companies and had the following data about each:

	Company A	*Company B*
	$	*$*
Sales	100,000	200,000
Net profit	10,000	15,000

Assuming that their product and activities are similar, a straight comparison would yield the information that Company B had more sales than A and made more profit than A. In other words, Company B is bigger than A – but that is easy to see and tells us very little about their relative efficiency.

However, a test of efficiency would be possible if we converted the information given to a ratio of profit to sales which would then tell us which company had the lower costs per unit of sales. This ratio is commonly used, and is sometimes called the 'profit margin ratio':

$$\frac{\text{Net profit}}{\text{Sales}} = \text{Profit margin ratio}$$

Applied to our example companies this yields:

Company A

$$\frac{10,000}{100,000} \quad * 100 = 10\%$$

Company B

$$\frac{15,000}{200,000} \quad * 100 = 7.5\%$$

By using a ratio we eliminate the size difference (the ratio expresses a relationship internal to each company) and are then able to make a meaningful comparison. We can see that Company A has a better performance than B; it makes a higher profit from its sales, so is more efficient than B, although smaller.

A practical point to bear in mind here is that the comparison is warped if the numbers used are not exactly the same. For example, if in the above comparison the Company A net profit was before tax, and the Company B net profit was after tax, the comparison of ratios would not be valid. The golden rule is that *like must always be compared with like*.

The use of just the one ratio would not be sufficient to make a final assessment of either company; we should certainly look for other ratios to indicate other perspectives on performance, such as sales to capital employed. It could be that A is more capital intensive than B, so that would qualify the efficiency assessment in the first ratio. In essence a good analyst will look for as many ratios as are meaningful, in order to build up a complete picture of the companies being examined.

Ratio analysis permits many comparisons, depending on the degree of detail available from the source data, and in general the analyst should always be free to construct whatever ratios seem appropriate in the context of the companies under review. However, some ratios are more commonly used than others and the following are generally useful for most companies.

Management performance ratios

$$\text{Return on equity} = \frac{\text{Net profit after tax}}{\text{Equity}}$$

$$\text{Return on capital employed} = \frac{\text{Net profit before interest}}{\text{Total assets}}$$

$$\text{Earnings per share} = \frac{\text{Net profit after tax, minorities and preference dividend}}{\text{Number of shares in issue}}$$

$$\text{Asset turnover} = \frac{\text{Sales}}{\text{Total assets}}$$

$$\text{Net profit margin} = \frac{\text{Net profit before tax and interest}}{\text{Sales}}$$

$$\text{Gross profit margin} = \frac{\text{Sales less cost of sales}}{\text{Sales}}$$

To an extent these ratios are self-explanatory. They all answer different aspects of the question as to how well management has performed. Net profit margin shows (in its change from year to year, or compared to another company) how successful the management is in creating profit from a given quantity of sales, while gross margin shows control of manufacturing or purchasing costs (depending upon the activity of the company). Return on equity is a slightly dangerous figure in that it is not a 'real' return and should not be compared with, for example, the rate of interest paid on a bank deposit account. It can be used in time series analysis to show whether profitability is improving or declining, viewed from the equity perspective, as opposed to all finance.

Taken in conjunction with the return on investment it shows whether the return to shareholders is changing better or worse than the return on overall financing (return on capital employed), which brings in the debt element of the company as well and affords a comparison between the efficiency of companies with different debt/equity ratios.

Earnings per share (eps) is another way of checking whether profitability is growing from a shareholder-only perspective. This ratio is given great importance by Anglo-Saxon companies and analysts and companies listed in London or New York are required to calculate this figure and show it in their annual report. It has taken on a major significance in the investment industry and is the single most commonly used measure. Many accountants, though, deplore its use as being too simplistic – it reduces a complex information set to a single figure, thereby destroying much of the message. There is even an IASC standard dealing with it – IAS 33.

Analysts also talk about 'quality of earnings' as well as the absolute number as being important (how sustainable are the profits? what activities are they derived from?). This is a question which needs further consideration in the light of accounting and other devices which are discussed later. The key question is the extent to which current profits are affected by special circumstances (e.g. asset sales) and to what extent they can be expected to continue for the foreseeable future.

The eps number is used as an input to a market ratio, the price/earnings or p/e ratio, which is relevant to companies listed on Anglo-Saxon stock exchanges:

$$\text{Price/earnings} = \frac{\text{Market price of share}}{\text{eps}}$$

We will come back to the p/e ratio later – this is another form of rate of return ratio, albeit inverted.

Net asset turnover shows how efficient a company is in using its assets – but the absolute ratio has little meaning; it is the comparison from one year to another or one company to another similar company which yields the interesting measure of efficiency. For example: does the company make less and less use of capacity? If so, it might indicate a dying market for the product, even if inflation were pushing up the sales price and the profits.

These are the major management performance ratios, albeit not the only ones. The definitions given are ones commonly found, but are not the only definitions possible – when discussing ratios it is sensible to check exactly what definition is being used. This is never more true than with the debt/equity or gearing ratio.

Financial strength ratios

$$\text{Debt/equity ratio} = \frac{\text{Debt}}{\text{Equity}}$$

This is also frequently computed on the basis of debt to total finance:

$$\text{Gearing} = \frac{\text{Debt}}{\text{Debt} + \text{Equity}}$$

$$\text{Interest cover} = \frac{\text{Profit before tax}}{\text{Net interest charges}}$$

$$\text{Dividend cover} = \frac{\text{Earnings per share}}{\text{Dividend per share}}$$

$$\text{Current ratio} = \frac{\text{Current assets}}{\text{Current liabilities}}$$

$$\text{Acid test (or quick ratio)} = \frac{\text{Current assets} - \text{Stock}}{\text{Current liabilities}}$$

These ratios indicate financial strength from different points of view. The debt/equity ratio is the one found most frequently in the financial press, and the relationship between loan finance and shareholders' funds, as we have discussed before, is an indicator of financial risk. A high debt/equity ratio implies substantial interest charges, and an exposure to interest rate movements: if interest rates are rising, this will imply lower profitability in the future. The existence of debt means that ultimately repayment must take place and a glance at the schedule of outstanding debt given in the notes to the accounts will indicate how early this may take place. Most agreements for the provision of long-term finance include stipulations as to the maximum debt/equity ratio the company may have ('loan covenants') – and this sort of covenant has been the driver of a certain amount of creative accounting designed to improve the debt/equity ratio.

The debt/equity ratio is sometimes computed in slightly different ways, for example debt as a proportion of total capital employed. Sometimes the computation of debt will include all liabilities, both short- and long-term. Occasionally debt repayable within one year is mixed in within short-term trade and operational creditors, thereby mixing a financing element with working capital. When computing the liability ratios, it is logical to look at the analysis of short-term creditors and include the pure financing element (normally indicated as 'borrowings' or debt in the note which analyses short-term creditors) in the debt/equity ratio, and the rest of short-term creditors (trade creditors, taxation, dividends etc.) as part of working capital.

The interest cover ratio is often used as a surrogate for the debt/equity ratio, or in addition to that ratio. This is partly as a response to creative accounting schemes which have reduced the reliability of the debt/equity ratio. Interest cover indicates the safety margin between profits and interest charges. In good times bankers and others like to see interest 'cover' of five times, but it is not unusual to see cover drop to as low as three times.

The current ratio and acid test (called the 'quick ratio' in the USA) are tests of the make-up of working capital. They measure in a crude way the relationship between assets which will shortly mature to cash, and liabilities which will require cash settlement. The acid test excludes stock on the basis that in some industries stock turns over very slowly and therefore should not be looked to for very quick maturity into cash.

As we discussed in Chapter 8 when looking at working capital management, interpretation of these ratios should be done with care since the working capital structure of companies varies considerably from one industry to another. Hotels and retail businesses often have acid test ratios of less than one (i.e. their short-term monetary assets are smaller than their short-term monetary liabilities) because (a) they have very few credit sales, so few debtors, and (b) they generate immediate cash from sales and have no need to keep large amounts of cash available at the bank to pay creditors.

As so often in ratio analysis, what is important is not the absolute number, but the direction and rate of change from one year to another. If a company's activity does not change, its working capital ratios should not change either. A sudden move in the working capital ratios means that something in the company's structure has changed, and further questions should be asked as to why this is – for example, an increase in the current ratio may be generated by an increase in stocks, so one should ask why have stock levels risen? has there been a sudden fall-off in demand for the company's products?

Another way of examining individual components of working capital is to compare the balance sheet value with the related annual turnover figure. For example, for a retail company, the ratio of stock on hand at the year end to annual cost of sales will tell you how many days' business would be required to sell the stock:

$$\text{Stock turnover (days)} \quad = \quad \frac{\text{Stock}}{\text{Cost of sales}} * 365$$

Similarly:

$$\text{Credit given} \quad \quad = \quad \frac{\text{Debtors}}{\text{Credit sales}} * 365$$

This tells you how many days' credit are given to customers (but note that you need to know either that all sales are on credit, or that a substantial proportion of these is on credit). Where a company is buying goods for resale, the ratio of trade creditors to cost of sales will show the days' credit taken from suppliers.

These ratios can also be useful even if you do not know that there is a high proportion of credit sales, or where most of the company's products are manufactured (so purchases from suppliers are only a small part of cost of sales), because while the absolute number of days is no longer a meaningful figure, a significant (say, more than 10 per cent) *shift* in the figure from one year to another will indicate a change in credit arrangements.

Analysing financial statements

It is very easy for people approaching ratios for the first time to go through a series of reactions, initially seeing the calculation of the ratios as an end in itself, and then later asking what use the ratios are. Essentially analysis is about decoding the messages which are built into financial statements, and using them to 'tell the story' of the company. Ratios are a means of throwing light upon certain aspects of a company, but not all ratios will be important for all companies, and often the calculation of ratios leads to a question rather than an answer. You must remember that ratio analysis is only part (even if important) of the investment appraisal process, and investors need to look at economic variables, information about the company's future plans etc. as well as decoding the information in the financial statements.

So how does one set about analysing a set of financial statements? The first question you must ask yourself is why you are making the analysis – is it for lending purposes, or for investing? Is it for a long-term involvement or short-term? In short, what is the nature of the decision which you need to make, and to inform which you are looking at the financial statements?

Having identified your analysis objective, you should gather what general information is available to you about the nature of the company and its activities – this will depend on whether you have a full annual report which will include much non-financial information, and under what circumstances you are carrying out the analysis.

Only then can you look at the accounts, and start work on calculating ratios. A normal process would be to compute the ten or so standard ratios which we have discussed above, for as long a time series as you have information available. Any one set of accounts will include previous year comparative figures, but in an ideal situation you would have more than one set of accounts, so that you can compile a longer time series.

Having computed your ratios, you should look to see if there are any patterns – which ratios are stable, which changing. If ratios are changing, you need to ask why they are doing so. This may be obvious from the accounts. For example, if the return on equity ratio increases, this might be because of an increase in profit, an increase in sales or a reduction in equity. If the net margin ratio (profit/sales) has gone up (say from 10 to 12 per cent), and you see that sales have remained static, this means that the amount of profit per pound of sales has increased, which probably means that the company is controlling its costs more efficiently, but on the other hand that poses questions as to why sales have not increased.

Key indicators SAS Group, SAS and SAS International Hotels

		SAS Group		SAS	SAS Int	Hotels
	1998	*1997*	*1998*	*1997*	*1998*	*1997*
Operating revenue, MSEK	40946	38928	38211	36769	2786	2304
Income after financial items	2829	2231	2588	2067	233	160
Gross margin %	10	11	10	10	33	32
Investments, MSEK	6112	3256	5554	2938	557	318
Return on capital employed %	13	12	12	11	14	12
Average employees	27071	25057	23992	22524	3041	2491

Source: Extract from Annual Report 1998,
The SAS Group

It may be that a picture gradually emerges of the activities of the company, and what you have to do is attempt to 'tell the story' of the company, based on what is available from its figures.

The next step is to do some cross-sectional analysis, if you have the necessary information – either data from another company in the same field, or industry data. You can then compare ratios and there may be further insights into your company from this process. If Company A has a gross margin of 35 per cent, why does Company B, in the same year and carrying out the same activities, have a gross margin of 40 per cent?

Worked example

In order to help put the use of ratios into some context, we will carry out basic analysis on a three-year time series of company data – note that we are not given any background information about the company's activities, so that will limit how far we can make deductions about what is going on, and we do not have any material for cross-sectional analysis. Also, the statements are simplified to the extent that we do not have a breakdown of fixed assets, and all debt is long-term.

Financial statements:

	20X7 $'000	20X8 $'000	20X9 $'000
Profit and loss accounts:			
Sales	620.0	745.0	762.0
Cost of sales	217.0	245.8	266.7
Margin	403.0	499.2	495.3
Distribution	204.6	260.7	266.7
Administration	95.1	97.2	101.4
	103.3	141.3	127.2
Interest	10.0	30.9	37.5
	93.3	111.3	98.7
Taxation	32.7	38.9	31.4
	60.6	72.4	67.3
Balance sheets:			
Net fixed assets	312.0	532.0	495.0
Stocks	43.4	49.2	66.7
Debtors	62.0	74.5	91.4
Cash	67.0	70.3	58.0
	484.4	726.0	711.1
Ordinary shares ($1)	120.0	120.0	120.0
Reserves	195.5	267.9	315.2
	315.5	387.9	435.2
Debt	100.0	250.0	200.0
Trade creditors	36.2	49.2	44.5
Tax	32.7	38.9	31.4
	484.4	726.0	711.1

Before starting on the ratios, let us just see if there are any trends visible from the financial statements as such. We can see that sales increased substantially from 20X7 to 20X8 (20 per cent) but the increase dropped to 2 per cent from 20X8 to 20X9. Profits increased in 20X7/X8 as you would predict from the sales, but dropped off in 20X9. An obvious explanation of this is the rapid increase in interest costs: from $10,000 in 20X7 to $30,900 in 20X8 and $37,500 in 20X9. Looking at the balance sheet, you can see debt going from $100,000 to $250,000 and then dropping to $200,000 (given the rising interest cost, it may well be that interest rates rose steeply during this period). We can see that fixed assets rose sharply as well, so already we can see some sort of story here: a company seems to have expanded capacity substantially in 20X8, leading to borrowing but also higher sales. In 20X9 sales growth has not continued at the same pace and interest rates have risen, causing the company's profits to fall.

Let us calculate some of the key ratios and see how this story is fleshed out:

Ratios:

	20X7	20X8	20X9
RoE	60.6/295.5 = 20.5%	72.4/367.9 = 19.7%	67.3/415.2 = 16.2%
ROCE	103.3/(312.0+ 43.4+62.0+67.0 = 21.3%	141.3/(532.0 + 49.2+74.5+70.3 = 19.5%	127.2/(495.0 + 66.7+91.4+58 = 17.9%
eps	60.6/120.0 = 50.5p	72.4/120.0 = 60.3p	67.3/120.0 = 56.1p
Asset T/O	620.0/484.4 = 1.28	745.0/726.0 = 1.03	762/711.1 = 1.02
Net margin	93.3/620.0 = 15.0%	111.3/745.0 = 14.9%	98.7/762.0 = 12.9%
Gross margin	403.0/620.0 = 65%	499.2/745.0 = 67%	495.2/762.0 = 65%
Gearing	100/295.5 = 33.8%	250/367.9 = 68.0%	200/415.2 = 48.2%
Interest cover	103.3/10.0 = 10.3	141.3/30.9 = 4.6	127.2/37.5 = 3.4
Dividend	60.6/20.0 = 3.0	72.4/20.0 = 3.6	67.3/20.0 = 3.4
Current	172.4/88.9 = 1.94	194/108.1 = 1.79	216.1/95.9 = 2.25
Acid test	129.0/88.9 = 1.45	144.8/108.1 = 1.34	149.4/95.9 = 1.56
Stock T/O	43.3/217 *365 = 73	49.2/245.8 *365 = 73	66.7/266.7 *365 = 91
Debtor T/O	62.0/620.0 *365 = 36.5	74.5/745.0 *365 = 36.5	91.4/762.0 *365 = 43.7
Creditor T/O	36.2/217.0 *365 = 60.9	49.2/245.8 *365 = 73.1	44.5/266.7 *365 = 60.9

Growth:		20X7/X8	20X8/X9
Sales		+ 20.2%	+ 2.28%
Profit		+ 19.3%	−11.3%
Capital employed		+ 51.2%	–
Net fixed assets		+ 70.5%	−6.9%

Interpretation

Overall, this looks like a company which has gone for a major expansion/replacement of capacity in 20X8 (fixed assets increased by 70 per cent), financed largely by an increase in debt. Overall, this has resulted in increased sales and improved margins in 20X8, but in 20X9 the expansion of sales has not continued and the company has also been hit by higher interest costs.

The effect of the heavy investment is to reduce return on capital employed from 21.3 to 17.9 per cent, and reduce asset turnover from 1.34 to 1.02 although a return to sales growth would easily correct this in the following year. The impression is that the market for the company's product slowed down in 20X9, causing an increase in unsold stocks (stock turnover time up from 73 to 91 days). Debtor turnover has also slipped, suggesting that the company may be chasing sales with extended credit offers (or its customers may be similarly hit by slowdown). Gross margin has also slipped, which suggests that the company may have cut sales prices in order to boost business.

The company has sensibly used its internal cash flow to contribute to financing the 20X8 investment (debt increased by $150,000 while fixed assets increased by $242,000 – although creditor turnover moved from 61 days to 72) and subsequently to reduce borrowing in 20X9. The gearing ratio moved from an unremarkable 34 per cent (and 10 times interest cover) to a rather more dangerous 68 per cent, although interest cover remained reasonable at 4.6. In 20X9 the repayment of $50,000 brought gearing down to 48 per cent but the higher interest rates and lower profits caused interest cover to decline further to 3.4. If the market does not drop further the company should be able to continue to reduce borrowing and diminish the exposure to interest costs, showing an improved return.

Overall, this looks like a company which has set out on a relatively ambitious expansion plan, financed by borrowing and internal cash flows, which has hit some difficulties with a slowdown in demand. While its gearing rose quite sharply in the expansion phase, the company looks as though it has a sensible policy of retrenching and reducing debt. It should be able to continue to trade satisfactorily and generate further cash to further reduce gearing.

Summary

Financial analysts, lenders and other users of financial statements are concerned to measure both the efficiency of a company's management and the financial strength of the company. They do this by extracting data from the published financial statements and either making comparisons or feeding the data into financial models.

The traditional approach to financial analysis involves making comparisons of a company's results over several years (time series) or comparisons between one company and another (cross-sectional). In order to make the analysis more meaningful, various devices are used to take away the disparity in size between companies.

The chief of these is the use of financial ratios, which express one accounting number in relation to another (economically linked) number. When making comparisons using ratios it is necessary to be sure that the ratios being compared have been calculated from the same basis, and that the companies being compared do indeed have broadly similar characteristics.

An examination of the patterns of ratios and the financial statements themselves can lead the analyst to deduce what the company has been doing, without any further non-financial information, although investors would normally take into account not only the results of financial statement analysis but also any other available information about the economy generally, the industry in which the company works etc.

Questions

1. The following is the income statement and balance sheet of a company. Please calculate four accounting ratios (e.g. return on equity, return on capital employed, gross margin, net profit margin, current ratio, gearing ratio) and supply the definition you have used with your answer.

Income statement

Sales	145,600
Cost of sales	(54,200)
Other operating costs	(49,400)
	42,000
Interest paid	(17,500)
Taxation	(14,500)
Net profit	10,000

Balance sheet

Assets		Financing	
Tangible	149,000	Share capital	50,000
Depreciation	(17,500)	Reserves	63,000
Stocks	82,300	Debt	100,000
Cash at bank	56,300	Owed to suppliers	57,100
	270,100		270,100

2. The following figures are drawn from the balance sheet of Medmove:

	20X1 $'000	20X2 $'000	20X3 $'000
Fixed assets (net)	2,350	2,900	3,800
Current assets			
Stocks	150	160	160
Debtors	310	300	310
Cash	55	—	235
Total assets	2,865	3,360	4,505
Financing			
Trade payables	220	600	200
Debt	—	—	1,500
Total liabilities	220	600	1,700

No fresh shares were issued during the period. The industry has an organization which publishes average financial data. The industry average balance sheet is:

Fixed assets	75	Equity	70
Stocks	10	Debt	20
Debtors	10	Payables	10
Cash	5		
	100		100

You are asked to:

(i) calculate whatever ratios you think may be useful in analysing Medmove's figures (but including current ratio, debt/equity);

(ii) using the analytical data which you have just computed, and the industry average balance sheet, comment on the company's position and development.

3. A company had the following financial statements:

	20X2 $'000	20X3 $'000	20X4 $'000
Profit and loss accounts:			
Sales	620.0	745.0	762.0
Cost of sales	217.0	245.8	266.7
Margin	403.0	499.2	495.3
Distribution	204.6	260.7	266.7
Administration	95.1	97.2	101.4
	103.3	141.3	127.2
Interest	10.0	30.9	37.5
	93.3	111.3	98.7
Taxation	32.7	38.9	31.4
	60.6	72.4	67.3
Balance sheets:			
Net fixed assets	312.0	532.0	495.0
Stocks	43.4	49.2	66.7
Debtors	62.0	74.5	91.4
Cash	67.0	70.3	58.0
Total assets	484.4	726.0	711.1
Ordinary shares ($1)	120.0	120.0	120.0
Reserves	195.5	267.9	315.2
	315.5	387.9	435.2
Trade creditors	36.2	49.2	44.5
Tax	32.7	38.9	31.4
Debt	100.0	250.0	200.0
Total financing	484.4	726.0	711.1

(a) You are asked to compute whatever ratios you think will be useful in analysing the above figures (but including eps, ROCE, gearing, current ratio, asset turnover, gross margin, net profit margin).

(b) You are asked to comment on the company's development and activity during the period covered by the financial statements.

4. The managing director of Bavarian Hypermarkets has been approached by the chief executive and majority shareholder of Black Forest Supermarkets, a medium-sized supermarket chain operating in southern Germany. Black Forest is looking for a partner: it feels it cannot grow any further without outside capital, and would like to sell 40 per cent of its shares to a larger supermarket operator who could inject more

capital and provide management expertise to expand the chain further. Black Forest is quite willing to contemplate selling a majority stake in due course.

Bavarian Hypermarkets is quite interested in the deal, because they think that the two businesses would be a good fit in operational terms. They hire your firm to carry out an analysis of Black Forest, and you are given the following financial statements, on which you are asked to comment:

Black Forest Supermarkets

Profit and loss account

	20X6 $'000	20X5 $'000	20X4 $'000
Sales	3,674	2,987	1,643
Cost of sales	2,718	2,151	1,133
	956	836	510
Distribution costs	412	392	242
Administration expenses	183	190	86
	361	254	182
Interest	315	243	0
Net profit/(loss)	46	11	182
Taxation	(15)	(3)	(65)
Retained profit	31	8	117

Balance sheets

	20X6 $'000	20X5 $'000	20X4 $'000
Fixed assets			
Intangible	2,100	2,200	0
Tangible	4,446	4,220	2,085
Investments			240
Current assets			
Stock	301	255	105
Debtors	38	42	29
Cash at bank	68	54	73
	6,953	6,771	2,532
Financing			
Ordinary shares	1,200	1,200	1,200
Retained profit	1,241	1,210	1,202
	2,441	2,410	2,402
Long-term debt	4,000	4,000	—
Trade payables	512	361	130
Total financing	6,953	6,771	2,532

Your report should identify and comment on all strengths and weaknesses of the company as revealed by its figures.

5. You work for the financial analysis section of a merchant bank and are asked to prepare a report on the following figures, which relate to a clothing retailer, who is looking to the bank to take a share stake:

	20X3 $m	20X4 $m	20X5 $m
Sales	589.4	601.2	604.1
Cost of sales	206.3	222.4	235.6
	383.1	378.8	368.5
Distribution costs	22.7	18.5	32.1
Administration expense	241.9	254.0	266.7
	118.5	106.3	69.7
Interest expense	49.5	63.0	72.0
Ordinary profit/(loss) before taxation	69.0	43.3	(2.3)
Taxation	22.8	14.3	(0.8)
Profit/(loss) after tax	46.1	29.0	(1.5)

Balance sheets

	20X3	20X4	20X5
Tangible fixed assets			
Land and buildings	620.0	620.0	620.0
Fittings and equipment	72.4	72.4	72.4
Depreciation	(37.2)	(44.4)	(51.6)
	655.2	648.0	640.8
Current assets			
Stocks	143.9	152.0	179.5
Debtors	5.7	6.1	5.9
Bank	12.7	7.3	
Total assets	817.5	813.4	826.2
Capital			
Ordinary shares	120.0	120.0	120.0
Retained profits	166.4	165.4	133.9
	286.4	285.4	253.9
Long-term debt	450.0	450.0	450.0
Trade payables	58.3	63.7	95.4
Tax	22.8	14.3	—
Bank overdraft			26.9
	817.5	813.4	826.2

You are asked to prepare:

(i) eight key ratios which are relevant to the analysis of this company;

(ii) a report which attempts to explain what has been happening to the company over the last three years, using ratios and trends as appropriate, makes recommendations as to the desirability of becoming involved and makes suggestions for the future management of the company.

10 Cash flow statements

Financial analysts make considerable use of cash flow information in their evaluation of companies. This chapter introduces the cash flow statement and its preparation. It starts out by reviewing the relationship between profits and cash flow, and then introducing the cash flow statement and finally showing how to construct one.

Introduction

Our focus so far has been on the preparation of the income statement and balance sheet, but in this chapter we are going on to consider the third of the annual financial statements, the cash flow statement. We first introduced this statement in Chapter 1 – it analyses the company's cash flows during the period covered by the profit and loss account. The statement presents, for the benefit of the external user, the cash generated by the company from its trading operations during the year, the company's investment in new fixed assets (increase in or renewal of its productive capacity) and the changes in the company's external financing from one balance sheet to the next.

Financial analysts have long used cash flows as a useful indicator of company performance, and not least when making comparisons between companies operating in different countries. One of the advantages of a cash flow measure is that it disregards charges such as depreciation or provisions, which may be applied differently by different companies, and focuses on actual revenue flowing in and costs being paid out. In this sense it filters out some of the differences which arise from accounting practices rather than operating practices.

Many analysts calculate their own cash flow statements. This is useful when making comparisons between companies since one must ensure that the information is presented in a comparable fashion. However, although company law in no country requires the disclosure of a cash flow statement, many accounting standards require it, and even where it is not required most companies provide one because that is now internationally accepted practice for a company of any size. In addition, corporate practice has settled more or less on what was originally the US model of presentation, and the International Accounting Standard (IAS 7) is widely used by companies (and is accepted by the SEC).

The utility of cash flow statements for small companies is contested. Most accounting standards on cash flow statements exempt small companies from its preparation; however, bankers, when lending to any size company, generally ask for a cash flow projection as part of any loan proposal. Many management consultants would also say that any business manager must be aware not only of profit and profitability but also cash flows.

A potential investor will want to know how successful the company is at generating cash, and what the company is doing with its cash flows. In as far as the object of preparing annual financial statements is to provide decision-useful information for investors and creditors, the cash flow statement shows what underlying cash flows have taken place during the year under review, while the profit and loss account provides information about the profitability of the company.

The profit and loss account concentrates on measuring profit from transactions irrespective of whether the associated cash changed hands during the accounting year or not; the cash flow statement shows what cash transactions did take place. In discussing balance sheet structure we have treated cash as being part of working capital, but of course the cash in the bank is simply the residual of a great number of different types of cash flows, not only operating cash flows, but also purchases and sales of assets, receipt of financing, reimbursement of old debt etc. In the cash flow statement, the net change in cash balances is the figure we are trying to explain, in terms of these different activities.

During the course of a year's operations a company will be generating cash flows from its trading, which will be used not only for materials, labour and other periodic costs but also for purchasing new assets or to pay off debt. It might also borrow fresh funds, sell off old assets and so on. All these activities will bring about a change in the various components of the balance sheet, and the cash flow statement analyses these changes for the shareholder. This analysis gives important insights into the company's success and its strategy. It shows what cash has been created by the company in a year – an important measure of performance, in an absolute sense, but also key to the company's potential for internally generated growth. What the company does with its cash (investing in productive capacity, paying off debt, paying dividends etc.) provides useful indicators of corporate strategy.

Going back to the balance sheet equation (total uses of finance = total sources of finance), the cash flow statement details changes in this equation during the year covered by the annual accounts. It therefore satisfies:

$$\text{Total changes in uses} = \text{total changes in sources}$$

The areas of change are presented in the cash flow statement in three broad categories: cash flows from operations, investment in long-term assets, and financing. In this chapter we will look first at the more straightforward issues of investment and finance, and then look at cash flow from operations, before going on to preparing cash flow statements.

Investment in assets and financing

In discussing the balance sheet we have pointed out that it is a basic tenet of financial management that long-term assets should generally be bought with long-term finance, in order to match the expected cash inflows from use of the asset with the outflows to repay the finance. Sometimes companies borrow short-term and arrange new finance when the short-term debt expires ('roll over' the borrowing), but this involves two risks, first that finance may be difficult to obtain in the second phase, and second that interest rates may have increased, making the cost of borrowing uneconomic in relation to the asset purchased. The cost of capital is normally an important factor in evaluating an asset purchase and companies expose themselves to an 'interest rate risk' if they do not match the borrowing to the investment cash flows. Matching investment with the borrowing is known as 'hedging' the interest rate risk, and the decision whether to do this or not is part of the company's financial strategy.

A company will generate long-term finance by retaining cash generated by its operations (increasing its equity through retained profits), but it would not necessarily wish to restrict its investments in new activities (or expanding existing ones) to the rate at which cash is generated internally. It will therefore often borrow outside finance or issue new shares.

Typically a company will wish to preserve a balance between the amount of capital borrowed and that obtained by issuing shares. That is, it will have a target balance between debt and equity. However, as we mentioned in Chapter 8, issuing shares is a costly business, so what companies often do is finance new projects purely from internal cash flows and borrowing and then once every few years issue a major block of shares which reduces the debt/equity ratio and enables them to pay off ('retire') some existing debt. Equally a company might sell off part of its operations which it no longer wants, as part of a rationalization programme.

A company which is expanding will also be buying new assets regularly, as well as selling off old ones which are worn out or which have been superseded by new technology. There will therefore be a pattern of regular change.

The long-term changes to be expected can be summarized as follows:

Uses of finance
Purchase of new assets
Retirement of existing debt

Sources of finance
Issue of new shares
New long term borrowing
Sale of assets

In a cash flow statement, these would be presented as:

Cash flow on investments
Purchase of assets (outflow)
Sale of assets (inflow)

Cash flow from financing
Issue of new shares (inflow)
Payment of dividend (outflow)
New borrowing (inflow)
Retirement of debt (outflow)

Note that we have slipped in the payment of dividends here in the financing section. We will discuss this below, but the IAS sees payment of dividend as an adjustment of equity, although some jurisdictions prefer it to be presented elsewhere in the cash flow statement, such as in cash flow from operations, as a distribution of the cash generated. (Where exactly it appears in the cash flow statement is not as important as checking when making comparisons that it is treated the same way in all statements being compared.)

Cap Gemini Group

Consolidated statements of cash flows for the years ended December 31, 1996, 1997, 1998

(in millions of French Francs)	*1996*	*1997*	*1998*
Operating activities			
Income of fully consolidated companies before tax	884	1660	2685
Adjustments to reconcile income of fully consolidated companies before tax to cash generated by operations			
Depreciation and amortization	336	489	536
Provisions	133	87	41
Profit on disposal of fixed assets	(84)	(252)	(25)
Other	(54)	(209)	15
Cash generated by operations	1215	1775	3252
Change in accounts and notes receivable, net	(575)	(456)	(1023)
Changes in accounts and notes payable, net	55	157	244
Change in other receivables and payables, net	(91)	272	226
Net movement in working capital	(611)	(27)	(553)
Net cash provided by operating activities	604	1748	2699
Investing activities			
Acquisitions of property, plant and equipment and intangible fixed assets	(591)	(614)	(858)
Disposals of property, pant and equipment and intangible fixed assets	20	91	208
	(571)	(523)	(650)
Acquisitions of investments	(44)	(509)	(104)
Disposal of investments	266	1093	20
	222	584	(84)
Net cash (used)/provided by investing activities	(349)	61	(734)
Equity financing activities			
Increase in share capital (incl. exercise of stock options)	26	127	3843
Minority interests in increase in share capital of subsidiaries	50	27	37
Dividends paid	(71)	(217)	(347)
Net cash provided /(used) by equity financing activities	5	(63)	3533
Net cash provided on a comparable Group basis before debt financing activities	260	1746	5498
Net cash/(net debt) at beginning of year	(2684)	(3027)	(1635)
Net change in borrowings	846	1521	1033
Net change in financial receivables, s/term investments and cash	(586)	225	4465
Net cash provided by debt financing activities on a comparable group basis	260	1746	5498
Effect of exchange rate movements on net debt	(8)	(85)	(74)
Net debt of companies acquired or sold during year	(595)	(269)	(2)
Net cash/(net debt) at end of year	(3027)	(1635)	3787

Source: Cap Gemini Group,
Consolidated financial statements 1998

Cash flow from operations

The profit and loss account and balance sheet are based on the accruals principle, which could be summed up as trying to present an economic analysis of profit by recording transactions when any relevant economic event takes place (sales, expenses, using up of assets etc.). Cash flows are only one type of event recorded, and while a company must manage its cash flows, it cannot manage the business just on cash flow information; it needs to know about economic profit and profitability. For example, a company might have more cash coming in from sales than going out on expenses, but if it is not also recording the consumption of its assets (depreciation), it could be making an economic loss even though generating a cash surplus in the short to medium term. Consequently, management focus has traditionally been on profits, but, in a healthy company, the reinvestment of cash generated is the main source of internal growth, and management should be looking how best to allocate this resource to increase the profitability of the company. The cash flow statement helps to show what wealth is being generated. Of course, over the life of the company the total of profits will equal the total of cash flows generated, but on a period-to-period basis this is not the case because of allocations of asset costs (depreciation) and timing differences from credit operations.

The simplest way to get at the operating cash flows for the year would be to look at the company's cash book (journal which records all receipts and payments) and remove cash flows relating to assets and financing. This can be done, and in the jargon is known as the 'direct' way of calculating cash flows. However, while this probably is easy enough for a small company, and may be the easiest way also for the small entrepreneur to envisage cash flows, in large companies it is arguably easier to calculate the cash flow by manipulating the profit and loss account and balance sheet. This is known as the 'indirect' method. Inevitably an external analyst must use the indirect method, because there is no access to the company's cash records, and in fact most companies present the information using the indirect method, so that is the one we will use.

The indirect method of calculating operating cash flows consists of taking the net accounting profit for the year and then making adjustments which deal with factors which influence profit but not cash flow (e.g. depreciation, provisions) and timing differences arising from the working capital cycle.

Depreciation, provisions

As we have seen above, the process of preparing annual accounts involves two kinds of adjustments: refinements to the profit to anticipate income and expenses which have not been included in the accounting database (such as accrued expenses); and adjustments to asset values (reflecting the using up of productive assets and extraneous value changes in assets). In the first case, these are short-term timing differences which will turn into cash flows after the balance sheet date, but in the second case, the associated cash flow (purchase of asset) has already taken place and we are simply showing that economically it has lost some value which should be taken into consideration when estimating the economic position of the company. From a cash flow statement perspective, the cash outflow on assets appears under 'investment' and is reported when the asset is acquired, therefore when depreciation is charged the investment cash flow has by definition already been reported. There is no operating cash outflow associated with depreciation or provisions for loss of value. Consequently, any charge to the profit and loss account for the year for these items should be added back to arrive at the underlying cash flow.

Provisions for risks and charges may turn into cash flows in due course, but their fate is uncertain and they too are added back here. Equally, where a provision is released, this will have the effect of increasing profit without increasing cash flows. Such releases must therefore be deducted from profit in calculating cash flow.

We can summarize as follows. The profit and loss account includes some charges which do not reflect current cash outflows or inflows, and these should be used to adjust the accounting profit and approach an approximation of operating cash flows:

Net profit or loss after tax	xxxxxxxxxxxxxx
Add back:	
Depreciation charge for the year	xxxxxxxxxxxxxxx
Provisions created in year	xxxxxxxxxxxxxx
Deduct:	
Provisions released in year	(xxxxxxxxxxxxxx)
'Free cash flow'	xxxxxxxxxxxxxx

Analysts frequently calculate this figure which is relatively easy to derive from the financial statements. It does not reflect the short-term timing differences which derive from credit operations, but is a valid approximation of cash flows from trading and is sometimes referred to as 'free cash flow'. It also has the advantage, in making comparisons between companies and particularly across national boundaries, that it excludes the most subjective elements of annual profit estimations, thereby providing more directly comparable figures.

Working capital movements

Working capital is generated by the operations of a company (see discussion in Chapter 4). There is a cycle of cash through the operation of the business in that a company buys materials (creating stock and creditors), processes the materials (in a manufacturing environment), pays the creditors, sells the finished goods on credit (creating debtors) and finally the debtors settle in cash, completing the cycle.

The exact needs of any business for working capital are dependent on the nature of the business. Some retailers, particularly supermarkets, keep very low stocks, and have little or no credit sales, so their working capital is largely negative – creditors. On the other hand, a manufacturing concern may have a long production cycle where it takes many months for raw materials to progress through manufacturing and be sold as finished goods. Such companies will have extensive stocks as well as debtors and creditors.

Movements in working capital items other than cash will affect cash flow from operations: increased debtors will mean that the cash from those sales will be received in the next accounting period; increased creditors means that the cash outflow to suppliers has been deferred to the next period. The cash flow statement will therefore need to take account of changes in working capital (excluding cash, which is the pivotal figure around which the cash flow statement is organized and whose changes we are trying to explain) in order to show the cash generated during the year from operations.

Let us just look at an example of how that works. Supposing that in its start-up year a company had no initial capital but had sales of $10,000, and it had purchased $8,000 of goods for resale. Its stock at the year end was worth $1,000, it owed $5,000 to its suppliers and its credit clients owed $2,000. The business had therefore the following profit and loss account:

	$
Sales	10,000
Cost of sales	(7,000)
	3,000

Its balance sheet at the end of the period was:

Current assets	
Stock	1,000
Debtors	2,000
Cash	5,000
	8,000

Financing	
Equity – Profit	3,000
Creditors	5,000
	8,000

The business has made a profit of $3,000, but its cash generated was $5,000. How was this possible? The answer is in the movements in non-cash working capital:

Cash owed to suppliers	5,000
Cash held in stocks	–1,000
Cash not yet paid by clients	–2,000
Non-cash working capital	2,000

The $2,000 difference represents timing differences, and if the business stopped trading and disposed of its stocks, its cash position would in a few weeks equal its profit as clients paid their accounts and the company paid its suppliers.

If we now move forward into the second accounting period, we can show how the change in net working capital affects cash flows. Let us say that the business has grown by 50 per cent and that the profit and loss account for period 2 gives the following result:

	$
Sales	15,000
Cost of sales	(10,500)
Profit	4,500

Assuming that credit sales and purchases had grown proportionately, debtors at the end of period 2 would be $3,000, stock $1,500 and creditors $7,500. We can display the balance sheets at the ends of periods 1 and 2 alongside each other and see not only how the cash position has changed, but also how the other balance sheet components have moved at the same time.

	End period 1 $	End period 2 $	Uses of finance $	Sources finance $
Assets				
Stock	1,000	1,500	500	
Debtors	2,000	3,000	1,000	
Cash	5,000	10,500	5,500	
	8,000	15,000		
Financing				
Creditors	5,000	7,500		2,500
Equity				
Accumulated profit	3,000	7,500	—	4,500
			7,000	7,000

In the two right-hand columns we have analysed the change in each balance sheet component that has taken place during the second year. If you look at the changes, you can see that the inflow of cash is related to the accounting profit through the changes in the other elements of working capital.

	$
Accounting profit	4,500
less uses of finance:	
• increase in debtors	(1,000)
• increase in stock	(500)
plus sources of finance	
• increase in creditors	2,500
Increase in cash	5,500

The example given is much simplified in order to highlight the changes in working capital – in many companies the increase in creditors would not be so high as to finance the increase in debtors and stocks entirely, and there would of course be some capital subscribed to start with. Accrued expenses and similar items have been ignored, but would be included here.

The IASC cash flow statement computes its cash flow from operations number by including an adjustment for changes in non-cash working capital:

Net profit after tax	xxxxxxxxx
Add back	
Depreciation for the year	xxxxx
Provisions created	xxxxx
Deduct	
Provisions released	(xxxx)
Free cash flow	xxxxxxxxx
Net change in non-cash working capital	(xxxxx)
Cash flow from operations	xxxxxxxxx

Constructing a cash flow statement 1

Let us now do a practical example. The working method is to take two consecutive balance sheets, calculate the difference between them and analyse these into inflows and outflows of cash.

	X2	X1	Δ	Outflow	Inflow
Fixed assets					
Cost	980	740	240	240	
Depreciation	−350	−265	85		85
Stocks	180	171	9	9	
Debtors	115	98	17	17	
Cash	92	110	18		18
	1017	854			
Financing					
Equity					
Capital	600	600	—		
Reserves	90	90	—		
X2 profit	50	—	50		50
Creditors	62	59	3		3
Debt	215	105	110		110
	1017	854		266	266

In the current example, the first step may be redundant, but this is useful where the analyst has to research more data to complete the analysis, as we shall see later. The cash difference is the figure we are trying to explain, and is entered onto the worksheet to ensure that one can make a mathematical control of the differences – when taking one balance sheet from another, the difference must be in equilibrium, since the two original balance sheets are in equilibrium. The cash figure is entered on the basis that an increase in assets is an outflow, and a decrease of assets is an inflow, even though this is obviously counter-intuitive. It should be thought of simply as the balancing difference.

Having calculated the inflow/outflow data, we can proceed to lay it out according to the type of activity with which the cash flow is associated (operations, investment, financing), as follows:

Operations

Net profit after tax	50
Add back depreciation	85
Free cash flow	135
Changes in non-cash working capital	−23
Net cash flow from operations (A)	112

Investment

Purchase of assets (B)	−240

Financing

New debt (C)	110
Net change in cash (A+B+C)	−18

Cash balances

At beginning of year	110
At balance sheet date	92
Difference	−18

Taking the cash flow statement line by line, the net profit figure is the profit for the year in the balance sheet (and in the profit and loss account, of course). The depreciation charge for the year is the difference between accumulated depreciation at the beginning and end of the year. The change in non-cash working capital is:

Increase in stocks	−9
Increase in debtors	−17
Increase in creditors	+3
Net change	−23

All that is left after that is the increase in assets of 240 and the increase in debt of 110. You should check off the differences identified in the worksheet against the cash flow statement to be sure you see where the information comes from.

Having drawn up the cash flow statement, the next question is: what useful information does that give us about the company?

Essentially here the message is simple – the company has acquired a substantial new asset, and has financed it approximately half by the cash flow it has generated in the year, and half by increasing its debt.

The increase in capacity is a good sign indicating increased future profits (provided the company can manage the asset successfully, of course). The degree of debt financing is out of line with the company's prior debt/equity ratio. In 20X1 the ratio was 105/690 or 15 per cent, and the financing of a new asset 50 per cent by debt must change this significantly. In fact the new ratio is 215/740 = 29 per cent. Of course the company may be planning to reduce the debt in 20X3 when it has generated more cash, or may simply have decided to adopt a more aggressive financing stance.

Disposal of assets

The use of raw balance sheet data in constructing a cash flow statement is complicated when there are both inflows and outflows under the same heading in the course of the year. This is frequently the case with fixed assets where companies are not only expanding capacity but are replacing old equipment with new. As regards the cash flow statement, asset disposals lead to two adjustments: (1) to separate out the disappearing book value of the old asset from the newly acquired assets, and (2) to remove the gain or loss on disposal from the operating profit and put it into the investment section, since all asset acquisitions and disposals should appear there.

Suppose that a company had assets at cost of 540 and accumulated depreciation of 235 at the beginning of the year. During the year it sold for 140 some equipment which had cost 275 and had accumulated depreciation of 160. It replaced this with an asset which cost 400. The depreciation charge for the year was 132.

The balance sheet analysis would give the following picture:

	X2	X1	Δ	Outflow	Inflow
Fixed assets	665	540	135		
Depreciation	−207	−235	28		

On the face of it the company has acquired a new fixed asset which cost 135, and there was a depreciation credit for the year instead of a charge. This is of course hardly likely, and would send the analyst immediately to the notes to the accounts for an analysis of movements on fixed assets, where it would quickly be discovered that there had been a disposal and an acquisition. Consequently the analysis can be completed more fully:

	X2	*X1*	*Δ*	*Outflow*	*Inflow*
Fixed assets	665	540	135	400	275
Depreciation	−207	−235	28	160	132

On the fixed assets line, the 135 represents the difference between the acquisition at 400 and the original cost of the asset disposed of, 275. For the purposes of the analysis we will put both the gross cost and the accumulated depreciation of the asset which has been sold into our worksheet, so that it is clear what is happening. The accumulated depreciation on this asset was 160, which, taken with the difference of 28 between balance sheet dates, means that the charge for the year was 132 (160–28=132).

The analysis therefore now includes all the elements which have intervened during the year: sale of a fixed asset, acquisition of another one and depreciation charge for the year. In the cash flow statement the depreciation charge of 132 will be added back to profit in the calculation of operating cash flows. The purchase of the new asset at 400 will appear under investments, and there too we must put the asset sold. The book value of (275–160) 115 should go there, but it should be adjusted by the amount of the gain or loss. In this case it is a gain of 20 (135–115), which we should remove from operating cash flows and add to the book value of the asset in investments. We would therefore have 'asset disposal 135' (115 + 20) which is the cash flow arising from the acquisition.

Had the resale price received been (say) 100, this would have resulted in an accounting loss of 15. For cash flow statement purposes, this loss of 15 should be removed from the operating result, and be deducted from the disposal under investments: 'asset disposal 100' (115–15).

We can restate our check list for operating cash flow as:

Net profit after tax	xxxxxxxxx
Add back	
Depreciation	xxxxxx
Provisions created	xxxxxx
Loss on disposal of assets	xxxxxx
Deduct	
Provisions released	xxxxxx
Gains on disposal of assets	xxxxxx
+/– change in non-cash working capital	xxxxxx
Net cash flow from operations	xxxxxxxxx

Constructing a cash flow statement 2

Unlike the preparation of the profit and loss account and balance sheet, there is no one tried and tested way of preparing a cash flow statement, any more than there is a unique format for presenting the data. We shall continue to use the system of comparing opening and closing balance sheets. This direct comparison has the merit that it produces a table of differences where (given that the two balance sheets do balance to start with) the differences in outflows will equal the differences in inflows. It gives a good starting point by providing a framework of change for that particular company. Let us do a new example. The profit and loss account follows and the balance sheet has been laid out as a working paper.

Connecticut River Co. Ltd

Sales		500
Cost of sales	148	
Salaries	105	
Depreciation	116	
Other expenses	95	(464)
		36
Profit on disposal of asset		3
Interest cost		(9)
		30
Taxation		(11)
Net profit after tax		19

Balance sheets

	X2	X1	Δ	Outflow	Inflow
Land	105	105	—		
Buildings	235	235	—		
Depreciation	−113	−107	6		
Plant	441	397	44		
Depreciation	−356	−282	74		
Stock	82	75	7		
Debtors	243	216	27		
Cash	73	62	11		
Trade creditors	190	195	5		
Debt	160	150	10		
Share capital	200	200	—		
Reserves	141	156	15		
Profit for the year	19	—	19		

The worksheet shows the crude differences between the two years' balance sheets, and the next step is to go in search of explanations of these differences.

The first one is an increase of accumulated depreciation on buildings. There is nothing inherently unusual in this – presumably this is the depreciation charge for the year, which we can verify in a real-life situation from the analysis of fixed assets given in the notes. The profit and loss account shows us that the total charge for the year was 116, so there remains another 110 to explain. This 6, anyway, can be put into the inflow column as part of cash flow from operations.

Moving on to plant, there is a net difference of 44. However, there is an asset disposal in the profit and loss account (gain 3). As there is no change in any fixed assets other than plant, this disposal must occur here, so the difference of 44 must be the difference between an acquisition and a disposal. The fixed asset analysis in the notes to the accounts will reveal that the company bought a new plant asset for 85, and disposed of one whose original cost was 41, which enables us to reconcile the difference:

Plant acquired	85
Plant sold	41
Balance sheet difference	44

We will therefore complete the plant assets line by showing an outflow of 85 and inflow of 41.

Of course this sale will impact upon the depreciation line for plant as well, since the accumulated depreciation on the plant which has been sold must be removed. The net difference on depreciation is 74, but we know from the other depreciation lines that the depreciation charge for plant during 20X2 was likely to be 110 (116 in profit and loss account, less 6 depreciation on buildings). This would give the following:

Depreciation for the year on plant   110
Balance sheet difference   74
Depreciation on plant sold   36

We should be able to verify this from the fixed assets analysis in the notes, in a real-life case. We would show 110 as an inflow, being part of the net cash flow from exploitation, and 36 as an outflow. Of course the 36 is not an 'outflow' in a real sense, but it is a deduction from the book value of the asset which was sold, and it is arithmetically convenient to note it here in this way, bearing in mind it is a deduction from an inflow. The 41 gross cost less 36 accumulated depreciation represents the accounting disposal value of the plant which has been sold (5) to which we will eventually add the gain of 3 (from the profit and loss account) to arrive at the sale proceeds which must have been 8.

After that we have routine increases in debtors and stocks, analysed as outflows. The difference in cash is 11, and we will analyse this as an outflow, to preserve the balance sheet equilibrium (in effect it is the difference between the inflows and the outflows, of course). (If you are unhappy with this treatment of the cash difference, another way to deal with it is just to leave it out. If you do that, when you add up the inflows and outflows you will obviously have a difference, which will be the amount of the cash difference. If these two differences agree, your analysis is arithmetically correct, if not there is a problem).

The trade creditors have actually reduced from 20X1 to 20X2, which is fairly unusual (but not impossible) where the stocks and debtors have increased, since these three are all linked in an operational sense to the same variable – sales – and therefore should tend to move together. From an analytical perspective a decrease in trade creditors is a decrease in financing, and therefore an outflow.

The Debt line shows an increase of 10. A review of the notes to the accounts will in many jurisdictions show a breakdown of debt, and in this case we understand that a new debt has been taken out for 70. This means therefore that an old debt has been retired, if the net variation is only 10:

New debt   70
Retirement of old debt –60
Net movement   10

The new debt is an inflow, repayment of the old debt an outflow.

There is no change in share capital, but reserves have gone down by 15. The most obvious explanation for this would be the payment of a dividend, which in most jurisdictions flows directly from revenue reserves (in the UK it is shown on the profit and loss account). A review of the analysis of movements on equity in the notes would confirm this. This is then analysed as an outflow.

The final difference is the profit for the year of 19. This will start off our cash flow statement, but we must bear in mind that it includes a disposal gain of 3 which must be reallocated in the cash flow statement to the investment section. The completed worksheet with the analyses on it is reproduced on the following page.

Balance sheets

	X2	X1	Δ	Outflow	Inflow
Land	105	105	—		
Buildings	235	235	—		
Depreciation	−113	−107	6		6
Plant	441	397	44	85	41
Depreciation	−356	−282	74	36	110
Stock	82	75	7	7	
Debtors	243	216	27	27	
Cash	73	62	11	11	
Trade creditors	190	195	5	5	
Debt	160	150	10	60	70
Share capital	200	200	—		
Reserves	141	156	15	15	
Profit for the year	19	—	19		19

We can now proceed to layout the cash flow statement in the formal way:

Cash flow statement for the year ended 31 December 20X1

Operations

Net profit for the year	19	
Add back		
Depreciation	116	
Deduct		
Gain on asset disposal	(3)	
	132	
Net change in non-cash working capital	(39)	
Net cash flow from operations		93

Investment

Purchase of plant	(85)	
Disposal of plant	8	
Net cash from investment		(77)

Financing

Loan received	70	
Retirement of debt	(60)	
Dividend	(15)	
Net cash from financing		(5)

Net change in cash during year		11
Cash balance 1 January 20X2	62	
Cash balance 31 December 20X2	73	

Note:
1. The net change in non-cash working capital is the total of stock (outflow 7), debtors (outflow 27) and trade creditors (outflow 5).
2. The figure for disposal of fixed assets is the book value of the plant sold (gross cost 41 less depreciation 36) plus the gain on disposal of 3 moved down from operations.

Interpretation

The cash flow statement is an interesting summary of a company's changes in financial structure during the course of a year, and can often give clues to business strategy which are not so readily apparent from the balance sheet.

Different elements will have more or less importance from one company to another, but major considerations which should be taken into account when interpreting company statements are:

1. How successful is the company at generating cash from operations? To what extent does this internally generated cash flow provide finance for expansion, and to what extent is it used up in providing dividends for shareholders?
2. Is the company disposing of many fixed assets? If so, does this mean a run-down of the business? Are assets being renewed, or new assets being acquired for expansion?
3. Is the company borrowing extensively, and if so, for what purpose? Is it restructuring its debt by replacing old debts with new; is it borrowing for new expansion; is it issuing new equity?
4. Is there any hidden message in the changes in working capital? For example, is a company acquiring higher stocks and higher debtors without any corresponding increase in creditors? Or, conversely, are creditors growing very quickly while other working capital elements are stable (possibly implying a cash shortage or at least an attempt to delay outflows)? Has there been a sudden drop in cash?

The cash flow statement can potentially provide a useful picture of the structural changes which a company is undergoing and it should be examined with care for any hidden messages.

If we look at the cash flow statement we have just constructed, the messages there are relatively simple.

Most of the company's operational cash flow comes from depreciation; the profit is relatively small in percentage terms. The main outflow has been on the purchase of new assets, but these at 85 are less than the depreciation of 116. In a crude sense this means that the company's total assets are getting smaller. This would prompt an analyst to ask the company if this is significant. It may not be; the company may depreciate its assets very quickly, for tax or prudence reasons, but it is curious.

The increase in working capital is relatively high in relation to profits as well, and one should check (the figures are not given here) whether there has been a substantial increase in sales to justify the change in working capital or if not, what is going on. The increase in working capital is twice the net profit, which means that profits are being swallowed up to finance expansion. This may be a good thing which will give a better return the next year, but at this point it looks a bit doubtful.

The company seems to have 'rolled over' debt by repaying some but replacing it. Again this is perfectly normal. On the whole the cash flow statement reveals that the company is investing in working capital more than fixed assets. This may be a good sign, meaning higher sales the next year and more efficient use of plant, but an analyst would be looking for further information to explain this. Aside from the growth of working capital, the picture is one of little change.

Presentational differences

While most companies of any size publish a cash flow statement, and these are now closely based on the US/IASC model, there are sometimes differences at the level of detail as to how the statement is constructed. In particular, our model here assumes that interest payments and taxation are included in the net profit measure, while dividends are treated as a financing item. Not everyone agrees with that presentation, and you may find that taxation, interest and dividend flows are separately identified in the statement and shown as part of operating flows – returns to stakeholders from the current year's cash.

Another difference is in the definition of 'cash' for cash flow statement purposes. Many companies, when they have excess cash, lend this out short-term on the money market or buy shares. These are sometimes called 'treasury' investments and are regarded as being so liquid as to be the same as cash, but not all jurisdictions define what is meant by cash, or if they do, they do not necessarily agree on the definition.

In all cases the analyst should either make his or her own cash flow statement on a uniform base, or read the notes to the accounts carefully to see how the company one has been constructed and take care about items such as dividends so that the statement can be adjusted to be comparable with others.

Summary

Most companies produce a cash flow statement as well as the profit and loss account and balance sheet. This statement analyses the change in financial position from one balance sheet to the next and generally companies use one variant or another of the IASC cash flow statement which analyses flows between operations, investment and financing.

Companies generate funds internally from their profit-making activities, but the extent of these funds differs from accounting profit in so far as the accounting profit includes non-cash adjustments such as depreciation and provisions, and to the extent that there have been changes in the working capital of the company derived from trading.

Companies' finances are also affected by acquisition of new assets, sale of old assets, borrowing funds and issuing new shares. The payment of dividends and taxation is another drain on company cash flows. The cash flow statement regroups all these elements of change for the information of shareholders and other accounts-users. The statement provides useful information about the company's financial management and underlying changes in structure.

There are no special rules for the workings necessary to construct such a statement, but we have approached this using one specific method. The method used depends upon an analysis of the net change in position between one balance sheet and the next. This basic analysis provides a framework from which one may systematically extend the full outflows and inflows by correcting for net movements in each of the important balance sheet categories.

Questions

1. Seurat Ltd commenced business on 1 January 20X1, having acquired an existing trading concern. The company's opening balance sheet was:

	$
Leasehold premises	5,000
Stock	1,200
Cash	1,800
	8,000
Ordinary share capital	8,000

During the year it traded successfully and had the following profit and loss account:

	$
Sales	25,000
Cost of sales	17,500
	7,500
Expenses	4,500
Net income	3,000

Its balance sheet as at 31 December 20X1 was as follows.

	$	$
Five-year lease		5,000
Accumulated depreciation		(1,000)
		4,000
Stock	1,800	
Debtors	2,300	
Cash	4,300	8,400
Total assets		12,400
Share capital		8,000
Profit		3,000
		11,000
Creditors		1,400
		12,400

Calculate the company's cash flow for 20X1, and reconcile this with the profit (assuming there is no taxation or dividend for 20X1).

2. During 20X2 Seurat Ltd (see question 1) continued to trade successfully, and also expanded. It acquired a second shop lease for $8,000, and borrowed $5,000 in order to help finance the transaction. Its profit and loss account for 20X2 is shown below and its balance sheet as at 31 December 20X2.

You are asked to prepare a cash flow statement for 20X2.

	$
Sales	57,500
Cost of sales	36,300
	21,200
Expenses	11,000
Profit before tax	10,200
Provision for taxation	3,000
	7,200

	$	$
Leases		13,000
Accumulated depreciation		(2,800)
		10,200
Stock	4,400	
Debtors	2,900	
Cash	11,900	19,200
Total		29,400
Financing		
Ordinary shares		8,000
Retained profits		10,200
		18,200
Creditors		3,200
Taxation		3,000
Creditors due in more than 1 year		5,000
Total net assets		29,400

3. Seurat Ltd (see question 2) continued to develop in 20X3. It acquired new shop premises for $15,000 and sold its original premises for $3,500 (they had a net book value of $3,000 at the time of sale). The company also paid off its bank loan and paid a dividend of $2,000. Its trading results for 20X3 are given below and its balance sheet as at 31 December 20X3.

You are asked to: (a) prepare a cash flow statement for 20X3; (b) comment on the company's financial position.

	$
Sales	69,700
Cost of sales	41,300
	28,400
Expenses	13,500
	14,900
Profit on sale of premises	500
Net profit before tax	15,400
Provision for taxation	4,620
	10,780

		$
Leasehold premises		23,000
Accumulated depreciation		(3,100)
		19,900
Stock	4,800	
Debtors	3,200	
Cash	7,400	15,400
Total		35,300
Financing		
Capital:		
Ordinary shares		8,000
Retained profits		18,980
		26,980
Creditors		3,700
Taxation		4,620
Total		35,300

4. (i) **You are given below successive balance sheets for a company (as at 31 December 20X6 and 20X7) and are asked to prepare a cash flow statement for 20X7.**

	20X6 $'000	20X7 $'000
Property at valuation	2,350	3,850
Plant and equipment	980	1,560
Depreciation	(423)	(572)
	2,907	4,838
Stocks	841	923
Debtors	1,213	1,297
Cash	106	73
Totals	5,067	7,131
Financing		
Ordinary shares	430	460
Share premium	802	892
Revaluation reserve	435	935
Retained profits	551	771
	2,218	3,058
Trade creditors	1,432	1,675
Taxation	217	198
LT creditors	1,200	2,200
	5,067	7,131

You are advised that no assets were disposed of during 20X7 and that taxation ($217,000) and dividends ($105,000) which related to 20X6 were paid out during 20X7.

(*Comment*: you should note that this case includes fixed assets held at valuation rather than historical cost. A valuation change does not involve any cash flows.)

(ii) **Explain briefly the utility of the cash flow statement to external users of accounts, including a discussion of the difference between cash flows and profits.**

Part Four

The accounts of multinational companies

11 The annual report

In this part we switch from an approach anchored in the accounts of individual companies to one where the focus is the multinational group of companies, whose shares are listed on one or more stock exchanges. While all the rules which we reviewed in the earlier parts hold good, there are additional factors which need to be taken into account. In particular the figures of international groups are so highly aggregated that they need to provide further analysis to enable users to understand them better. Equally there are public interest issues such as transparency and controls on management behaviour which come into play when looking at a group which employs thousands of people and whose actions affect many different economies. This first chapter reviews the annual report of the multinational.

Introduction

As was discussed in the first chapter of the book, it is widely recognized now that there are at least two quite different types of company in any developed economy: small and medium-sized enterprises (SMEs) and large, listed multinationals (MNCs). Where exactly one draws the line between the two is not clear, and in any event probably varies from economy to economy, but we can identify two models which represent the contrasting poles: first, the SME is a company whose shares are held by a small number of individuals and are not publicly traded; its managers are usually shareholders, it employs few people, its financing is oriented towards bank loans, and the main users of its annual reports are the tax authorities, the management and the bank.

The second pole is the MNC, which is listed on several stock exchanges; it has no one shareholder with a significant proportion of its equity, has professional managers, is active in many countries, and employs thousands of people. Its main objective is to generate returns for shareholders which it does by generating ever larger profits and trying to push up the share price. Generally its annual report will have to satisfy a wide range of users: the analysts in the financial markets – so that they can encourage institutional funds to buy the shares; the general public – in the sense of creating a public image of responsibility; and governments – to reassure them that the company is honest and meets its commitments (and does not need further statutory surveillance).

Transparency in reporting is essential because uncertainties lead investors to demand higher returns and generate tensions with governments and the general public.

From a financial reporting perspective, the two are quite different animals. The SME has narrow reporting needs, closely linked to taxation, while the MNC has a wide audience and needs to use the annual report as a major publicity tool both to inform and reassure the world about the activities of the company. Equally, the scope of activities is different: the SME typically has few or only one line of business, its scale of activity is small and usually based in one country, and therefore it is relatively easy to see what is going on from its accounts. The MNC on the other hand has many different activities, works in many different currencies and many languages. A kind of report is needed which can make some attempt to bring together all these different elements and convey some impression of them to users – technically a very demanding challenge!

In terms of regulations, the difference between SME accounting and MNC reports is usually articulated through the difference between individual accounts and group accounts (although you should not forget that many small or micro-businesses are not organized as limited liability companies and may only have the most rudimentary of accounts). An MNC is usually very many individual companies, often in a range of product areas and in different countries, operating under some kind of unified management structure. Typically such a group has sophisticated accounting systems which are capable of providing detailed internal information on a timely basis for management purposes, while maintaining all the usual functions of a financial reporting system as well.

Each individual company has to prepare accounts which are used, amongst other things, for tax purposes, and then the group prepares what are called 'consolidated' or group accounts which aggregate the data from the individual companies. These group accounts are what we shall look at from here on. It is in their nature that they present an approximation of an economic entity, not a legal one, and the accounts serve the purpose of giving an economic picture, which is not used for taxation, and is therefore free of tax constraints. In many countries the rules for drawing up consolidated accounts are separate from those for individual company accounts (although they build on these), and in international circles, the rules used are typically either those of the International Accounting Standards Committee (IASC) – which we use here – or of the US capital markets.

The group accounts are published each year, generally in a glossy document, often running to a hundred pages, and are frequently reproduced on the corporate website as well. This document includes both legally required information and public relations material. It is often known as the annual report, or the corporate report.

The corporate report

The contents of the annual report will differ from one company to another – as a result of the non-regulatory parts, but in general, and you should make sure you study some examples to see this, the average annual report contains the following:

1. *Corporate publicity material*, which is not statutory and not checked. Often this is described as the chairman's statement, or review of operations. It might run to fifty or more pages, will have lots of photographs and is designed to give a good image of the company. This information should not be discarded by the user – much of it is highly

informative and relevant – you should just not expect it to contain too much bad news, albeit some companies try to be much more transparent than others.

2. *Management report.* This can be very confusing, because the publicity material may also include items which are described as a director's report. Different countries have different regulations and different traditions about non-accounting disclosures alongside the accounts. Companies listed in the US have to provide something called 'Management's Discussion and Analysis' which discusses the year's results in relation to the previous year and future prospects. The IASC recommends that a company includes a financial review (see box).

IAS 1 *Presentation of financial statements*

8. Enterprises are encouraged to present, outside the financial statements, a financial review by management which describes and explains the main features of the enterprise's financial performance and financial position and the princicpal uncertainties it faces. Such a report may include a review of:

    (a) the main factors and influences determining performance, including changes in the environment in which the enterprise operates, the enterprise's responses to those changes and their effect, and the enterprise's policy for investment to maintain and enhance performance, including its dividend policy;
    (b) the enterprise's sources of funding, the policy on gearing and its risk mangeement policies; and
    (c) the strengths and resources of the enterprise whose value is not reflected in the balance sheet under International Accounting Standards.

9. Many enterprises present, outside the financial statements, additional statements such as environmental reports and value added statements, particularly in industries where environmental factors are significant and when employees are considered to be an important user group. Enterprises are encouraged to present such additional statements if management believes they will assist users in making economic decisions.

Company law in the UK calls for something called the 'directors' report' which calls for disclosures about diverse items such as directors' shareholdings, the company's main activities, amounts spent on research and development, number of disabled people employed – a real mixture of information. German companies provide a lot of information as well.

3. *Income statement.* This we are already familiar with, but there are extra ramifications of this which are relevant to large companies with a shifting portfolio of subsidiaries, which we shall examine later in this chapter.
4. *Reconciliation of movements in shareholders funds* is not exactly a main statement but provides, as it says, a bringing together of information from different places to help the shareholder understand the changes in accounting equity. The IASC talks about 'changes in equity' and IAS 1 *Presentation of financial statements* specifies that an analysis should be provided of changes in equity during the year, to include payment of dividends, details of all classes of equity and any changes in these, the net profit or loss for the period, and any charges or revenues taken directly to equity without passing through the income statement.

5. *Balance sheet*. At last, you may say, back to familiar ground! – this is as you would expect from your studies to date.
6. *Statement of cash flows*, as introduced in Chapter 10, is a very useful analytical tool, not mandated by company law in any country but required by IAS 7 and published voluntarily, usually in a form which approximates to IAS 7, by most large companies.
7. *Statement of accounting policies*. Actually a statutory note to the accounts but often placed separately by large companies, usually in close proximity to the profit and loss account and balance sheet. Essential first reading when an analyst looks at a set of accounts because this specifies what set of rules (e.g. IASC standards, US GAAP etc.) have been followed in preparing the accounts.
8. *Notes to the accounts* provide essential further analysis of main statement items. For large companies a lot of very useful information is to be found in the notes to the accounts and they should always be read very carefully.
9. *Auditor's report*. Sometimes found at the beginning of the accounts, sometimes at the end, but should always be checked first, in case there is anything unusual.

It would be a good idea to look at some examples of corporate reports and try to split them up into these categories – identify the different components – just to make sure you can do so. If you are able to locate the annual report of an SME, this would be a helpful comparative tool. In many countries the SME has much lighter disclosure requirements than the MNC and most SMEs prefer not to show their accounts to anyone. In France and the UK any limited company has nonetheless to file a copy of its annual accounts with a public registry, and so they are in theory available to anyone who wants to look (although late filing is endemic amongst SMEs). In Germany SMEs are supposed to file but many do not, while in Switzerland the file is not open to the public. Generally, therefore, SME accounts are much more difficult to find and, when you have them, contain much less detail than the accounts of multinationals.

Publicity document

For the MNC, however, the annual report fulfils a quite different role. As far as statutory and contractual requirements are concerned, the MNC has obligations to publish because of its economic importance and usually because it is listed on several stock exchanges. These obligations are usually very stringent. Thereafter, the MNC wishes to influence investors, and any signs of opacity or failure to disclose what is regarded as key information will cause investors to become suspicious. When they get suspicious they either do not invest, or demand a higher return for their money to compensate the increased risk which is attached when there is uncertainty surrounding the company. For example, if an MNC has potentially polluting manufacturing activities but says nothing about its pollution control in the annual report, investors may fear that there is potential bad news awaiting for the future with, say, a big bill to reinstate a polluted river, or compensate a poisoned community.

The annual report of an MNC has come to be a major publicity document. It has great authority as the major formal communication between the group and the outside world, and MNCs build on that to use it to present the company in as positive a light as possible and to explain what the company is doing. In some ways it represents the company's passport. Aside from its statutory and investor role, it is widely used when making major sales pitches to potential clients, when talking to governments, even when taking on new staff – it is a way of establishing the company's identity, its size, its range of activities, its financial strength.

It is a key document and many large companies automatically include it on their website. This last is potentially a trap for the analyst or student. For the moment there is no regulation as such of financial information on corporate websites. While company law usually requires that, say, income statements and balance sheets are never published without the audit report and the accompanying explanatory notes about accounting policies and so on, it is not clear that these constraints apply to the Internet. Some companies may put only extracts of key financial data on the Internet, and the analyst should be wary of missing information and if in doubt obtain the published hard copy. That said, of course the Internet is a great way of obtaining corporate data rapidly. You can even access MNCs' filings with the SEC in the US which are all made available on the SEC's EDGAR database (www.sec.gov). This gives access not only to the annual report information but also all other data required by the SEC, including Management's Discussion and Analysis. For a detailed review of a US listed company, this is a good tool.

Analysis

Generally speaking, when you first look at a company's report, with a view to analysing the accounts, we would suggest that you follow this routine:

1. Read the publicity material to get an idea of the company's activities and how it sees them.
2. Check the auditor's report to see if there are any warnings. There usually are not because disagreements have been worked out before finalizing the accounts, or the auditors have made sure that adequate information is available elsewhere.
3. Read the accounting policies to see which set of accounting principles has been used and whether there is anything special you should note about the methods used. The IASC specifies that companies should not claim they use IASC rules while not conforming with all of them. However, companies do sometimes allow themselves to make exceptions. Such exceptions should normally be indicated either in the audit report or the note on accounting policies, and should be considered to be a warning light for the analyst.
4. Look at the main statements: income statement, balance sheet and cash flow statement to get the overall accounting picture.
5. Look at the statement of movements on shareholders' funds and the notes to the accounts to get more detail.

The extract from IAS 1 which talks about a management discussion of the company's situation is quite a good guide to what the analyst is trying to do – to flesh out the company's strategy, the risks it faces, its investment stance etc. The analyst should be trying to provide this kind of strategic overview by analysing the accounts and related material.

Summary

This chapter is a short introduction to the world of the financial information of large, multinational companies listed on several stock exchanges. These companies use the annual report as a major publicity document and it also has to satisfy many legal disclosure requirements. While the basic statements are exactly the same as those you already know, the MNC publishes 'consolidated' figures – which bring together the sum of all its subsidiaries – to give a world overview. We will look at the techniques for putting these together in the next chapter. Their statements also include much more supplementary information both by way of detail behind the accounts and of other matters concerning company strategy and activities.

Questions

1. Identify the users and uses of a multinational group's financial statements as opposed to those of a small company.
2. To what extent do you think it is reasonable to allow a group to publish unregulated public relations information in the same document as statutory accounts which are subject to audit?

12 Group accounts

This chapter introduces the concept of consolidated accounts – known as group accounts – which are the basis of figures published by multinational corporations. The chapter deals successively with issues such as consolidating wholly owned subsidiaries, goodwill, minority interests, and merger accounting.

Introduction

As discussed in Chapter 11, MNCs publish an annual report whose accounting numbers are *consolidated accounts*, often known as group accounts. These are an attempt to represent the whole economic entity which is the MNC. In effect they are based on the assumption of an Anglo-Saxon pyramid style of management structure. That is to say that there is a 'head office' management team at the top of a chain of command which extends to the furthest subsidiary. The central management's authority must be respected in all the companies owned by the group. In practice, modern group structures do not always correspond to this model in all their arrangements. In individual operations they may have all sorts of shifting arrangements with other companies. There are often alliances with other groups in particular areas. For example, oil companies may form alliances with each other to exploit oil wells or build pipelines, while fighting it out with each other in the high street for retail sales of petrol. These kinds of involvement mean that, at the margin, group accounts have some difficulty in reflecting the economic realities, but they are still the best implement we have for measuring MNC activities.

Your strategy and economics courses will, if they have not already done so, give you ideas about why companies are organized in groups. However, it is worth just reviewing quickly the main practical reasons. Traditional theory notes that companies tend to develop on either a horizontal or vertical basis. The vertical basis is that a typical production chain for a product involves:

1. extraction of raw materials;
2. transport to manufacturing markets;
3. manufacture of products;
4. distribution through wholesale outlets;
5. retailing to consumers.

The description 'vertical' relates to the progress from basic raw materials to final retailing to the consumer. In theory a company in the manufacturing sector might well expand its activities up and down to control both its raw materials and its retailing, and this would be called a vertical group. Examples of this would indeed be the major oil companies who not only extract the oil but also own tanker fleets, refineries and filling stations.

A horizontal group, by comparison, expands into different industries united by some similar process or product. For example, a company might manufacture plastic mouldings for motor manufacturers, and would expand sideways by moving into the manufacture of plastic mouldings for the toy industry. Oil companies may sprout chemical offshoots to exploit the by-products of the oil refining process.

These two directions are natural lines of development for companies that wish to expand. However, there is a third type of group, the conglomerate. The conglomerate diversifies into non-related fields, on the basis of building up a profitable group which draws strength from the fact that it consists of many diverse elements which are operating in different economic environments. (Finance theory has the concept of a 'portfolio' where diversification across a minimum number of different investments reduces the overall risk of the total holding.)

The fact of being in several different areas should mean that when one product is having a bad year, other products are not so affected. A particular disadvantage of the vertical group is that if demand for the final product is depressed, it follows that the whole chain of production is similarly depressed. However, it should be noted that while the diversified conglomerate looks like a good idea on paper, there are few managements that have been equally successful at managing all parts of such groups. But again, this is a question to pursue within your strategy courses.

If a company is going to expand, there are three main ways in which the group may be built up: the development of new subsidiaries by a company, the acquisition by takeover of other companies and mergers between companies. Expansion by takeover has for long been a common practice amongst Anglo-American companies and is much more common now in Europe (as witness the battle between Deutsche Telekom and Olivetti for control of Telecom Italia), even if the rules in different countries are sometimes an obstacle. There has for some time been a polarization of business with large companies needing to become gigantic in order to compete on a global scale. The 'global' business can command lower costs than smaller, national businesses, through economies of scale.

It does also happen that companies form joint ventures with other companies – for example, Airbus Industrie is the classic example of different national companies coming together to compete with a large competitor. This provides a different kind of vehicle which has its own special accounting rules.

Companies have a need to find new products – business theory suggests that products and businesses have a life cycle. When a company's main product is at a 'mature' stage (market is static or beginning to decline, margins have been pared to the limit) it is well time for it to be using the cash generated to look for new products, or it will decline and disappear. Large, international companies are therefore constantly buying new companies which either help to build global market share, or are an attempt to find growth products.

Cadbury Schweppes

Reasons for the acquisition

The acquisition of A&W Brands would represent a further step forward in the Group's development of its beverage interests. The United States carbonated soft drinks market is the largest in the world with estimated retail sales of $47 billion. The acquisition of A&W Brands would increase Cadbury Schweppes' share of this market from 3.4 per cent to 5.6 per cent. The combination of A&W Brands with Cadbury Schweppes' exiting soft drinks interests in the United States would provide Cadbury Schweppes with greater influence in the United States bottling systems and would result in operating efficiencies.

Source: Extract from circular to shareholders

The simplest case of group expansion is where a company forms a subsidiary to expand its trading. This may be done for a variety of reasons. For example, it may be that the holding company wants to take on borrowing specifically for a project, and that can most easily be done by putting the project's assets and the associated lending within a separate subsidiary. It gives the lender a clearer sight of the project independently of the rest of the group.

It is often quite useful for management purposes to organize business operations into separate subsidiaries, since one can delegate management responsibility by making the manager of a specific project a director of that subsidiary, thereby giving him or her the legal power to operate the subsidiary effectively, whereas if there were no subsidiary the manager would have to be a director of all the group's activities, extending his or her legal authority beyond the required point.

Once a company extends its trading beyond its home country base there are other powerful reasons for forming new subsidiaries in foreign countries. Where a company has a foreign operation it will be subject to foreign tax on the earnings of the foreign operation. That in itself is a highly complex issue, but if there is no local subsidiary, the question of the profit attributable to that operation is even more complex. In a foreign environment the limitation of liability is still more important, and since the operation is likely to be more remote than a domestic subsidiary, the necessity for clear lines of management responsibility is even stronger. A foreign operation will have to keep records of its transactions in the local currency, and this is sometimes more easily done through a chain of subsidiaries.

The more noticeable development of groups occurs when one company takes over another pre-existing operation. The reasons for a company to do this are also many and various. If a company is bent on rapid expansion, and has the finance available, there are obvious advantages in acquiring another company which is already trading in the field rather than starting up a totally new company. By takeover the expanding company gains in one stroke an established market position, working assets and experienced management in that field. Against that it may have to pay a premium to persuade the shareholders of the acquired company that they would benefit by the takeover.

An established public company with a good profits record can frequently take over another company simply by offering to give the shareholders of the acquired company shares in the public company in exchange for their existing shares. If it succeeds in persuading them that this is worthwhile, it has only to issue more shares rather than actually raise additional finance – a very effective way of expanding.

> **Roche Group**
>
> **Consolidation policy**
>
> The consolidated financial statements of the Group include Roche Holding Ltd and the companies which it controls (subsidiaries). Control is the power to govern the operating and financial policies of an enterprise so as to obtain benefits from its activities. This control is normally evidenced when the Group owns, either directly or indirectly, more than 50% of the voting rights of a company's share capital. The equity and net income attributable to minority shareholders' interests are shown separately in the balance sheet and statement of income, respectively. All intercompany transactions and balances with companies included in the consolidation are eliminated. Companies acquired during the year are consolidated from the date on which operating control is effectively transferred to the Group, and subsidiaries disposed of are included up to the date of disposal.
>
> *Source:* extract from Annual report 1998, Accounting policies, F Hofmann-La Roche Ltd
> www.roche.com

The third form of expansion is that of a merger. Since this is the least common form we will not devote a great deal of time to considering it, but it differs in an essential way from acquisition. Under acquisition Company A buys Company B; in effect it is simply acquiring a new asset in the same way as it might buy a new factory but at the same time raising all the usual questions about the valuation of the asset. Under a merger Company A and Company B are combining their assets to form in effect a new, expanded company whose assets and liabilities are the sum of A and B.

We have implied so far that when a company expands, the new companies it acquires will be fully under its control. However, this is not necessarily the case. A company may have different levels of influence over another company in which it has invested. If Company D buys more than 50 per cent of the shares of Company B, the implication is that, since the shareholders elect the directors and the directors run the company, Company A can fully control Company B by exercising its majority vote. It follows from this that 'control' can exist well short of having 100 per cent ownership of the shares in a subsidiary.

It also follows, however, that if Company A has only 40 per cent of the shares in Company B and the remaining 60 per cent are owned by Company C, Company A may well have no influence at all, since Company C has a voting majority. By contrast, if Company A had 40 per cent but the remaining 60 per cent was widely dispersed with no one having more than 2 or 3 per cent, Company A would have effective control except where all the other shareholders joined together to frustrate A, which rarely happens in practice.

At the other extreme Company A might have only a token shareholding of 10 per cent and have no effective influence whatsoever on Company B. You can see that outside a situation where an investor company owns a clear majority of the shares in a second company, the question of the degree of influence exerted by one company over another is difficult to assess.

Rationale for group accounts

If we take the basic case of a group which has wholly owned subsidiaries, which is the most common situation, the question arises: 'What is the purpose of producing group accounts?' Consolidated accounting for groups was not put forward as a technique until the early part of the twentieth century, by contrast with much of basic accounting which stems from the second half of the nineteenth century. It originated in the USA, and spread fairly quickly through the world of Anglo-Saxon accounting from the 1920s. Its adoption in mainland Europe was slower, with Germany requiring consolidation of domestic subsidiaries of listed companies from 1965, and all companies from 1985, while France adopted only from 1986 and Switzerland from 1992. Consolidated accounts are the subject of the Seventh EC Directive, passed in 1983.

The main argument for consolidated accounts is that, although a group may operate through a whole network of theoretically independent legal entities, the fact of real control by a central holding company means that economically, there may well be only one real entity. (Note, though, that the rationale for consolidated accounts depends upon the pyramid concept of management structure where there is centralized control. It does not work for groups of linked companies with no central economic control, such as Japanese Keiretsu.) It follows that to appreciate the strength of this economic entity it is not sufficient to look only at the holding company, but one must look at the total assets and liabilities under the unified control and disregard the legal entities.

A potential investor who looked only at the holding company accounts might very easily be misled as to the strength of the group. To take a very simple case, Company W, a holding company, might be constituted so that all its trading operations were channelled through a single subsidiary, Company X, which also contained all the operating assets and liabilities. The figure below shows how the balance sheets of the two companies might look.

	Co. W $'000	Co. X $'000	W Group $'000
Tangible assets	500	1000	1500
Investment in subsidiary	500		
Current assets	250	350	600
Total	1,250	1,350	2,100
Shares	500	500	500
Reserves	300	(50)	250
	800	450	750
Long-term debt	300	700	1,000
Trade creditors	150	200	350
Total	1,250	1,350	2,100
Debt/Equity	37.5%	155%	133%

If a potential investor looked only at Company W's balance sheet, he or she could have no idea of the underlying asset and liability structure. The company has a 37.5 per cent debt/equity ratio, so the potential investor would probably regard it as a relatively low-risk company. However, if the accounts are consolidated (and in essence this just involves adding together the statements of all the companies in the group: the investment cost of the subsidiaries in the parent company balance sheet is replaced by the assets and liabilities actually acquired), and the 'investment in subsidiary' of $500,000 is replaced by the assets and liabilities of Company X, the balance sheet looks very different. From the consolidated accounts, the investor could see that in fact the group is very highly geared, that is, it has a large amount of debt outstanding, and the losses made by Company X are reflected in the group profit and loss.

The view which an investor might have of Company W is quite different, according to whether it is the consolidated accounts or simply those of the holding company which are seen, and this is the reason for preparing consolidated accounts. They give a picture of the economic entity rather than the legal entity: they provide information which is more useful in investment decision-making.

Current practice

Since implementation of the Seventh Directive, consolidated accounts are the norm for large companies in Europe, and many companies produced them on a voluntary basis well before. One will now commonly find that the annual report of a company includes two sets of accounts: the group (or consolidated) accounts and the parent (holding) company accounts. The consolidated accounts have no tax consequences, and in some countries, notably France, companies are required to draw up the group accounts on a different basis from the parent accounts, excluding tax depreciation and similar adjustments.

The essence of the accounting treatment is that the assets and liabilities of holding company and subsidiaries should be treated as though they were a single entity. The rationale is that, if the holding company controls the assets and liabilities of other companies, then the difference between the individual legal entities should be set aside and the economic whole should be treated as though it were a single company.

This means that instead of showing in the holding company's balance sheet the amount invested in subsidiaries, we substitute the assets and liabilities of the subsidiary companies. In essence this is simple enough, but it gives rise to certain problems where the holding company's investment is different in value to the net worth (net value of assets less liabilities) in the subsidiary, or where the holding company owns less than 100 per cent of the shares in the subsidiary.

We will illustrate the accounting solutions in a series of examples which will deal with the individual aspects of different situations, and will concentrate on the balance sheet effects (and deal with the profit and loss later). First, let us look at the basic case, where the holding company's investment in the subsidiary (S Company) exactly coincides with the value of the equity in the subsidiary. This would happen where the holding company has formed a subsidiary and subscribed to the shares at par (i.e. paid the nominal value of the shares exactly).

In order to prepare consolidated accounts the investment by the holding company is eliminated and replaced by the assets and liabilities of the subsidiary (see below).

	Holding $m	S Co. $m	Elimination $m	Group $m
Net fixed assets	100	20	—	120
Investment in subsidiary	25	—	(25)	
Current assets	30	10	—	40
Totals	155	30	(25)	160
Share capital	70	25	(25)	70
Reserves	30	—	—	30
	100	25	(25)	100
Current liabilities	15	5	—	20
Long-term liabilities	40	—	—	40
Totals	155	30	(25)	160

The elimination column shows how the investment in S Company has been cancelled out against the net worth of the subsidiary (in this case entirely represented by the share capital of the subsidiary) and then the assets and liabilities have been added across – thus effectively substituting the assets and liabilities of S, which have a net value of $25m, for H's investment in S of $25m. This kind of working paper is classic for consolidation – of course it lends itself easily to a computer spreadsheet application.

Acquisition accounting

This is used after the classic takeover, where one company buys the shares of another and takes over the management of the acquisition. From a consolidation perspective, this presents a technical problem: so far the value of the 'investment in subsidiary' in the parent company has always agreed with the initial capital of the subsidiary, because the parent started the subsidiary so we are indeed looking at two ends of the same transaction. However, when a company buys the shares of an existing company, it is usually paying the existing shareholders to hand over their shares – the money does not go to the acquired company, and there is no link between the value of the investment as it appears in the parent's balance sheet, and the book value of equity in the subsidiary. They will be different amounts, and that leaves us with a difference between the two which is an awkward problem in group accounts.

IAS 22 *Business combinations*

An acquisition is a business combination in which one of the enterprises, the acquirer, obtains control over the net assets and operations of another enterprise, the acquiree, in exchange for the transfer of assets, incurrence of a liability or issue of equity.

(definition of an acquisition)

When one company takes over another, it usually pays a price for the shares which is related to its expectations of future profit potential and not to the book value of the shares. Consequently, the book value is usually different from the purchase price and an adjustment is required when preparing group accounts to deal with this difference. It is known as consolidation difference, or goodwill arising on consolidation. What exactly is the appropriate treatment of this goodwill is a bone of contention. Not all accountants are convinced it is meaningful.

By way of note, when a holding company buys another company which has accumulated reserves, these reserves (even though they may be revenue reserves within the subsidiary) are no longer available for distribution. They are known as 'pre-acquisition reserves' and must be offset against the investment in the subsidiary in preparing the consolidated accounts.

In the following example, we have the balance sheets of the Holding company and S Co. at the date of acquisition. Holding has paid $38m for 100 per cent of the shares in S Co., whose book value is $25m. The consolidation adjustments are as follows:

	Holding $m	*S Co.* $m	*Elimination* $m	*Group* $m
Fixed assets	100	20	—	120
Investment in subsidiary	38	—	(38)	
Goodwill	—	—	13	13
Current assets	17	10	—	27
Totals	155	30	(25)	160
Share capital	70	20	(20)	70
Reserves	30	5	(5)	30
	100	25	(25)	100
Current liabilities	15	5	—	20
Long-term liabilities	40	—	—	40
Totals	155	30	(25)	160

Note that the $13m 'goodwill' figure is simply the difference between the investment in the subsidiary at its worth in the parent company's accounts and the accounting value of the equity of the subsidiary in its balance sheet at the time of acquisition. Note also that the $5m of reserves included in equity at that time are frozen for group accounting purposes at that moment as pre-acquisition reserves. Reserves generated later from profits after acquisition will flow through to the group balance sheet and increase group reserves, but the $5m at the moment of acquisition will always disappear in the consolidation adjustment.

The question remains as to whether the goodwill figure should be treated as an asset, and if an asset, whether it should be depreciated. If you take the view that there is no relationship between the cost of the investment (the cost which the new parent incurred in buying the subsidiary) and the accounting value of the subsidiary, goodwill is a meaningless figure. It is almost as though you said the distance from Zurich to Vienna is 600 kilometres, while the distance from Zurich to Geneva is 400 kilometres, so what is the difference of 200? But whatever it may be, it is not the distance between Geneva and Vienna. If goodwill is just a meaningless difference, then it should be labelled as such in the balance sheet, perhaps, and left alone.

However, the standard rationale for accounting for goodwill is that the purchase price of the new subsidiary's shares represents the cost of acquiring a bundle of assets and liabilities. This cost should be allocated over all identifiable assets and if there is an excess, this is goodwill and represents 'intangible' assets such as know-how, client goodwill etc. to which no accounting value can be reliably attributed.

The second question is whether, having identified this as an intangible asset, it should be subject to depreciation. Generally, the answer to this is held to be yes, since whatever intangibles were acquired with the subsidiary are thought to be replaced over time. For example, clients' loyalty to the company will be modified by their experience of the new management. The old asset disappears and the new asset is not recognized in historical cost accounting.

Goodwill – j'accuse

If goodwill was a person, she/he would probably stand trial around the world on numerous counts of complicity in undesirable or criminal acts. In the UK, over the past decade alone, the issue of accounting for goodwill might stand accused on at least three charges: being an accessory to the act of obtaining money under false pretences by distorting the competitive position of companies; contributing to, or concealing, the mismanagement of corporate and national resources by creating incentives for companies *not* to invest internally in their businesses; and involvement in revolutionary activities in terms of being a major contributor to the demise of the Accounting Standards Committee.

Linda Kirkham and John Arnold
Source: Goodwill accounting in the UK – a fresh approach to an old problem, *European Accounting Review*, December 1992

The Seventh Directive prefers goodwill to be treated as an asset and be amortized over five years. However, it permits amortization over 'useful life' and also allows member states to permit immediate write-off against reserves.

IAS 22 *Business Combinations*(extracts)

27. Individual assets and liabilities acquired should be recognised separately as at the date of acquisition when:
    (a) it is probable that any associated future economic benefits will flow to or from the acquiror; and
    (b) a reliable measure is available of their cost or fair value to the acquiror.
33. The assets and liabilities recognised in accordance with paragraph 27 should be measured at their fair values as at the date of acquisition. Any goodwill or negative goodwill should be accounted for in accordance with this standard. Any minority interest should be stated at the minority's proportion of the fair values of the assets and liabilities recognised in accordance with paragraph 27.
38. The fair values of identifiable assets and liabilities acquired in an acquisition are determined by reference to their intended use by the acquirer. The intended use of an asset is usually the asset's existing use unless it is probable that the asset will be used for some other purpose.
40. Any excess of the cost of the acquisition over the acquirer's interest in the fair value of the identifiable assets and liabilities acquired as at the date of the exchange transaction should be described as goodwill and be recognised as an asset.
42. Goodwill should be amortised by recognising it as an expense over its useful life. In amortising goodwill, the straight-line basis should be used unless another amortisation method is more appropriate in the circumstances. The amortisation period should not exceed five years unless a longer period, not exceeding twenty years from the date of acquisition, can be justified.

Cap Gemini Group

Notes to the consolidated financial statements

d) Intangible assets

Market share

When the acquisition of companies allows the Group to obtain a significant share of a specific market, part of the excess of purchase cost over the fair value of assets acquired is allocated to the market share acquired.

Such market share is valued as at the date of acquisition in relation to economic data with reference to activity and profitability indicators.

In view of its nature, acquired market share is not amortised. However, at each accounting date, it is reviewed in accordance with the same criteria used as of the date of acquisition and a provision is set up if there is any impairment in value.

Goodwill

Goodwill consists of the excess of cost over the group's equity in the fair value of the underlying net assets as of the date of acquisition of companies consolidated or accounted for by the equity method, after allocation of purchase cost to identified tangible or intangible assets, such as market share. Goodwill is amortised on a straight line basis over a maximum period of 40 years.

Computer software

Computer software and user rights acquired on an unrestricted ownership basis, as well as software developed for in-house purposes, which have a positive, lasting and quantifiable effect on future results, are capitalised and amortised over their estimated useful lives. They are stated at the power of cost or fair value to the Group.

Source: Cap Gemini Group Financial report 1998

The goodwill problem has been such that companies have had strong incentives to look for alternative solutions, and one such has been found in the area of fair value adjustments, which is the next aspect we should consider.

When first preparing the accounts of the new subsidiary for consolidation, the parent must revise the individual assets and liabilities of the acquired company to 'fair value'. What this means is that the bundle of assets and liabilities is valued as at the date of the takeover, and then any difference between the revalued assets and the investment by the parent is goodwill.

The rationale for revaluing the acquired assets and liabilities is that they are being purchased by the new parent company and historical cost, viewed from the parent, runs as from the date the parent acquired them, not the date at which they were acquired by the company which the parent has acquired. This seems perfectly reasonable, and up to a point the user is safeguarded in as far as companies are now required to disclose the basis of their revaluation of acquired assets as a note to the accounts.

However, it has given rise to a number of what are sometimes termed 'agressive' accounting techniques. A number of major companies have paid very high prices in takeovers to acquire brand names, which do not appear in the accounts of the company that has created them. These companies argue that if goodwill is acquisition cost less net tangible assets, they have very high goodwill, but this really represents the value of the intangible assets in the shape of brands which have been acquired. They have therefore attributed a value to the brands, which reduces the goodwill write-off substantially.

For example, Company G pays $200m for Company H whose book value is $100m. Company H has a single product, HHH, which is a household name. For consolidation purposes the goodwill might be $100m, and if written off over ten years, would give an annual depreciation charge of $10m. However, if G recognizes the H brand as an asset in the consolidated balance sheet at $75m, this means goodwill becomes $200m less tangible assets $100m less brand $75m = $25m, a much more manageable figure, and annual depreciation drops to $2.5m. (Note that the depreciation charge for goodwill can only appear in the group accounts; it is not entered into the books of the parent, for example. Similarly, asset revaluations in this context are only a consolidation adjustment and are not reflected in the ledger of the subsidiary.)

Thus far there might be a valuation problem, but in essence the goodwill intangible is being swapped for a brand intangible, so credibility is not pushed too far. However, the argument then advanced is that the brand does not require depreciation because its value is being maintained by advertising. This neatly deals with the goodwill problem because there is no subsequent depreciation to reduce the future earnings.

To pursue the mechanics of this with our basic example, let us assume that a fair value for the assets and liabilities of S involves recognizing an intangible asset worth $10m. This would give the adjustments shown below.

	Book value of S $m	Adjustment $m	Fair value balance sheet $m
Fixed assets			
– intangible	—	10	10
– tangible	20		20
Current assets	10		10
Totals	30	10	40
Share capital	20	—	20
Reserves	5	10	15
	25	10	35
Current liabilities	5	—	5
Totals	30	10	40

When the revised figures are built into the consolidated accounts with the holding company, this will give rise to a different goodwill value.

	Holding $m	Revised S $m	Elimination $m	Group $m
Fixed assets				
– goodwill			3	3
– other intangibles		10		10
– tangible	100	20	—	120
Investment in S	38	—	(38)	
Current assets	17	10	—	27
Totals	155	40	(35)	160
Share capital	70	20	(20)	70
Reserves	30	15	(15)	30
	100	35	(35)	100
Current liabilities	15	5	—	20
Long-term liabilities	40	—	—	40
Totals	155	40	(35)	160

Note: In this consolidation we have left the balance of goodwill, $3m, still as an asset in the group balance sheet.

Some countries in Europe, notably the UK, but also the Netherlands and Germany, have allowed companies an alternative treatment of goodwill. Instead of being treated as an asset and then amortized, it can be removed from the balance sheet at the time of takeover by deducting it from reserves. This method has now been outlawed in the UK and is progressively disappearing elsewhere, not because there is fundamentally a flaw in it necessarily – as we have noted, goodwill is something for which there is no satisfactory accounting treatment, but because most countries capitalize and amortize, and comparability and comprehensibility are improved if everyone does the same.

If the goodwill is regarded as a capital expense, this justifies it being deducted against the accumulated reserves of the holding company. If our example above were treated that way, it would give rise to the group balance sheet shown below.

	Before $m	Elimination $m	After $m
Fixed assets	120	—	120
Goodwill	13	(13)	
Current assets	27	—	27
Totals	160	(13)	147
Share capital	70	—	70
Reserves	30	(13)	17
	100	(13)	87
Current liabilities	20	—	20
Long-term liabilities	40	—	40
Totals	160	(13)	147

Clearly, if goodwill is capitalized and depreciated, an aggressive company will find that its measured profits from an acquisition are being reduced by the depreciation charge. This is not popular with managements who are trying to justify a takeover by showing enhanced profitability (research into takeovers actually shows that practically all acquirers pay too much money and the people who gain most are the original shareholders in the acquired company).

Against this, a company which mounts a series of takeovers and writes off the goodwill against reserves will find that its equity is steadily eroded. This is good for management in terms of enabling the company to show an improved return on equity, but has disastrous effects on a company's gearing ratio, which may be linked to loan agreements, quite apart from altering the user's perception of the riskiness of the company.

Another problem from the analyst's point of view is that it becomes increasingly difficult to make cross-sectional analyses when companies treat goodwill in different ways. To add to the problem, a goodwill write-off is clear in the year it takes place and will appear in the following year's comparative figures, but thereafter will disappear from the accounts, unless, as some companies do, it is left as a cumulative negative balance within reserves. Many analysts prefer to add goodwill back to equity if they have the information, in order to treat all companies the same.

Minority interests

In preparing our consolidations so far we have used an example where the holding company owns 100 per cent of the shares of S. Although this is often the case, it is not always so – companies may sometimes have less than 100 per cent of the shares in the subsidiary. The reason might be political: in some foreign countries the governments insist that where a multinational wishes to set up a local operation it should be done in partnership with either the foreign government or with local business people. Another reason might be operational – the company wishes to work in partnership with someone else in order to have access to their technical expertise, etc.

IAS 22 Business combinations

Minority interest is that part of the net results of operations and of net assets of a subsidiary attributable to interests which are not owned, directly or indirectly through subsidiaries, by the parent.

As far as accounting treatment goes, ownership of less than 100 per cent of the shares presents a problem. If the basic idea is to present an economic picture which gives an overview of the group activities, consolidating 60 per cent of a factory where one owns 60 per cent of the company which runs it does not really give the whole picture. Showing that the factory is part of the group but is financed in part by outside shareholders gives a more complete picture of the situation.

The accounting standard takes the view that where a company has control of another, then it has effective control of all the assets and liabilities, even though the ownership of some part of the company is in other hands. Accordingly the procedure is that the holding company consolidates all the assets and liabilities, but acknowledges the outside interest with a separate component of group equity, called 'minority interests'.

Assuming that the acquiring company L had bought only 80 per cent of the subsidiary M, paying $600,000, the consolidation would be:

	L Co. $'000	M Co. $'000	Elimination $'000	Group $'000
Intangibles	—	—	280	280
Tangibles	1200	300		1500
Investment	600	—	(600)	—
Current assets	550	225	—	775
Total	2,350	525	(320)	2,555
Share capital	800	300	(300)	800
Reserves	1150	100	(100)	1150
Minority interests			80	80
	1950	400	(320)	2030
Current liabilities	200	125	—	325
LT Creditors	200	—	—	200
	2350	525	(320)	2555

Pre-acquisition equity in the subsidiary is worth $400,000, so L Co's share is $320,000 [80 per cent] and minority interests are worth $80,000 [20 per cent], based on the split of share ownership. L Co. actually paid $600,000, so it must recognize (or write off) goodwill of $280,000 ($600K – $320K). In the consolidation adjustments we cancel the pre-acquisition equity of M Co. as usual, but the counter-adjustment is to create a new line called minority interests of $80,000, as well as offsetting L's part of the equity against its investment.

Uniting of interests   walton (2000) § 2.3.

Up until now this chapter has treated all business combinations as though they were 'acquisitions' in the jargon – i.e. that one company has bought a controlling interest in another company, and as a consequence, the management of the acquiring company controls the management of the acquired company. It is, however, possible for two companies to merge their activities and managements, even if sceptical regulators are disinclined to believe that large companies ever work this way. We will just make a short detour to consider mergers and their accounting, before getting back to the detail of acquisition accounting.

We can recognize two kinds of merger in terms of their technical outcomes. One type, largely restricted to continental Europe, is a 'fusion' and this is usually, but not exclusively, done by SMEs. Under a fusion, two or more companies are merged into a single company. For the sake of comparison, we could say that the typical fusion is that Company A and Company B transfer all their assets and liabilities into Company C. Companies A and B are dissolved and their shareholders become shareholders in C. Of course, such a fusion involves some potentially difficult valuations of the underlying assets and liabilities in order to determine the value of shares to be issued, but this is also a tax question and special rules apply in each country where it is used. Since there is only one company left at the end of the exercise, there is no group and no consequence in terms of consolidated accounts.

The other kind of merger is much practised in the US, where it is known as 'pooling of interests' (the IASC prefers 'uniting of interests') and technically remains very close to an acquisition. Under a pooling or uniting, Company A acquires the shares of Company B (in exchange for shares in Company A) and the two companies continue to exist but under a united management. In this context there is indeed a 'group' and a consequent requirement to prepare consolidated accounts. However, what makes the pooling very interesting to companies is that there is rarely any goodwill created in consolidated accounts prepared under this method because the new shares issued are recognized at face value, and any difference between the value of the shares issued and the assets and liabilities acquired (valued at book value) is adjusted against equity. In addition, there is no distinction betweeen pre-acquisition and post-acquisition activities: previous year consolidated comparisons can be calculated as though the two companies had always been together.

IAS 22 Business combinations

Definition

A *uniting of interests* is a business combination in which the shareholders of the combining enterprises combine control over the whole, or effectively the whole, of their net assets and operations to achieve a continual mutual sharing in the risks and benefits attaching to the combined entity such that neither party can be identified as the acquirer.

The following example will illustrate the point. Suppose that Company A agrees to unite with Company B. Company A's shares were trading at $3 before the merger, while those of Company B were trading at $5. The merger terms were therefore an exchange of five Company A shares for three Company B shares.

	Company A before merger	Issue shares	Co. A after	Company B	Adjust	Group
	$m	$m	$m	$m	$m	$m
Assets						
Tangible fixed	1200		1200	900		2100
Investment in B		+500	500		−500	
Current assets	420		420	350		770
Totals	1620	+500	2120	1250	−500	2870
Financing						
Share capital	300	+500	800	300	−300	800
Reserves	420		420	730	−730 } +530	950
Debt	600		600	—		600
Trade payables	300		300	220		520
Totals	1620	+500	2120	1250	−500	2870

As you can see, this slightly changes the composition of the combined equity, but does not change its value. New shares in A are issued and accounted for at face value ($1 per share, even though their market value is $3). When these are offset against the equity of B, this creates a surplus $530m (300m + 730m − 500m) but does not change the overall value of group equity. There is no goodwill created or recognized and all assets and liabilities retain their previous values.

If we accounted for the same transaction as an acquisition, it would give the following picture:

	Co. A before merger $m	Issue shares $m	Co. A after $m	Co. B $m	Adjust $m	Group $m
Assets						
Goodwill					+470	470
Tangible fixed	1200		1200	900		2100
Investment in B		+1500	1500		−1500	
Current assets	420		420	350		770
Totals	1620	+1500	3120	1250	−1030	3340
Financing						
Share capital	300	+500	800	300	−300	800
Reserves	420	+1000	1420	730	−730	1420
Debt	600		600	—		600
Trade payables	300		300	220		520
Totals	1620	+1500	3120	1250	−1030	3340

Under the acquisition method the issue of shares by A is recognized at market value ($3 per share, treated as $1 face value and $2 share premium) and so the investment is valued at $1,500m. On consolidation (assuming no revaluation of B's assets and liabilities), this provides a goodwill figure of $470m, and of course group equity is that much greater. From the company's point of view the goodwill must be amortized against profits, giving rise in this case to a charge of at least $23.5m a year under IASC rules. This charge would not arise under a uniting of interests.

Clearly the accounting picture and the subsequent evaluation of the group is potentially affected substantially. Supposing the above group had a profit of $200m after tax but before amortization of goodwill (which has no tax effect), an analyst looking at the rate of return on equity would have two different results:

Uniting of interests
Profit   200
Equity 1750
Return on equity 11.4 per cent

Acquisition
Profit (200–23.5 =) 176.5
Equity 2220
Return on equity 7.95 per cent

You can see that here is another case where the choice of accounting treatment has a substantial effect on the perceived performance of the group. Sometimes analysts, when comparing across companies, remove the goodwill from the assets and make a compensating deduction from equity, while also adding back amortization charges. This also explains why some MNCs go to a little trouble to detail the goodwill amortization charge in the accounts.

Regulators are not enthusiastic about uniting of interest methods. The IASC says 'in exceptional circumstances, it may not be possible to identify an acquirer'. For uniting of interests to be allowed, it requires that there is a 'mutual sharing of risks and benefits' by the shareholders of both companies and 'the managements of the combining enterprises participate in the management of the combined entity'.

IAS 22 (extract)

16. In order to achieve a mutual sharing of the risks and benefits of the combined entity:
    (a) a substantial majority, if not all, of the voting common shares of the combining enterprises are exchanged or pooled;
    (b) the fair value of one enterprise is not significantly different from that of the other enterprise; and
    (c) the shareholders of each enterprise maintain substantially the same voting rights and interest in the combined entity, relative to each other, after the combination as before.

One of the problems which regulators experience is that it is sometimes possible for the companies to structure a deal so that it looks like a merger, while unwinding it later to be more clearly the takeover that it always was. For example, those exchanging their shares in Company B for Company A shares may be given a put option to sell their A shares to a merchant bank or some other intermediary, so that they exchange and then later sell, hence requirements that the underlying balance between shareholders should not change.

This kind of manoeuvre is usually only found in group accounts and must be specified in the notes when it takes place. It is most often practised in the US and there the regulators have taken a decision in principle to do away with the practice. However, we are still a long way from that actually taking place.

Group profit and loss account

We have so far concentrated primarily on the balance sheet, since this is perhaps the more difficult aspect of group accounts to understand, but the consolidated profit and loss account also has its own technical challenges. You will have seen that the group profit and loss account *includes* charges such as the amortization of goodwill which do not appear in the accounts of the individual companies which make up the group. At the same time, the group result *excludes* a number of expenses and revenues which are to be found in the individual companies – essentially all those which involve trading with another group company.

Most groups have quite a large number of transactions which are with other members of the same group. If these were not eliminated, the group accounts would potentially include the same transaction many times over. Imagine a vertically integrated company which (i) grows coca beans in subsidiary A, (ii) manufactures chocolate in subsidiary B, and (iii) then sells this through wholesaler C in another country. You might have the following figures:

Subsidiary A

Expenses	1,200		
Sales to B		1,500	
Profit			300

Subsidiary B

Purchases from A	1,500		
Other expenses	5,000		
Sales to C		7,500	
Profit			1,000

Subsidiary C

Purchases from C	7,500		
Other expenses	500		
Sales to retailers		8,500	
Profit			500
Totals	15,700	17,500	1,800

If you aggregate the figures, you would have a group profit and loss account like this:

Sales	17,500
Expenses	15,700
Profit	1,800

However, a large part of the sales and the expenses are within the group and are double counted:

Sales from A to B	1,500
Sales from B to C	7,500
Total	9,000

These appear both in the aggregate expenses and the aggregate sales, so are artificial from the perspective of the group as a single economic entity. Had the group been a single legal entity, the internal transactions would have no meaning. It is only the external transactions which should be retained in the consolidated profit and loss account. This should be:

Sales (outside the group)	8,500
Expenses (outside the group)	6,700
Profit	1,800

Notice that this does not change the profit, just the turnover and expenses. From the perspective of an outsider, the internal transactions have no meaning and result in a false set of figures. For example, the profit margin before eliminations would be:

Profit	1,800
Sales	17,500
Margin	10.3 per cent

After elimination of intra-group transactions:

Profit	1,800
Sales	8,500
Margin	21.2 per cent

The intra-group transactions only exist because of the group structure, and cause the double-counting problem. If they were not eliminated they would mislead investors (some famous frauds have been engineered this way) and analysts would have difficulty comparing figures between groups.

Note that for the accounts of the individual companies the sales and expenses are valid and for tax purposes, the profits are still dealt with as part of the individual companies. Subsidiary A would be taxed on 300, subsidiary B on 1,000 and subsidiary C on 500, which is a factor we shall come back to in relation to taxation of groups later (see Chapter 15).

You can see that the group financial accounting system must be able to distinguish between transactions with fellow subsidiaries and transactions with outside interests, so that the internal transactions can be included in the individual company accounts but excluded from the group accounts.

Another adjustment which should be made is to ensure that the accounting policies used for the group accounts are reflected in the results of the individual companies which make up the group – the consistency principle applies to group accounts. When a group has subsidiaries in different countries, they will be subject to different tax rules, which may in turn influence policies such as depreciation or provisions. Equally, all the subsidiaries in the same country may not necessarily follow the same rules, although they usually do. This sometimes results in a situation where, in the consolidation process, the depreciation rates and other aspects of measurement in individual companies have to be adjusted so that the same accounting principles are applied consistently throughout the group. To keep this process as simple as possible and ensure comparable figures for management purposes throughout the group, some companies apply uniform accounting rules worldwide, and then prepare local variants for tax purposes.

In broad terms, the preparation of the group accounts (which can be done on a spreadsheet) involves the following stages:

Aggregation of financial statements of all subsidiaries

↓

Remove investment in subsidiaries and equity of subsidiaries, identify goodwill

↓

Remove intra-group transactions

↓

Adjust measurements to uniform principles

↓

Deduct amortization of goodwill

↓

Group accounts

The accounting principles used in the group accounts are traditionally those of the parent company. This aligns with the idea that the group accounts have the effect of treating all transactions as though they had been carried out within the parent. However, the influence of taxation and the pressure to align group accounting on the principles used in the major financial markets means that in many countries a multinational may in fact draw up the group accounts on principles other than those used in the parent, and in that case the measurement adjustments ('restatement' of figures in the jargon) may be substantial, and sophisticated information systems are required to permit the collection of the necessary data.

Associated companies and joint ventures

At the beginning of the chapter we pointed out that there are different kinds of relationship possible between an investor company and a company it has invested in (the investee company). Accounting recognizes three different categories:

1. The investor has a 'controlling' or dominant influence: i.e. the investor can dictate the strategy of the investee company, appoint its management and so on. In this situation, the investee is consolidated, as we have just examined.
2. The investor is not able to determine strategy, but has 'significant influence' – the investor's views are considered in determining the strategy.
3. The investor is not able to determine strategy and has no influence whatsoever.

It should be noted that the distinctions between these categories are not always very clear cut, and depend a lot on the surrounding circumstances. As we have discussed, a shareholding of 40 per cent could put the investor in a dominant position if there are no other major concentrations of ownership. However, it would be more likely to put the company in a position of significant influence. It could even leave the company with no influence – for example, in 1999 LVMH, the French luxury goods company, made a contested takeover bid for Gucci. The bid was foiled by concerted action by the other shareholders which eventually left LVMH with a large minority holding but no participation whatsoever in the management of the company.

The choice of accounting method can have a major effect on the group accounts, and in some cases is quite subjective, because of the need to consider the context. It represents a difficult area for auditors and preparers and the analyst should approach it with caution!

Roche Group

Investments in associated companies are accounted for by the equity method. These are companies over which the Group exercises significant influence, but which it does not control. This is normally evidenced when the Group owns 20 per cent or more of the voting rights of the company. Interests in joint ventures are reported using the line-by-line proportionate consolidation method. Other investments are carried at cost after deducting appropriate provisions for permanent impairment and are included in other long term assets.

Source: extract from Annual report 1998, Accounting policies, F Hoffmann-La Roche Ltd
www.roche.com

The last case is the easiest to account for. The financial asset is held in the investor's books at historical cost. If its current value falls below historical cost, then the investment should be written down (and the expense would normally appear in the financial result part of the profit and loss account). In some jurisdictions, if the current value exceeds historical cost, this information would be disclosed as a note to the accounts. If the investor receives a dividend from the investee company, then this is treated as financial income.

It is the second case which is the more interesting, and which creates the most problems for accounting and therefore in interpretation. Anglo-Saxon multinationals typically prefer full ownership of any venture, while continental European companies have a greater tradition of operating in coalitions and different kinds of partnership. It is these joint ventures or interests in coalitions which present a difficult technical problem in group accounting.

For example, suppose you are a French company that sells bottled non-alcoholic beverages, and you want to expand in Russia. The market is difficult, the risk high, so you decide to go into a joint venture with another soft drink company and a Russian entrepreneur. You each take a one-third stake in a new bottling plant in Moscow which will be managed by the Russian partner with technical assistance from the two multinational partners. How is this going to appear in your group accounts?

Since you do not own or run the plant, it will not be consolidated; on the other hand, you have a significant input into the decision-making and a significant investment which impacts upon the future expansion of your company in that market. You could certainly just treat the investment as a financial asset, but this does not convey the much closer economic relationship you have in it. What can you do?

Essentially there are two basic methods, known as 'equity accounting' and 'proportional consolidation' (sometimes 'proportionate consolidation'). Under equity accounting the investor shows its investment in its consolidated accounts at the accounting value of that investment in the investee's books. If, for example, the investor has 25 per cent of the shares in the investee, it shows that investment at 25 per cent of the book value of equity in the investee's financial statements and not at historical cost to the investor. Under proportional consolidation, the investor takes a proportion of all assets and liabilities of the investee into the consolidated accounts.

These two different approaches are probably best understood through a detailed example. Suppose that Company A buys 20 per cent of Company C, whose balance sheet at the moment of acquisition is as follows:

	$m
Assets	
Tangible fixed assets	600
Current assets	300
Total	900
Financing	
Shares	400
Reserves	50
	450
Debt	250
Payables	200
Total	900

The book value of C's equity in C's books is $450m; A owns 20 per cent of that, which is therefore worth (450*0.2=) $90m. Under equity accounting, the investment in C which appears in A's group accounts should therefore be $90m, and any difference between that and historical cost of the investment is considered as goodwill. The adjustments to bring C into A's group accounts at equity value would be as follows:

	Company A	Company C	Group
Assets			
Goodwill		+60	60
Tangibles	1050		1050
Cost of			
investment in C	150	−150	
Equity value		+90	90
Current assets	420		420
Total	1620	—	1620
Financing			
Shares	300		300
Reserves	420		420
	720		720
Debt	600		600
Payables	300		300
Total	1620		1620

The goodwill should be depreciated in the normal way. On subsequent consolidations, the book value of C would normally have changed, and all changes must also be reflected in the A accounts. So if, for example, C made a net profit of $50m in the year after A had acquired its 20 per cent stake, A would show 'income from associates' $10m in its income statement and would increase the carrying value of its investment by $10m. Any subsequent dividend would decrease the carrying value and increase cash at bank.

If, on the other hand, C were dealt with on a proportional basis, the consolidation would look like this:

	Company A	Company C (20%)	Adjust	Group
Assets				
Goodwill			+60	60
Tangibles	1050	120		1170
Cost of				
Investment in C	150		−150	
Current assets	420	60		480
Total	1620	180	−90	1710
Financing				
Shares	300	80	−80	300
Reserves	420	10	−10	420
	720	90	−90	720
Debt	600	50		650
Payables	300	40		340
Total	1620	180	−90	1710

Under the proportional accounting method a part of the underlying assets and liabilities of C appears in A's balance sheet, as in a normal consolidation, and in future years any profits or losses post acquisition will flow through to the group income statement.

Critics of the equity method point out that only the book value of the equity is shown, and this may conceal a company which is heavily indebted. Indeed, associated companies have been used as a means of shifting debt off the main balance sheet. In addition, the method involves recognizing income from the associated company which has not been paid to the investor and over which the investor does not exercise control – something an analyst would be wary of (see 'quality of earnings' in Part Five).

Critics of proportional consolidation, on the other hand, say that a mathematical fraction of assets and liabilities has no economic significance – an investor cannot sell 20 per cent of a factory in case of difficulty, for example – and that the resulting consolidation is meaningless.

It is clearly a difficult issue because the relationship between the investor and its investment may be highly significant (e.g. the investors in the Airbus consortium draw significant economic benefit from that relationship but none has a majority holding) and should therefore not be missing from the group accounts. From an analyst's perspective, the equity method is easier to decode because profits and losses are separately identified (income from associates) in published statements and can therefore be considered on their own merits in relation to the particular company. Evaluating the effect of proportional consolidation on the accounts is not usually possible.

IAS 28 Accounting for Investments in Associates

8. An investment in an associate should be accounted for in consolidated financial statements under the equity method except when the investment is acquired and held exclusively with a view to its disposal in the near future in which case it should be accounted for under the cost method.

The IASC recommends the use of the equity method for associated companies, which are defined as those where the investor has 'significant influence', which is assumed to be the case where the investor holds at least 20 per cent of the shares. However, the IASC also has a standard which specifically addresses joint ventures, IAS 31, and the provisions of that intersect with those for associates.

Joint ventures

The IASC defines a joint venture as 'a contractual arrangement whereby two or more parties undertake an economic activity which is subject to joint control'. This might be the case where, for example, two or three oil companies build a pipeline for shared use. The IASC recognizes three kinds of arrangement:

1. *Jointly controlled operations.* Here the 'venturers' each devote certain assets to a joint exploitation and perhaps split the profits – for example, when two airlines both operate on the same route and agree to share revenues. Here each venturer has its own assets involved and all that is required is a correct accounting split of revenues and expenses under the terms of the agreement.
2. *Jointly controlled assets.* Here the venturers both put specific assets into the joint venture but retain direct ownership of those assets. No special legal vehicle is created.

Again each venturer accounts for its own assets and revenues and expenses are allocated on a contractual basis.

3. *Jointly controlled entities*. This case intersects with associates – a company or other legal vehicle is created, the venturers make investments in this entity which in turn owns assets and undertakes operations. In this case the IASC recommends use of proportionate (the IASC does not use the word proportional) consolidation for the consolidated statements of the venturers. IAS 31 specifies, however, that where the venture is subject to long-term restrictions which 'significantly impair its ability to transfer funds to the venturer' it should be accounted for as a financial investment under the terms of IAS 39 (financial instruments).

Summary

In this chapter we have reviewed the techniques of preparing group accounts. In particular, this affects analysis by introducing the 'asset' of goodwill arising on consolidation, as well as providing the opportunity for groups to bring into the balance sheet intangibles such as brands which are typically missing from individual company balance sheets. We have noted the necessity of removing transactions within the group since these will distort ratios and turnover and that of ensuring that accounting policies are harmonized. The group accounts give a wider economic picture than individual company accounts. The accounts of a single subsidiary of a group are always open to distorsion.

Questions

Practical case

1. Dickens Enterprises formed a new subsidiary in March 20X4, called Great Expectations. At 31 December 20X4 the balance sheets of the two companies were as shown below. **You are asked to prepare group accounts as at 31 December 20X4.**

	Dickens	GE	Elimination	Group
Net tangible assets	5200	750		
Investment in GE	500			
Stocks	700	49		
Debtors	800	60		
Cash	1200	25		
	8400	884		
Ordinary shares	3000	500		
Reserves	1900	—		
Profit for 20X4	700	31		
Sub-total	5600	531		
Debt	1000	300		
Short-term creditors	1800	53		
	8400	884		

2. Company A has set up a subsidiary to deal with the distribution of its products by mail order. At 31 December 20X6 their respective balance sheets were:

	Parent $m	Subsidiary $m
Assets	980	340
Investment	180	
Loan to subsidiary	50	
Current assets	360	195
	1570	535
Equity/Liabilities		
Share capital	800	180
Reserves	360	
Loan from parent		50
Debt	300	250
Current liabilities	110	55
	1570	535

Draw up a consolidated balance sheet at that date.

3. You work in the mergers and acquisitions department of a merchant bank and have spotted what you consider to be an attractive acquisition. Northeast Foods plc is a small, listed food-manufacturer based in Leeds. It has for many years sold a well-established range of tinned speciality foods. The market regards it as rather sleepy and lacking the management edge necessary to convert to modern technology, bring in new products and compete generally. The company is slowly losing market share as supermarkets bring in own-label products of the kind which were Northeast's strength. The $1 ordinary shares currently trade at $5.25.

   You have also identified Wearside Products plc, a relatively young company which grew rapidly as a result of the success of its tortilla chips. It has broadened its product range but is hungry for more brands and needs to grow to be able to compete more effectively in international markets. Northeast would be a good fit for Wearside, and is reasonably cash rich.

   You are about to have a meeting with the chairman of Wearside to discuss mounting a takeover. You are going to suggest that Wearside offers one of its $1 ordinary shares (market value $4.50) plus $1.50 cash for each Northeast share, giving Northeast shareholders a profit of 75cts at present prices. You are prepared to take less than 100 per cent if necessary but would regard a 60 per cent stake as the minimum acceptable. For 60 per cent you would be willing to offer one Wearside share plus $1.20 cash.

	Wearside $m	Northeast $m
Fixed assets		
Intangible	200.1	—
Tangible	180.2	67.1
Investments	—	10.5
Current assets		
Stock	37.4	20.2
Debtors	41.8	19.3
Cash	5.9	39.2
Total assets	465.4	156.3
$1 Ordinary shares	68.5	24.0
Reserves	123.9	79.7
	192.4	103.7
Creditors due in less than one year	48.3	21.6
Creditors due in more than one year	224.7	31.0
	465.4	156.3

(a) You are asked to draw up a post-takeover balance sheet for the group in order to illustrate the effects of the proposed takeover, assuming that Wearside would borrow short-term to meet the cash element of the bid (and subsequently repay from Northeast's cash reserves). You should draw up alternative balance sheets on the basis of

(i) capitalizing goodwill;
(ii) capitalizing goodwill, but recognizing a brand worth $40m;
(iii) treating the transaction as a uniting of interests.

(b) You are also asked to draw up a balance sheet on the basis of taking only 60 per cent of the shares and using historical cost as fair value.

(*Note:* this is a fairly tough case and is designed to introduce you to the realities of mergers and acquisitions thinking.)

13 Foreign operations

Up until now we have assumed that the accounts of a group's subsidiaries were all kept in the same currency, but this is rarely the case for a multinational. In this chapter we address the special accounting problems of working in several currencies. The analyst does not necessarily need to be able to convert accounts for consolidation purposes and in any event cannot break out conversion effects from published accounts. However, conversion or translation from several currencies potentially brings in a number of distortions, of which the analyst should be aware. In addition, year-on-year comparisons are likely to be affected by value shifts in currencies in which a multinational has major operations, assets and liabilities. Often companies will bring these to the attention of the analyst.

Introduction

The modern multinational corporation typically trades in many countries of the world and in many currencies. Usually it will have subsidiaries in many foreign countries and will also have raised finance outside its national base. Quite often multinationals not only borrow money outside their home market but are also listed on several stock exchanges in different parts of the world. When preparing consolidated accounts it is obviously necessary that all items are expressed in a single reporting currency. Given that the values of a group's assets and liabilities may be stated in foreign currencies, and that the exchange rates between currencies are changing constantly, there is therefore a considerable accounting problem in converting ('translating') amounts expressed in foreign currencies into the reporting currency. In addition, different stock exchanges may have different reporting rules.

Clearly this situation is bound to pose a number of problems, both in interpreting such aggregated data and in expressing annual group accounts in a single currency. We shall look first at the problems of being listed on several stock exchanges, then at the provision of further analysis of company activities, and finally at the accounting problems of converting to a single currency.

Stock exchange requirements

Multinational companies increasingly see a stock exchange listing on all major markets as a strategic issue, not necessarily connected with the company's financing. A listing gives local credibility, increases awareness of the company and its products, and makes it possible to make takeover bids which involve share exchange rather than necessarily cash.

Advantages and disadvantages of foreign markets

For many large corporations the expansion of their international activities is one of the most important goals, if not a condition for continuing success in international competition.

… Developments in the markets for goods and factors are paralleled by developments in the financial markets. More and more companies are actively engaged in the world's most important capital markets, ranging from holding foreign investment accounts or foreign securities to issuing debt and equity. The decision to establish or expand a presence on a foreign capital market allows a company to extend its position as a global financial player as well as to underline its commitment to that foreign market. This signal is strongest when the shares of the company are quoted on the local stock exchange. These apparently rather abstract aims bring with them a number of concrete advantages that support foreign ventures and listings.

Wolf Bay and Hans-Georg Bruns, Daimler Chrysler

Source: Extract from 'Multinational companies and international capital markets', in Walton, P., Haller, A. and Raffournier, B. (1998) *International Accounting*, London: Thomson Learning (previously International Thomson Business Press).

Over time the effect of internationalization has been to drive both markets and then companies to attempt to harmonize the kind of accounts which they use and the information disclosures. The IASC rules which we are using in this book are accepted by most stock exchanges and are as a consequence used by many multinational companies.

Companies using IASC standards

The IASC listed 817 international companies using its standards in September 1999. Amongst these were the following:

Australia	*China*
BHP	China Southern Airlines
TNT	Guangdong Electrical Power Co
Austria	*Czech Republic*
Boehler-Uddeholm Group	Komercni Banka
Voest Alpine Stahl AG	Prague Breweries
Belgium	*Denmark*
Baekert	Borealis
Powerfin	Danisco
Canada	*Finland*
Alcan Aluminium	Nokia Group
NOVA Corporation	Nordisk Investment Bank

▶

(continued)

France	*Norway*
Aerospatiale	Kvaerner
Cap Gemini Sogeti	Statoil
Germany	*Russia*
Adidas-Solomon	Gazprom
Bayer	Uneximbank
Hong Kong	*South Africa*
Jardine Matheson Holdings	Barlow Rand
Mandarin Oriental International	South African Breweries
Hungary	*Sweden*
Fotex	Esselte
Hungarian Development Bank	Saab-Scania
Italy	*Switzerland*
Benetton Group	Nestlé
Olivetti	Roche
Japan	
Fujitsu	*Source:*
Nissan Motor	IASC website: www.iasc.org.uK

However, the major exception to this harmonization is the United States. At the moment the Securities and Exchange Commission (SEC) requires that foreign companies that wish to be listed on any of the US exchanges must either prepare accounts according to US rules, or may use their normal accounts but must then provide a reconciliation between these and US measurements as far as the profit is concerned and owners' equity.

Many jurisdictions (e.g. France, Germany, Switzerland, Italy) permit their multinationals to draw up consolidated accounts on a basis other than domestic measurement rules. As a consequence some companies, such as Peugeot, use US measurement rules (US generally accepted accounting principles – US GAAP) while others (e.g. Nestlé, Hoffman la Roche) use IASC rules and if listed in the US provide a 'US GAAP reconciliation').

Volvo Group

Note 31 Profit for the year and Shareholders' equity in accordance with US GAAP

A summary of the Volvo Group's approximate profit for the year and shareholders' equity determined in accordance with US GAAP, is presented in the accompanying tables.

Application of US GAAP would have the following approximate effect on consolidated profit for the year and shareholders' equity:

Profit for the year	1996	1997	1998
Profit for the year in accordance with Swedish accounting principles	12,477	10,359	8,638
Items increasing (decreasing) reported profits for the year			
Foreign currency translation (A)	(89)	(4,994)	535
Income taxes (B)	494	122	(201)
Tooling costs (C)	(312)	—	—
Business combinations (D)	(529)	(529)	(530)
Shares and participations (E)	176	—	90
Interest costs (F)	15	28	20
Leasing (G)	49	46	(118)
Debt and equity securities (H)	(147)	123	116
Items affecting comparability (I)	—	—	1,178
Pension and other post-employment benefits (J)	(95)	65	313
Tax effect of above US GAAP adjustments	178	1,336	(609)
Net increase (decrease) in profit for the year	(260)	(3,803)	794
Approximate profit for the year in accordance with US GAAP	**12,217**	**6,556**	**9,432**
Approximate profit for the year per share, SEK in accordance with US GAAP	**26.40**	**14.50**	**21.40**
Weight average number of shares outstanding (in thousands)	463,558	452,540	441,521

Shareholders' equity	1996	1997	1998
Shareholders' equity in accordance with Swedish accounting principles	57,876	60,431	68,056
Items increasing (decreasing) reported shareholders' equity			
Foreign currency translation (A)	3,660	(1,163)	(628)
Income taxes (B)	1,398	1,520	1,319
Tooling costs (C)	—	—	—
Business combinations (D)	2,558	2,029	1,499
Shares and participations (E)	(90)	(90)	—
Interest costs (F)	503	531	551
Leasing (G)	(91)	(51)	(177)
Debt and equity securities (H)	1,604	3,962	133
Items affecting comparability (I)	—	—	1,178
Pension and other post-employment benefits (J)	786	851	1,548
Other	(203)	(224)	(226)
Tax effect of above US GAAP adjustments	(1,726)	(1,184)	(774)
Net increase in shareholders' equity	8,399	6,181	4,423
Approximate shareholders' equity in accordance with US GAAP	**66,275**	**66,612**	**72,479**

Source: Extract from Annual Report 1998, Volvo Group
www.volvo.com

This is often provided as an item in the notes to the accounts of multinational companies. Analysts, when making cross-sectional comparisons, need to check whether companies are using IASC rules or US rules for their accounts, and decide whether to use the figures in the reconciliation for a US GAAP- based comparison or whether to make an IASC-based comparison.

Segment reporting

While consolidated accounts have the advantage of measuring the whole economic group, they also have the disadvantage of providing highly aggregated data which may be difficult to interpret when a group has several disparate types of trading activity and works in several different economies. This problem is addressed by requiring companies to disclose information by line of business and by geographical area. Defining what is an identifiable *segment* of a company's activity is notoriously difficult. The US defines it as contributing at least 10 per cent of sales, net assets or profits.

The IASC (IAS 14 *Segment reporting*) says that companies should give information about the different products and services provided by a company and the different geographical areas in which it operates in order to help users of financial statements:

1. better understand the enterprise's past performance;
2. better assess the enterprise's risks and returns; and
3. make more informed judgments about the enterprise as a whole.

Breaking with previous Anglo-Saxon standards, IAS 14 was revised in 1998 and now specifies that the company should identify what is the 'primary reporting format' which is useful. It considers that product and geographical information do not necessarily both have equal importance in assessing risk and return. It therefore asks the company to identify 'the dominant source and nature of an enterprise's risks and returns', either products and services or geographical areas, and concentrate analysis on that kind of segment (with nonetheless some limited information on the other type). If both are important, it suggests a matrix approach.

In general terms, IAS 14 does not use the objective criteria favoured by the US in the past but suggests that it is up to the company to exercise judgment in identifying segments which are significantly different from each other in terms of how they affect the performance of the enterprise. Standards of disclosure vary enormously from company to company. The matrix style of disclosure (combining both geographical and line of business analysis) is little used – most companies give the two types independently. The Seventh Directive calls for disclosure of turnover by product and geographical area, but many companies go beyond that. However, it is one of the obstacles to clear analysis of the accounts of multinational companies.

Logic suggests that forecasters need both geographical and industry segments in order to forecast future results, since the fact that, for example, the US economy is depressed will probably affect all lines of business carried out there, but will carry no implications for the same businesses in other economies. Curiously, though, the research into the subject tends to suggest that forecasts based on industry segment have a better correlation with actual results than those based on geographical segments.

When analysing the accounts of multinational companies it is well worth trying to assemble as long as possible a time series of industry segment data to work out growth

Nokia

Segment information

	Telecom-munications	Mobile phones	Other operations	Elimi-nations	Group total
Net sales					
1998, MFIM	26,103	47,984	6,029	−885	79,231
1997, MFIM	18,826	27,643	7,239	−1,096	52,612
Operating profit/loss, IAS					
1998, MFIM	5,706	9,158	−65	—	14,799
1997, MFIM	4,053	3,837	564	—	8,454
Capital expenditure					
1998, MFIM	1,291	2,899	337	—	4,527
1997, MFIM	1,037	886	479	—	2,402
Identifiable assets, IAS					
1998, MFIM	17,378	22,055	39,630	−19,403	59,660
1997, MFIM	14,426	12,659	26,608	−11,955	41,738

	1998 MFIM	1997 MFIM
Net sales by market area		
Finland	2,763	2,557
Other European countries	41,011	26,914
Americas	16,740	9,520
Asia-Pacific	16,873	12,105
Other countries	1,844	1,516
Total	79,231	52,612

MFIM = millions of Finnmarks

Source: NOKIA Financial Statements 1998, Notes to the consolidated financial statements

trends by product. This will then provide a picture of which products are expanding, which contracting and so on.

Analysts would like more segment data. They complain that it is very difficult to forecast future profits of companies if they do not know the relative profitability of different product lines, and are unable to judge what proportion of turnover is generated by each. Companies on the other hand do not like giving too much detailed analysis because they feel it gives away competitive advantage, and some argue that analysts do not understand the artificiality which can be induced by segment analysis. Where a company trades across the world, there are many transactions between subsidiaries, and these take place at relatively artificial prices which are fixed by the company.

For example, if a new product is developed in the German parent company, but the product is manufactured in South Africa, does the African subsidiary pay a royalty on the development cost to the German parent? How do you allocate worldwide advertising costs? If you have several different product lines, how do you allocate all the costs of running the head office, including preparation of group accounts, stock exchange listing costs, investor relations etc.? There are many factors that impinge upon these decisions, including tax, and the resulting allocations of cost are not necessarily economically meaningful (see Chapter 15 on taxation).

Analysts should look closely at the segment data provided by a company, but remember that allocations distort the overall picture, and that no two groups necessarily make their allocations in the same way. Segment data is probably more useful for time series analysis than cross-sectional.

Currency translation

It is worth considering the behaviour of exchange rates briefly in order to understand the environment within which the accounting decisions have to be made. In the early part of the twentieth century, exchange rates were relatively stable and governments attempted to reinforce this stability by promoting 'fixed parities' between currencies or against the price of gold. Later, economic pressures, particularly inflation, made it very difficult to maintain such fixed exchange rates. One solution was to go for 'pegged' rates, where currencies were allowed to move within a narrow tolerance, but this too proved impossible in the economic conditions of the 1960s and 1970s.

Today we have a situation where most currencies are allowed to 'float', that is, they have no fixed exchange rate, and can change rapidly from one day to another. This creates a number of severe financial management problems, as well as accounting problems, and these are not the least of the reasons for the introduction of the euro. As we will show in this chapter, having to deal in many currencies introduces very many measurement problems into accounting, quite apart from uncertainties in decision-making because values are not stable.

For example, an asset can be bought for $10,000 one day when £1 = $1.75, and can be stated at £5,710 in the UK accounts, but next day the rate might move to £1 = $1.60. Is the asset then worth £6,250 and if the rate goes to £1 = $1.80 the day after, do you change the asset once more to £5,550? Rates do not normally move quite as dramatically as in the example, but they do move quickly, and the movements are not necessarily consistently in one direction. A sharp drop in value one day does not mean that next day or two years later the value will not gain.

Our purpose in addressing these questions is to consider their impact on the financial statements of public companies. This impact can be seen in two different areas:

1. translation of the accounts of subsidiaries for inclusion in annual financial statements;
2. translation of individual assets and liabilities of companies which are denominated other than in sterling.

Translation of subsidiaries

The problems arise because we need to consolidate the accounts of the subsidiary with those of the parent in order to publish group accounts. So our first step should be to consider the objectives of consolidation. Some accounting regulators describe group accounts as presenting the information contained in the separate financial statements of the holding company and its subsidiaries as if they were the financial statements of a single entity. In other words, we are removing the separate legal status of each company in the group and treating them as one company.

One implication which we might draw from that is that we should treat all the transactions of the foreign subsidiary as though they had been carried out by the parent company. That would indeed be treating the group as a single entity. If we did that, we should then look at the individual assets and liabilities of the subsidiary as though they were part of the parent, and logically we should use the exchange rate for each which we would have used if the transactions involved had been carried out directly by the parent. The approach would be something like that shown in Table 13.1.

Table 13.1   Consolidation exchange rates

Balance sheet item	Rate
Assets	
Fixed assets	Rate at time of acquisition
Debtors	Rate at balance sheet date (best estimate of likely proceeds)
Stock	Rate at time of acquisition
Cash	Rate at balance sheet date
Financing	
Equity	
Shares	Rate at time of subscription
Retained profit	Rate ruling at successive balance sheet dates when each slice of retained profit was added to the balance sheet
Creditors	Rate at balance sheet date
Long-term debt	Rate at balance sheet date

This arrangement seems quite logical – it treats every element as though the transaction had been carried out by the parent and converted into parent company currency as though the parent had bought foreign currency to meet each transaction. Of course it means that, since different rates are used for different elements of the balance sheet, the balance sheet will not balance. A new item, translation difference, has to be added. That in itself poses a further problem: is the translation difference (gain or loss) something which should flow through the consolidated profit and loss account? If the result is a gain, this must be an unrealized gain because the parent still owns the subsidiary, and prudence requires that this should not be recognized in the profit and loss account. Against that, unrealized gains on long-term liabilities are recognized.

Then again, is this translation adjustment truly a gain or loss? In so far as rates of exchange may fluctuate both up and down, there is no real reason to suppose (on first principles) that the translation difference may not be purely temporary, and an accident caused by the timing of the balance sheet. For example, if the rate of exchange at balance sheet date is £1 = \$1.60 and the next week £1 = \$1.70, how valid would it be to recognize a gain or a loss as at balance sheet date, when the position has already changed at the time the statements are being prepared? If the gain or loss is temporary, then is it useful to include it in the profit and loss account? You can see that there are some close analogies here with inflation accounting; both issues pose questions of valuation of assets and liabilities, and whether or not changes in value should be recognized in the balance sheet and in the profit and loss account.

The other question which we must pursue is whether the agreeably logical solution of translating the balance sheet of the foreign subsidiary as though the assets and liabilities had been acquired directly by the parent provides useful information for investment decisions and for users generally. For example, is it an entirely accurate view of the economic relations between a subsidiary and parent that the transactions of the subsidiary are seen as relating only to the parent and not having their economic basis in the activities of the subsidiary itself?

The answer to that question must depend to a large degree on the facts in any particular case. For example, if a British manufacturing company sets up a Spanish subsidiary whose sole purpose is the marketing of the finished goods manufactured in Britain, there is a strong case for treating the Spanish subsidiary as nothing other than part of the parent's distribution costs. The separate legal status can be seen merely as a convenience, and the entity has no independent existence outside its marketing function. Translation of its balance sheet (consisting perhaps of a warehouse, stock of finished goods and debtors, with its main creditor being the UK manufacturing company) as though the transactions were those of the parent would probably reflect the economic substance.

However, what if the Spanish subsidiary were a rather more complex business which manufactured its own finished goods (under the group brand name perhaps), sold these independently throughout the world (perhaps using other group subsidiaries in countries where these existed) and also sold products manufactured in other countries by other members of the group (a structure used by Philips, for example)? What if, as is often the case, there were local Spanish minority shareholders in the company, and also that in order to finance its operations the Spanish company also borrowed on the local capital market? The situation here is rather more complex, since the Spanish subsidiary is arguably a complete and independent trading entity in its own right and to account for its transactions as though they were carried out by the parent is a denial of that. It would not reflect the economic reality of the situation.

Looking at the mechanics of translation, we can argue a case that the assets and liabilities of the complex subsidiary have an economic relationship with each other, rather than with those of the parent. For example, the stock does not derive from external manufacturing operations; the manufacturing plant is not an extension of an operation by the parent; the long-term loans borrowed on the Spanish market relate to the Spanish operation and its assets, not to the parent's global financing needs. If we translate the assets at the rate ruling when they were acquired, but the long-term liabilities at the rate ruling on balance sheet date, we are using different rates to translate two items whose economic existence is interdependent. We are arguably distorting the economic relationships and therefore it is questionable whether such an approach does give some approximation of the economic relationship. There seems a good reason here for using the same rate for both assets and liabilities to preserve their interrelationship.

In practical terms the 'independent' subsidiary could be recognized as a set of interrelated assets and liabilities which were translated for group accounts purposes at the rate ruling at the balance sheet date when consolidation is taking place. In other words, the value used would merely represent a mathematical conversion from one currency to another to enable the group accounts to be stated in a single currency.

Critics point out, though, that there is a major conceptual flaw in this approach: by consolidating the subsidiary using the current exchange rate, one is importing current values into historical cost accounts and this represents some form of hidden revaluation. According to Purchasing Power Parity theory, exchange rates move in response to inflation, and the use of current rates for fixed assets would mean that an inflation adjustment was automatically being built into the group accounts. This is not acceptable within the context of pure historical cost, but also it would be inconsistent to revalue some assets and not others, and revaluation should be worked out systematically and not on the haphazard basis of currency and differential inflation. The correct rate must be the historical rate.

To illustrate the effect of this, suppose that a German subsidiary of a UK parent bought plant for DM300,000 on 1.1.X1 when £1 = DM3.00; at that point the asset, if translated, would be worth £100,000. During 20X1 inflation is 10 per cent in the UK and 5 per cent in Germany. According to Purchasing Power Parity theory the exchange rate at the end of the year should be £1*1.1 = DM3*1.05, or £1 = DM2.86. If the asset were translated at the current rate at the year end, it would appear in the group accounts as £104,895.

Accounting techniques

Over the years a number of different translation approaches have been used, but current regulation typically proposes a choice of two methods, based largely upon the rationale we have considered above. In effect the standard-setters seem to take the view that no one method is defensible under all circumstances, so companies have the choice of two methods, depending upon the actual conditions for which they are accounting. The method which takes the subsidiary as an extension of the parent is known as the 'temporal' method, while that which takes the subsidiary as a whole is known as the 'net investment' method (also the current or closing rate method).

IAS 21 *The effects of changes in foreign exchange rates* requires that companies review the way in which foreign subsidiaries operate in relation to the parent, and the way in which they are financed. It distinguishes between 'foreign operations that are integral to the operations of the reporting enterprise' and 'foreign entities'.

It says that where the operations of the subsidiary are in effect an extension of those of the parent, a change in the exchange rate in which the subsidiary accounts will have immediate effects upon the parent's cash flows, and it is appropriate to use a translation methodology which treats its transactions as though they had been undertaken by the parent – the temporal method.

On the other hand, where the foreign subsidiary generates sales and pays expenses primarily in local currency, there is little direct effect on the parent when there is a rate change: 'The change in the exchange rate affects the reporting entity's net investment in the foreign entity rather than the individual monetary and non-monetary items held by the foreign entity.' In this case the 'net investment method' is appropriate.

In order to demonstrate the implications of the choice of method on the picture presented in the group accounts we shall now translate the accounts of a foreign subsidiary using each of the methods.

Temporal method

The temporal method is based on the assumption that the best way of translating the balance sheet and profit and loss account of a foreign subsidiary is by treating the transactions as though they were carried out by the parent, and thus using rates which relate to the time when the transaction took place (hence 'temporal'). Assets which are carried in the books at historical values are translated at the rate ruling when the asset was acquired, while assets having a current value (i.e. debtors, cash) are translated at the current rate. The broad lines used are shown in Table 13.2.

Current monetary assets will be received after the balance sheet date, while current liabilities and long-term liabilities will be payable after the balance-sheet date, so all are stated at the closing or current rate as being the best approximation. Other assets are translated at the historical rate which obtained at the time of acquisition.

Table 13.2 Exchange rates – temporal method

Balance sheet component	Exchange rate
Fixed assets	Historical
Depreciation	Historical
Current assets	
Stock	Historical
Monetary assets	Current
Current liabilities	Current
Long-term liabilities	Current
Equity	
Share capital	Historical
Retained earnings	Average

Worked example

The European Trading Co. plc invests Sw.Fr.3,000,000 in a Swiss subsidiary. The subsidiary borrows a further Sw.Fr.2,000,000 locally and buys a factory for Sw.Fr.5,000,000. At the time the subsidiary was set up (1 January 19XI) the exchange rate was £1 = Sw.Fr.4.00, so the European Trading Co. plc invested £750,000 in the share capital of its new subsidiary. During I9XI the Swiss company traded successfully and achieved profits of Sw.Fr.500,000. The exchange rate had been slipping against the pound during the year and at the end of the year had reached £1 = Sw.Fr.3.00. The average rate during the year was £1 = Sw.Fr.3.50. The balance sheets of the Swiss subsidiary (as expressed in local currency) are shown on the following page.

	1 Jan 20X1 SF'000			31 Dec 20X1 SF'000
Fixed assets	5,000			5,000
less Depreciation	—			(250)
Current assets				
Stock	—		500	
Monetary	—		750	
Current liabilities	—	—	(500)	750
	5,000			5,500
Long-term liabilities	(2,000)			(2,000)
	3,000			3,500
Financed by				
Equity				
Share capital	3,000			3,000
Retained profits	—			500
	3,000			3,500

During the year the net asset value of the Swiss subsidiary has risen from Sw.Fr.3m to Sw.Fr.3.5m. If we now take the balance sheet position of the subsidiary at the beginning and end of the year and use the temporal method to translate it into sterling in order to prepare group accounts, the relationship of assets and liabilities within the subsidiary will change as shown below:

	1 Jan 20X1 £'000		31 Dec 20X1 £'000	Rate used £ =
Fixed assets	1,250		1,250.00	4.00
less Depreciation	—		(62.50)	4.00
Current assets				
Stock*	—	142.86		3.50
Monetary	—	250.00		3.00
Current liabilities	—	(166.67)		3.00
	—		226.19	
	1,250		1,413.69	
Long-term liabilities	(500)		(666.67)	3.00
	750		747.02	
Equity				
Share capital	750		750.00	4.00
Retained earnings	—		142.85	3.50
Translation adjustment**	—		(145.83)	
	750		747.02	

*This rate is assumed: the temporal method requires use of the actual rate at the time the stock was acquired, for simplicity the example assumes that stock was acquired uniformly throughout the year.
**Under the temporal method the translation adjustment is charged against net income and is only shown separately in this example in order to highlight its existence.

In applying the temporal method, different exchange rates are used for different elements of the balance sheet, and in this case we can see clearly the dilemma which emerges: in Swiss franc terms the subsidiary has grown by 16.67 per cent in value, but when translated back to sterling using this method the net asset value has fallen slightly. Which is the more useful picture from the point of view of users?

Probably your immediate reaction will be that this translation method must be wrong – but you need to think carefully about it. The major difference between the sterling result and the Swiss franc result derives from the fact that the long-term liability is translated at the current rate, while the major asset is translated at a historic rate. As in this example the rate has moved against sterling, the liability has risen considerably in sterling terms while the asset has remained at its historic sterling value. This is exactly what would happen if the parent had borrowed in Switzerland for repayment ultimately from sterling resources.

The dilemma arises from the fact that the assets and liabilities are being viewed from the parent company standpoint, and the application of the prudence principle requires that the growth in current value of the liability is recognized while the assets are at historical cost. So the question arises as to whether one should ignore the prudence principle and state the liability also at a historical cost, or whether the asset might be revalued. Revaluation of the asset, though, would be inconsistent if other assets owned by the group were not revalued as well.

The strict application of accounting rules designed for accounting within one country and one currency to a multi-currency problem leads to this situation, and one should consider whether such rules can reasonably be extended in that way. The application of the rules ignores the economic reality, which is that the Swiss franc loan was negotiated in order to purchase a Swiss franc asset, and it is expected that the loan will be repaid out of Swiss franc earnings derived from the use of that asset. Does this have anything to do with the parent company other than to the extent of its investment?

This use, in the example, of a local loan to back up the purchase of a local asset is a classic technique in international business. If the parent company had not borrowed any capital but had invested Sw.Fr.5m, its economic exposure to rate changes would obviously be much greater than for the investment of Sw.Fr.3m. In effect, it has acquired an asset of Sw.Fr.5m with a currency risk of Sw.Fr.3m. Economically the loan element is balanced by the asset, since a rate change affects both asset and liability in the same way. This is known as a currency 'hedge'. The major difficulty with the temporal method is that it fails to recognize the economic existence of the hedge – the rate change is reflected in the accounts only in so far as it affects the liability, and not where it affects the asset.

Net investment method

This approach approximates to the alternative view of the parent/subsidiary relationship. It assumes that the subsidiary should be considered as an entity and the assets and liabilities translated at the same rate, thereby in effect showing the results of rate changes on the parent company's net investment in the subsidiary.

If we apply the net investment approach to the same Swiss subsidiary, the translation would be made at the rate ruling on balance sheet date: in this case therefore the opening balance sheet would be translated at £1 = Sw.Fr.4.00, while the closing balance sheet would be translated at £1 = Sw.Fr.3.00.

	1 Jan 20X1 £'000			31 Dec 20X1 £'000
Fixed assets		1,250		1,667.67
less Depreciation		—		(83 33)
Current assets				
Stock	—		166.67	
Monetary	—		250.00	
Current liabilities	—		(166.67)	250.00
		1,250		1,833.34
Long-term liabilities		(500)		(666.67)
		750		1,166.67
Equity				
Share capital (initial)		750		750.00
(translation diff.)		—		250.00
Retained earnings		—		166.67
		750		1,166.67

Note: The original share capital has been translated at the historic rate, with the difference between that and the closing rate shown separately as a translation adjustment. The closing rate has been used for retained earnings, although some theorists would say that this should have been done at an average rate, reflecting the growth over the year.

Use of the net investment method ties in the rate change to both assets and liabilities, reflecting a current exchange value for both. The precise differences in the results of the two methods may perhaps best be viewed if we now compare the sterling translation of the closing balance sheet under each method.

	Temporal 31 Dec 20X1 £'000		*Net investment* 31 Dec 20X1 £'000	
Fixed assets		1,250.00		1,666.67
less Depreciation		(62.50)		(83.33)
Current assets				
Stock	142.86		166.67	
Monetary	250.00		250.00	
Current liabilities	(166.67)		(166.67)	
		226.19		250.00
		1,413.69		1,833.34
Long-term liability		(666.67)		(666.67)
		747.02		1,166.67
Equity				
Share capital		750.00		750.00
Translation adjustment		(145.84)		250.00
Retained earnings		142.86		166.67
		747.02		1,166.67

The difference in result between the two methods is quite dramatic and emphasizes a point we hope you have now fully realized, that the measurement of profit is subject to all kinds of quite subjective decisions on accounting principles.

The essential difference in result derives from the fact that the net investment method has recognized the increase in sterling value of the asset as a result of a rate change, while the temporal method has not done so. Either view of the sterling result of the subsidiary is justifiable, depending upon how you interpret the economic relationship between the parent and the subsidiary.

In the example chosen, the rates of exchange used presented a picture where sterling was weakening against the foreign currency, and the effect of that on the translation was to show up an increased liability under the temporal method. If the rate movements had been the opposite, however, the picture would have been the exact reverse. Under the temporal method, the asset would have remained at its old sterling value while the liability would have diminished, thereby showing a positive translation adjustment. Under the net investment method both asset and liability would have declined, giving a negative translation adjustment. Do not fall into the trap of supposing that the net investment method always gives a more profitable result.

One implication of the differences thrown up by translation methods is that when assessing the performance of a subsidiary from a parent company viewpoint, care must be taken to distinguish the currency effects in the sterling results from the real underlying operating results. Using the relationship which profit bears to the investment in an operation as a yardstick (return on equity), the results for the Swiss operation could be interpreted three different ways:

	Growth in equity	*Opening equity*	*Percentage growth in year*
Swiss Fr. accounts	500	3000	16.67 per cent
Temporal	(2.98)	750	(0.40 per cent)
Net investment	416.67	750	55.56 per cent

Precisely the same economic situation can yield three different measures of success or failure, depending on the perspective chosen. This is clearly a problem for the analyst. The effect of translation differences can be highlighted in two ways: firstly, it will be reflected to an extent in the analysis of fixed assets – when the net investment method is used (and most European corporates use it) the translated value of assets will change, as we discussed above. The amount of this change will be reflected in the fixed asset note, and the analyst can check whether this is material in relation to total assets, or whether a portfolio effect applies (what accountants call 'swings and roundabouts'!) and translation gains on some items are balanced by losses on others. Secondly, the analyst should look at the translation difference taken to reserves – is this material? If possible, a five-year or more time series should be constructed (back copies of the accounts would be required) in order to see whether there is a definite trend.

Pirelli Spa

The financial statements expressed in foreign currency have been translated into Italian lire at rates prevailing at year-end for the balance sheet and at average exchange rates for the statement of income, with the exception of the financial statements of companies operating in high inflation countries, whose statements of income have been translated at rates ruling at the year-end.

The differences arising from the translation of beginning shareholders' equity at year-end exchange rates have been recorded in the consolidation reserve.

Source: extract from 'principles of consolidation', Pirelli Spa, Notes to consolidated financial statements

The method used to translate foreign subsidiaries must be disclosed in the accounting policies note and the amounts written off must also be disclosed, including details of what has gone through the profit and loss account and what has been taken directly to reserves (and appears in the statement showing movements on reserves?).

Individual balance-sheet items

The other element of foreign currency which impacts upon the published balance sheet is the translation of individual group assets and liabilities, other than subsidiaries, which are denominated in other currencies. The most important single category here is borrowing in foreign currencies – loans may be negotiated for a period of several years and need to be restated in several balance sheets between initial receipt and final repayment.

For example, suppose a company borrowed $5m on the Eurodollar market for five years, and the current value of the liability moved as shown in Table 13.3. The accounting question that arises is: what value should be given to the loan liability in the interim balance sheet between receiving the loan (1.1.X1) and repaying it (31.12.X5)? In this transaction the company has to repay more than it borrowed and the difference will also need to be recognized as a loss at some point. How and when should the loss be recognized?

Table 13.3   Movements in value

Balance sheet date	Exchange rate £=	Sterling equivalent
1.1.X1	$1.60	3.125m
31.12.X1	$1.55	3.226m
31.12.X2	$1.40	3.571m
31.12.X3	$1.25	4.000m
31.12.X4	$1.30	3.846m
31.12.X5	$1.40	3.571m

In terms of providing useful information for shareholders, the only really useful information is the final repayment value and the total loss over the loan period. However, this information is only available at the end of the period. Should the exchange differences be recognized only at that point?

Potentially there could be a number of responses to the question, but the accounting standard takes the view that such items should be translated at the current rate on each balance sheet date, and the resultant difference be taken to the profit and loss account. The rationale for this is that the current rate provides the best available (if poor) approximation of the future repayment date and represents the best available information. A particularly interesting aspect of this is that the standard requires that any difference in translation value between succeeding balance sheets should be closed to the profit and loss account *irrespective of whether it is a loss or a gain*. Such gains are unrealized until the loan is repaid, and this recognition of them in the profit and loss account is one of the only two cases where an unrealized gain is taken to the profit and loss account.

There is, though, a major loophole in the standard which concerns dealing with currency hedges. A multinational company has investments in many countries which are therefore denominated in many currencies. This potentially creates many exchange exposures and a multinational usually tries to minimize this by borrowing in foreign currencies. So if a company wants to buy a US subsidiary for $100m it will try to borrow US$ to finance the deal, rather than sterling. The investment will yield a dollar cash flow which can be used to pay interest and ultimately repay the debt. With a US$ loan, any move in exchange rates has no effect on this closed circuit, while a sterling loan would have fluctuating results (see example later in this chapter).

Companies therefore hedge their investments and borrow in currencies which reflect the currencies of their future expected cash flows. These debts have notwithstanding to be translated into sterling at balance sheet date at the closing rate, while the underlying investment is held in the parent at the historical rate. Following normal rules this would mean that the two were not balanced, but the standard allows that translation gains and losses on loans which are hedges of investments may be taken directly to reserves, without flowing through the profit and loss account. This is very rational, but has a flaw in that complex multinationals tend not hedge individual transactions, but rather take out a basket of currency loans to hedge a basket of investments, so one cannot tie down individual assets to individual debts. Consequently, it is rather in the hands of the treasury department at year end to say which items are trading debts (gains and losses to the profit and loss account) and which are hedges (have no effect on profit), and one does not have to be unduly suspicious to see that this system is open to abuse!

Short-term transactions

By way of background information in this area, we should also mention other aspects of dealing in foreign currencies which affect profit measurement but which are less immediately germane to an understanding of corporate reports.

One of the ways in which companies minimize the risk of changes in exchange rates causing losses is to take out 'hedges' against individual transactions. For example, where a company wants to buy (say) a French machine tool for Fr. 10,000 and places the order at a time when the exchange rate is £1 = Fr.10 for delivery in six months' time, there is a risk that the rate could move to (say) £1 = Fr.8 by the time delivery takes place, with the result that the expected sterling cost rises from £1,000 to £1,250. The company can avoid the risk by buying francs in advance ('buying forward') and so fixing the rate actually paid. This sort of technique is known as 'hedging'. When such a transaction takes place, the asset would be recognized in the buyer's books at the exchange rate built into the forward contract, not at the rate ruling when the asset was delivered.

Receivables and payables

Receivables and payables in foreign currencies other than the recording currency of the individual companies are adjusted to the year-end exchange rates or the agreed exchange rates under hedging contracts; related exchange gains or losses are recorded in the statement of income.

Source: Pirelli Spa, extract from Notes to the consolidated financial statements

---

In the absence of a hedge, individual transactions are translated at the rate ruling when the transaction took place. Supposing the French machine was delivered on 30 June, when the rate was £1 = Fr.8, but three months' credit was allowed. Settlement was made on 30 September when the rate was £1 = Fr.8.5. The accounting transactions would be:

1. Recognize asset 30 June at £1,250 and create creditor.
2. Settle creditor 30 September at £1,176 and recognize exchange gain in profit and loss account of £74.

Contingent liabilities

Companies are required to disclose any material contingent liabilities in the notes to the accounts – any areas where some claim might be made on the company based upon a past event, but for which it is uncertain that a claim will ever materialize. Many companies enter into forward exchange deals or interest rate swaps or options on either interest rates or currencies which perhaps should be disclosed under this heading. This is something of a grey area where the external user has very little idea of the potential problems. Allied Lyons treasury dealers famously lost about $130m on US dollar dealings over a three-month period. While there have been few losses on such a scale, very little is actually disclosed in this area and the contingent liabilities note should be checked. (See Chapter 14.)

Summary

The analysis of multinational operations faces problems of highly aggregated data and of accounts denominated in many currencies. Corporates are required to provide some analysis of industry and geographical segments to help the analyst.

Fluctuating exchange rates pose a major accounting problem when it comes to preparing consolidated accounts which include foreign subsidiaries. Accountants have to decide on the appropriate exchange rate to use in order to convert the foreign subsidiary's accounts to parent company currency.

If the subsidiary is translated as though the transactions were those of the parent, its accounts are translated at different rates appropriate to the category of asset or liability concerned. This is known as the *temporal method*. The translation difference is seen as either income or expense for inclusion in the consolidated profit and loss account.

Alternatively, if the subsidiary is considered to be economically a whole entity in its own right, its financial statements are translated at the rate ruling on balance sheet date. This is known as the *net investment* (or *closing rate* or *current rate*) method. The use of this method preserves the relationships between assets and liabilities within the subsidiary's balance sheet. It does, however, risk including assets which have, in effect, been revalued, within a historical cost balance sheet on an unsystematic basis.

The International Accounting Standard recommends the use of either the net investment method where a foreign subsidiary is dependent on the parent, or the temporal method. The translation difference arising on consolidation is treated as a direct adjustment to shareholders' equity when using the net investment method and flows directly through reserves.

Long-term balance sheet items must be translated at the rate ruling on each successive balance sheet date, as providing the best approximation of their ultimate settlement value. Differences arising from translation of such items, whether gains or losses, are taken to the profit and loss account.

Questions

1. Norwood Ltd contracts to buy a new machine tool from Illinois Tools Inc. at a price of $85,000 on the following terms of payment: 10 per cent on delivery, 50 per cent after one month and the balance after a further two months. The machine is ordered on 1 September 20X1, leaves the Illinois factory on 1 October and reaches Norwood on 30 November. Norwood makes its payments on 1 December 20X1, 1 January 20X2 and 1 February 20X2. The £/$ exchange rates during this period were:

1 Sept. 20X1	£1 = $ 1.20
1 Oct. 20X1	£1 = $1.25
30 Nov. 20X1	£1 = $1.20
1 Dec. 20X1	£1 = $1.20
1 Jan. 20X2	£1 = $1.15
Feb.20X2	£1 = $1.10

   (a) On the assumption that the invoice was denominated in US dollars, show the balance sheet entries for Norwood at 31 December 20X1 and the profit and loss account items for 20X1 and 20X2 which relate to this transaction.

   (b) On the assumption that the invoice was agreed in sterling at £70,000, show the same financial statement items for Illinois Tools Inc.

2. Continental Holdings borrows Sw.Fr.20m on 1 July 20X1 for a five-year term, at a time when £1 = Sw.Fr.4.00. **Show the relevant balance sheet and profit and loss account items relating to this loan for the years 20X1 to 20X6 inclusive, given the following exchange rate information:**

31 Dec. 20X1	£1 = Sw.Fr.4.25
31 Dec. 20X2	£1 = Sw.Fr.4.10
31 Dec. 20X3	£1 = Sw.Fr.3.50
31 Dec. 20X4	£1 = Sw.Fr.3.25
31 Dec. 20X5	£1 = Sw.Fr.3.60
30 June 20X6	£1 = Sw.Fr.4.10

3. Voltaire Industries SA set up a UK subsidiary, Candide Ltd, on 1 July 20X1 with an investment of Fr.12m. The subsidiary borrowed £500,000 on the UK market and purchased a leasehold factory for £300,000 and plant for £1.0m. The draft balance sheets of the two companies as at 30 June 20X2 are given below. The exchange rates which applied during the year were:

Date	£ = Fr
1 July 20X1	12.00
30 June 20X2	10.00
Average for year	11.00

   Candide purchased its closing stocks at a time when £1 = Fr.10.50.

   You are required to prepare group accounts for Voltaire Industries as at 30 June 20X2. Any foreign currency adjustments should be shown as a separate component of equity, and an indication given by note of its treatment in the profit and loss account. Two sets of accounts should be prepared, using both possible methods of translation.

	Voltaire F'000	Voltaire F'000	Candide £'000	Candide £'000
Fixed assets				
Tangible				
Leaseholds	320,000		300	
Depreciation	(75,000)	245,000	(30)	270
Plant	850,000		1,000	
Depreciation	(375,000)	475,000	(200)	800
Investment				
in Candide		12,000		
		732,000		1,070
Current assets				
Stock	85,000		175	
Debtors	120,000		250	
Cash	163,000		250	
	368,000		675	
Creditors due in				
less than 1 year	(250,000)	(125)		
Net current assets		118,000		550
Creditors due in				
more than 1 year		(100,000)		(500)
		750,000		1,120
Capital				
Ordinary shares		400,000		1,000
Reserves		250,000		—
Profit for year		100,000		120
		750,000		1,120

14 Issues in financial reporting by multinationals

The object of this chapter is to review what are currently considered to be problems either in understanding corporate reports or in the quality of the information given in them. A financial analyst is likely to encounter some of these in looking at different companies. The subjects are not necessarily related to each other, and you might regard this as a reference section for advanced problems in financial reporting.

Investor relations

A problem for the financial markets is that although stock exchanges require companies to publish widely any information that is likely to affect the market price of a share (this is often done by sending a release to the stock exchange itself), in practice not all investors have access to the same information. The bulk of investment in the market comes from collective investment vehicles and not directly from private individuals. Many people save for retirement by buying shares in a unit trust or investing in a life assurance policy or an independent pension scheme. Employer schemes are frequently handed over to professional managers. Consequently, the individual intervenes less and less directly in the market and the vast majority of investment is channelled through different institutional investors. This means that a company seeking investors can address most of the market in effect by talking with professional fund managers and analysts.

This has given rise to the investor relations function. Large companies maintain a department whose job is to communicate, often on a one-to-one basis, with investment organizations. This department is somewhere between a public relations unit and a financial reporting unit. Their job is to maintain continuing relations with market professionals, to respond to their questions and to organize 'road shows': visits to different cities around the world to explain results and usually to enable investors to meet the chief financial officer or chief executive and talk about the company. Company websites often provide their financial data via a link on the home page entitled 'investor relations', rather than (say) financial statements. Analysts are invited to contact the 'Corporate Communications Director', not the finance director.

Investor relations meetings

The analysts sought to make the best qualitative judgment on the company. Factors of particular interest about the company which were said to make a strong contribution to this qualitative judgment may be summarised as:

- quality of management
- performance indicators
- quality of assets
- verification and assurance

What was clear from the analysts' comments was that relatively little of this information came directly from the annual report. Company meetings were the key source of qualitative information and the annual report was the confirmation in terms of financial outcomes.

Source: ICAS: *Corporate Communications: views of institutional investors and lenders*
(Research Committee, Institute of Chartered Accountants of Scotland, 1999)

At the same time, professional analysts will follow individual companies very closely, and aim to become a specialist in that company. They will attend company presentations but also make visits to company sites and will constantly be updating their knowledge of the company and their future expectations. Evidently such analysts have a much more detailed knowledge of the company than the average private individual, creating an imbalance of knowledge in the market.

That said, the Internet is modifying that a little. In the US particularly there are some brokers who now sell shares to private individuals on the Internet and there is developing a market where TV companies will screen business reports early in the morning, often with soundbites from well-known analysts. Private investors then turn to their computer and buy and sell on the basis of that morning's comments. They then check the market regularly through the day to see how their gamble is paying off – all the excitement of betting on horse races or whatever, with the added psychological boost that what you are doing is seriously managing your finances, not amusing yourself. Private investors are coming back to direct buying and selling, but they are taking advice from professional brokers and others. In some ways this is likely to bring further complications to regulating the market because most effort currently goes into ensuring quality information to the professional investor and regulators may yet feel they have to step in to regulate the advice being given to private individuals in order to protect them and preserve confidence in the market.

Income smoothing

There is a basic problem in financial reporting that the net earnings of a company are likely to vary from year to year because they are the result of many different factors, whereas the financial markets want earnings to increase progressively from year to year. This means that company financial executives are under some pressure to 'manage' the reported earnings so that they meet analysts' expectations.

Let us look at this proposition in more detail. Firstly, why are earnings important to analysts, secondly, why do they fluctuate and thirdly, how are they managed?

We talked in Chapter 9 about the price/earnings ratio. This is a ratio that reflects the degree of risk which the market considers inherent to a particular company within a particular business sector. The relationship is expressed:

$$\frac{\text{Market price of share}}{\text{Earnings per share}} = \text{p/e ratio}$$

This relationship is fundamental to the stock market. When investment managers are looking for shares to buy, what they are seeking is a share which is 'undervalued', i.e. whose market price is below its real value. The current market price is determined by analysts as a function of the historic p/e for that company multiplied by forecast earnings per share. If the share is undervalued, that means that the market is either underestimating future earnings, or overestimating the riskiness of the company (the higher the risk, the higher the return necessary to compensate investors for running the risk, and so the lower the p/e and price).

The p/e ratios for the sector often fluctuate together (many aspects of risk will affect all companies in the same sector similarly) but the p/e for the individual company within that tends to be fairly stable in relation to other companies in the same sector.

The accounts are now so complex that most users need someone else to explain them. But financial analysts are only interested in earnings per share and the price/earnings ratio. Les Cullen, a director of Inchcape, said "Standard-setters must realise there is a limit to the complexity which preparers can put up with". He added: "The City is not using the more complex information. It is still seeing the company as a sort of annuity". He explained that the markets are more interested in stable earnings patterns and this creates a pressure on preparers to smooth earnings, even though in the modern economy earnings are becoming more volatile. "There is a disconnection at present between accounting principles and the financial market".

Source: Accounting & Business July/August 1999, p.20

It is changes in expected earnings which are the more frequent cause of fluctuations in price which affect individual companies. During the accounting year, professional analysts will visit the company and will try to obtain information which will give them as good as possible an idea of the likely outcome for the year's earnings. A forecast increase in earnings will cause them to buy more shares (market currently undervalues shares) whereas a drop in forecast earnings will cause them to sell shares (market overvalues the company at current price). There is therefore a direct link between accounting earnings and the market price.

Why earnings fluctuate

The net profit after tax of a multinational is subject to an enormous number of different variables – temporary changes in turnover as a result of local conditions, the arrival of competing products on the market, unexpected losses as a result of, for example, civil unrest, tax changes and so on. A multinational may well be operating in over a hundred countries and selling many different types of products, so the number of factors which contribute to the shape of the consolidated profit and loss account is inevitably substantial. While there may be a 'portfolio effect' (i.e. if you have enough different risk factors they may cancel each other out), there are many circumstances which can influence the final outcome.

Another issue is that net profit after tax is a small percentage of turnover. For example, if you take the results of the EMI record group for 1999, the turnover was $2905.6m (1998: $2352.7m) but net profit due to shareholders was $122.6 (1998: $132.4m) which is

4.2 per cent (1998: 5.6 per cent). This means that operating expenses, interest and taxation amounted to 95.8 per cent of turnover. In this context a 1 per cent decrease in costs would bring a 25 per cent increase in profits and vice versa.

You can see that a small shift in costs has a major effect on profits. This has two consequences: firstly, that profits are likely to move up and down, year on year, in an apparently arbitrary fashion; but, secondly, that management can influence profits by relatively small manipulations of costs. If management want the share price to rise steadily year on year, they have to ensure, given the market's dependence upon p/e ratios, that profits rise steadily year on year.

How do managers manipulate profits?

There are a number of classic ways in which this can be done legally, and they are all difficult for the analyst to recognize. The most difficult to detect is the management of what are sometimes called *discretionary costs*. These are costs which the group can stop incurring without having any immediate effect on profitability, such as research and development, staff training, advertising. Of course, it is suicide for the company in the medium to long term and also has a bad effect on company morale in the short term, but it is frequently practised. Most groups operate an internal monthly reporting system which compares actual performance with budget, and many add to that a forecast for the year-end profit which is updated every month. If this forecast shows that the target profit for the year is unlikely to be achieved, it is possible that the call will go out from head office to abandon advertising campaigns or halt product development, or simply defer these until the start of the next accounting year. Any of these tactics will increase short-term profits, and there is little or nothing visible on the outside to warn the analyst. Where a company discloses its annual research and development expenditure, this may show a decrease. But even here, the classification as to what is development expenditure and what ordinary running costs is not that clear, and a little creative redefinition could hold the figure up even when real expenditure has dropped.

A second area of action is closure of loss-making divisions. Suppose that a company has five divisions with forecast results as follows:

Division	Profit
A	140
B	(120)
C	80
D	75
E	50
Group	225

If you close division B, group profit jumps immediately from $225m to $345m. This may or may not be a good idea. It may just hasten the demise of a division which had no future – the product was near the end of its life cycle and could no longer make an adequate contribution. On the other hand, it may cause the company to close a unit which is in a start-up situation. Many operations lose money in their early days – you have only to look at companies like Amazon and other very visible Internet start-ups to see that. The very difficult trick for central management is to decide how long to continue to nurse a start-up (potentially up to five years) and when to decide to cut one's losses and stop the experiment. In this situation, pressure to help the group profit can result in a start-up being abandoned too early, because its losses are causing aggregate group profit to suffer. This tactic is usually not all that difficult to spot because there is likely to be some mention of the closure in the notes to the accounts or the management report, but there may be only hints which require interpretation.

A variant on this involves an accounting manipulation: most consolidated accounting rules allow the group to exclude from the consolidation any subsidiary which is to be disposed of. Flagging division B as a disposal would mean that it could be held out of the group result without even closing it down.

IAS 27 *Consolidated financial statements and accounting for investments in subsidiaries*

13. A subsidiary should be excluded from consolidation when:

(a) control is intended to be temporary because the subsidiary is acquired and held exclusively with a view to its subsequent disposal in the near future; or

(b) it operates under severe long term restrictions which significantly impair its ability to transfer funds to the parent.

The third way of smoothing profits is what the SEC has called 'cookie jar accounting'. This involves making provisions when profits are higher than expected, and releasing them when times are difficult. The basic tactic is to create a provision by making a charge against profits, and carrying forward a credit in the balance sheet (go back to Chapter 6 if you want to review the basic technique). This charge will generally not be accepted for tax purposes, but that does not matter since its function is to deceive the market, not the taxman. The more difficult problem is to convince the group auditors, but this is often done by talking about future reorganization or restructuring costs, which are notoriously difficult to estimate ahead of actually deciding which plant is to close and whether workers can be found employment elsewhere in the group and so on.

The way this would work might be:

Year 1	Market expectations of profit	150
	Actual turnover	3,400
	Actual costs	3,200
	Actual profit	200
	Create provision	(45)
	Reported profit	155

When the results are announced, the slight increase against analysts' forecasts would generate a slight increase in share prices.

Year 2	Market expectations of profit	170
	Actual turnover	3,450
	Actual costs	3,300
	Actual profit	150
	Release part of provision	20
	Reported profit	170

Had the group reported the actual result for Year 1 of $200m, and a year later the actual result of $150m, the share price would first have rocketed, and the market might have expected profits of $250m in Year 2, leading to a steep decline in the share price once the actual result was announced.

Is this manipulation visible to the analyst? Well, up to a point. In the balance sheet, the manipulation would show up as a change in the balance for provisions for risks and expenses. Provided this is well enough analysed in the notes to the accounts, the analyst can see whether there has been a net increase or decrease in provisions, without necessarily having enough information to know what exactly has happened – but an analyst attending a road show could ask questions. Equally, the cash flow statement usually includes a reconciliation between accounting net profit and operating cash flows. The effect on the profit and loss account of changes in provisions will also be visible here, because they do not affect cash flows and have therefore to be highlighted in the reconciliation between profit and cash.

Cookie jar reserves

One of the accounting "hot spots" that we are considering this morning is accounting for restructuring charges and restructuring reserves. A better title would be accounting for general reserves, contingency reserves, rainy day reserves or cookie jar reserves.

Accounting for so-called restructurings has become an art form. Some companies like the idea so much that they establish restructuring reserves every year. Why not? Analysts seem to like the idea of recognizing as a liability today, a budget of expenditures planned for the next year or next several years in down-sizing, right-sizing, or improving operations, and portraying that amount as a special, below-the-line charge in the current period's income statement. This year's earnings are happily reported in press releases as "before charges". CNBC analysts and commentators talk about earnings "before charges". The financial press talks about earnings before "special charges". (Funny, no one talks about earnings before credits – only charges). It's as if special charges are not real. Out of sight, out of mind ...

The occasion of a merger also spawns the wholesale establishment of restructuring or merger reserves. The ingredients of the merger reserves and merger charges look like the makings of a sausage. In the Enforcement Division, I have seen all manner and kind of things that ordinarily would be charged to operating earnings instead being charged "below the line". Write-offs of the carrying amounts of bad receivables. Write-offs of cost of obsolete inventory. Write-downs of plant and equipment costs, which, miraculously at the date of the merger, become non-recoverable, whereas those same costs were considered recoverable the day before the merger. Write-offs of previously capitalised costs such as goodwill, which all of a sudden are not recoverable because of a merger. Adjustments to bring warranty liabilities up to snuff. Adjustments to bring claim liabilities in line with management's new view of settling or litigating cases. Adjustments to bring environmental liabilities up to snuff or in line with management's new view of the manner in which the company's obligations to comply with EPA will be satisfied. Recognition of liabilities to pay for future services by investment bankers, accountants and lawyers. Recognition of liabilities for officers' special bonuses. Recognition of liabilities for moving people. For training people. For training people not yet hired. For retraining people. Recognition of liabilities for moving costs and refurbishing costs. Recognition of liabilities for new software that may be acquired or written, for ultimate sale to others. Or some liabilities that go by the title "other".

It is no wonder that investors and analysts are complaining about the credibility of the numbers.

Source: Speech by Walter P. Schuetze, Chief Accountant, Enforcement Division, US Securities and Exchange Commission, 22 April 1999
http: www.sec.gov/news/speeches/spch276.htm

A variant on this technique is known as 'big bath' accounting. This is most frequently applied when a group takes over a new subsidiary but may also occur when there is a change of chief executive. The idea is that the acquiring group, or the new chief executive, identifies over-valued assets (and under-valued liabilities) and makes a once and for all provision for these. This involves a major charge against profits but is explained to analysts as an exceptional year where a major cleaning-up exercise (big bath) has been done.

The advantage of this is that future depreciation charges will be lower (and therefore profits higher), or that excess provisions are available to boost future profits, but at the same time the current share price is often not affected. In fact if analysts accept the argument they have been given, the share price may even rise despite the disastrous immediate effect on profit of the write-offs, because the market expects even better results in the future.

Is income smoothing a good thing or a bad thing?

This is difficult to say. On the positive side, theorists argue that 'clean surplus accounting' (profits after smoothing) are a very good guide to long-term profitability, even if the year on year result has been managed. They say that the management have the best grasp of the real underlying capabilities of the group, and they will manipulate the profits to fit into their view of the long-term growth of the group. Consequently the 'managed' profits are a reliable indicator of long-term performance.

On the negative side, people point out that the markets are misled by income smoothing. They claim that often when a company goes broke or is taken over in disastrous circumstances, this follows on a period of profit manipulation which built up market expectations well beyond the capabilities of the company. Some standard-setters work to correct this, and say that the market should have as much information as possible and be allowed to make up its own mind.

Supplementary information

Another debate which is different in principle, but where the issues are related, is the question of the extent to which corporate preparers should interpret their financial data and present their view of it, as against simply providing raw data and leaving the professional analyst to make a judgment about it. An example would be provisions for liabilities: supposing a company is being sued by a customer, it could either make a provision for its own best estimate of the likely cost outcome, or it could simply make a disclosure in the notes that a case had been brought against it and provide information about the nature of the case. The analyst could then decide what adjustment to make.

Sometimes supplementary disclosures are a way of dealing with something which is too difficult to measure reliably because, for example, not enough information is yet known. Sometimes the disclosure may also be a way of informing the investor by providing information which does not necessarily relate to the year on which the company is reporting but may have an impact on future years.

In jargon terms, accounting talks about 'contingent liabilities' and 'post-balance sheet events'. The IASC has a single standard, IAS 10 *Contingencies and events occurring after the balance sheet date*, which covers both these issues. IAS10 defines a contingency as 'a condition or situation, the ultimate outcome of which, gain or loss, will be confirmed only on the occurrence, or non-occurrence, of one or more uncertain future events'.

Generally speaking, any company has an ongoing bundle of obligations, contracts and operations. It is the fact that the company is a continuing business which makes the annual profit of necessity an estimate based on a number of assumptions about the future. The contingencies standard in effect says that, as long as future foreseeable events are expected to be profitable, there is no need to reflect them in the accounts, and indeed prudence requires that future profits are not recognized in advance. However, future losses are another matter entirely.

If a company has a loss-making division, then this would not generally qualify as requiring a contingency note disclosure, but one would expect that the chairman's statement or review of operations would make clear that this is the case, and what action is being taken to deal with it. However, the outcome of a legal case such as being pursued for anti-competitive behaviour by the European Commission would certainly qualify as something which needed treatment in the accounts.

IAS 10

8. The amount of a contingent loss should be recognised as an expense and a liability if:

   (a) it is probable that future events will confirm that, after taking into account any related probable recovery, an asset has been impaired or a liability incurred at the balance sheet date; and

   (b) a reasonable estimate of the resulting loss can be made.

9. The existence of a contingent losss should be disclosed in the financial statements if either of the conditions in paragraph 8 is not met, unless the possibility of a loss is remote.

The question which next arises is, if there is a foreseeable future loss, should we disclose it in the accounts, or do we need actually to recognize the amount of the loss in the accounts ? This is dealt with in IAS 37 *Provisions, contingent liabilities and contingent assets*. Broadly, the standard recognizes four different situations where some event has already taken place (e.g. signing a contract), and a loss may arise:

1. **Executory contract.** An executory contract is one where the company has entered into an agreement but fulfilment of the terms has not been completed (and perhaps not started). Most businesses have many of these, and if the business is continuing, you would expect at any given moment that there would be sales agreements, purchases etc. at varying stages of completion. IAS 37 says these need no special treatment except if such a contract is particularly 'onerous' – i.e. where the expected costs of meeting the contract are greater than the expected benefits, in which case it would fall into one of the following categories.

2. **Clear liability, but where the amount and timing of costs is uncertain.** Here the company should make a provision – expense an estimated figure in the income statement and carry forward a provision in the balance sheet, against which the expense will be offset when it arises.

3. **Possible liability, or liability where the amount involved is so uncertain as to make an estimate impossible.** The company should disclose a contingent liability in the notes to the accounts.

4. A liability which is possible but unlikely to cause an outflow of assets – no disclosure.

This information is clearly important to the analyst in forming an opinion about the future profitability of the business. At the same time, it is sometimes quite sensitive information whose disclosure may have wider consequences for the company than simply influencing analysts' forecasts. A disclosure that the company is being pursued in the courts for causing environmental damage or infringing other company patents would have a considerable negative public relations impact.

Contingencies

The operations and earnings of the Group continue, from time to time and in varying degrees, to be affected by political, legislative, fiscal and regulatory developments, including those relating to environmental protection, in the countries in which it operates. The industries in which the Group is engaged are also subject to physical risks of various kinds. The nature and frequency of these developments and events, not all of which are covered by insurance, as well as their effect on future operations and earnings are not predictable.

Group companies are defendants in various legal actions. In the opinion of management, after taking appropriate legal advice, the results of such actions will not have a material effect on the Group's financial position.

Source: Extract: Annual Report, F Hoffmann-La Roche Ltd
www.roche.com

A more specialist disclosure is events occurring after the balance sheet date. While multinationals try to publish their accounts as quickly as possible after the financial year end, it is difficult to finalize the accounts of all subsidiaries, obtain auditor approval and then consolidate the accounts in under three months, and many companies take up to six months to do this. Potentially this means that events may take place between the financial year end and the publication of the accounts which have a bearing upon the future of the company. IAS 10 requires disclosure of any event taking place in this period which would affect users ability to make decisions or evaluate the company.

Financial instruments

A specific problem which has become increasingly important in the past decade is the ability of companies to enter into forward deals to buy or sell, to borrow or lend, to issue shares or buy back shares etc. This is the world of financial instruments where the markets are in theory being used to reduce risk because they enable companies to match their risk with a company which has an opposite risk. For example, your company has a US dollar loan to repay in five years, and has revenues in Deutschmarks. The market matches that with another company which has a Deutschmark loan to repay in five years and has revenues in US dollars – you agree an acceptable rate and swap the obligation to repay. This enables both companies to cancel the risk of the exchange rates moving against them. Certainly they lose the potential for gain at the same time, but this is normal – the lower the risk, the lower the potential gain (and the lower the potential loss).

However, this idyllic scenario is an oversimplification and the markets do not always work out the problems correctly. As far as commercial operating companies are concerned, sometimes they receive bad advice, and make losses (famously this happened to Procter and Gamble). Sometimes executives look at the upside potential of the currency or commodity markets and are tempted to think they could be making money for their company. They stop trying simply to reduce the company's risk and start trying to bet against the market, occasionally with disastrous results. Famously this happened with Sumitomo Corporation and its copper trader who tried to influence the copper markets by taking major positions, and lost the company millions of dollars in the end (as well as conducting various frauds to obtain the cash resources to pay for the trading). It happened with Metallgesellschaft and oil futures.

The position is much more serious with banks, although these are fortunately outside the scope of this book. The banks are often the intermediaries in the market place and sometimes accept to take on risks expecting to be able to find a counter-risk and not doing so, or occasionally just betting on the way the market was moving (e.g Nick Leeson and the collapse of Barings Bank).

Nokia

Fair value of financial instruments

The following table presents the carrying amounts and fair values of the Group's financial instruments outstanding at 31 December 1998 and 1997. The carrying amounts in the table are included in the balance sheet under the indicated captions, except for derivatives, which are included in amounts receivable and accounts payable and accrued liabilities. The fair value of a financial instrument is defined as the amount at which the instrument could be exchanged in a current transaction between willing parties, other than in a forced or liquidation sale.

MFIM	Carrying amount	1998 fair value	Carrying amount	1997 fair value
Financial assets				
Cash and cash equivalents	17,188	17,277	12,247	12,260
Receivables	17,691	17,691	10,637	10,637
Investments in other shares	445	885	453	548
Other non-current assets	202	202	195	195
Financial liabilities				
Accounts payable	7,831	7,831	5,188	5,188
Short term borrowings	4,158	4,158	3,008	3,008
Long term interest-bearing liabilities	1,530	1,683	1,348	1,473
Off balance sheet instruments				
Currency options purchased	133	133	41	41
Currency options written	−95	−95	−45	−45
Forward foreign exchange contracts	875	875	−152	−152
Interest rate swaps	7	33	10	30
Interest FRAs and futures	—	—	—	2

Source: NOKIA Financial statements 1998, Notes to the Consolidated financial statements (extract)

Fortunately most commercial companies are not heavily involved in financial instruments, but the publicity given to the major losses which have been run up in this sort of area have caused investors and analysts to call for much more information about company involvement. Unfortunately this has proved very difficult to regulate, not least because companies which make widespread use of commodity markets, for example, see it as unnecessarily onerous and potentially damaging in competitive terms, to disclose their dealings. Equally there are problems about (a) how to value futures contracts, and (b) whether a relevant current valuation should be brought into historical cost accounts. Preparers argue that the final settlement value of a futures contract cannot be known until settlement because the markets are volatile. Consequently, potential losses recognized prior to settlement may never be realized and are misleading. The current value of a contract is not necessarily any guide to its future value.

Another problem in this area is the question of whether a financial instrument has been entered into as a hedge for another transaction. For example, if a company has to pay a US dollar sum in two years, it could enter into a forward contract to buy US dollars. This would in effect be a hedge of its exchange rate risk and would enable it to lock into the exchange rate guaranteed by the forward contract. The economic argument is that transactions and their related hedges should be accounted for the same way and balancing gains and losses be offset against each other. This means that in regulating financial instrument disclosures one should potentially have one rule for financial instruments which are either entered into for speculative reasons or as part of general trading policy and another rule for those which are entered into as hedges of specific transactions. Regulators do not like rules which enable corporates to defer accounting for losses, even if there is a related profit due at the end of the contract, but corporates resent recognizing 'paper losses' when the overall arrangement is neutral in profit and loss terms.

The US has a measurement standard which is not yet in effect and a disclosure standard. The IASC similarly has a disclosure standard (IAS32) in effect and a provisional measurement standard (IAS 39) which comes into effect for years beginning on or after January 2001. A number of standard-setters are members of the Joint Working Group on financial instruments which is working towards agreeing a solution which can be applied by all countries.

IAS 32 *Financial Instruments: disclosure and presentation*

47. For each class of financial asset, financial liability and equity instrument, both recognised and unrecognised, an enterprise should disclose:

    (a) information about the extent and nature of the financial instruments, including significant terms and conditions that may affect the amount, timing and uncertainty of future cash flows; and

    (b) the accounting policies and methods adopted, including the criteria for recognition and the basis of measurement applied.

Some financial instruments, such as where a company receives a loan, have an immediate balance sheet effect, and are in the IASC jargon 'recognized' instruments. They may also have an 'unrecognized' or off balance sheet effect if, for example, they are denominated in a foreign currency, and therefore the future repayment amount is unknown. Other financial instruments, such as a contract to buy or sell commodities or currencies in the future, have no immediate balance sheet effect since no money changes hands when the contract is entered into, but they may involve a loss in due course.

In broad terms, financial instrument measurement rules argue that outstanding contracts, whether on or off balance sheet in historical cost terms, should be brought into the balance sheet as current value. This is known as 'marking to market' and consists of asking what is the buying or selling value of the contract at balance sheet date, and if that involves a gain or loss, bringing this into the result for the year for the company.

You can see that this is a difficult issue for companies because, amongst other things, it changes the notion of profit which they are used to. In the early part of the twentieth century, a profit was a simple enough concept – you bought sheet metal, you stamped it into ashtrays, you sold the ashtrays. The difference between the sales and your costs was your profits, after allowing for usage of machinery. In the twenty-first century the concept of profit is more complicated, involving a more sophisticated way of trading (e.g. using financial instruments to reduce risk) and a more sophisticated appreciation of the company's obligations and potential.

Environmental disclosures

Part of this change in attitudes involves the company's relationship with society in general and in particular how the company impacts upon the physical environment. Environmental disclosures by companies are at an early stage, but very few large companies do not make reference somewhere to their environmental policies. We can distinguish two kinds of environmental reporting:

1. information designed to reassure investors and others;
2. environmental costs brought into the financial statements.

Accounting standard-setters have so far not addressed this sort of issue, but a number of professional accounting bodies have produced guidelines and the United Nations inter-governmental group of experts on international standards of accounting and reporting (ISAR) published detailed recommendations in 1998 which remain the most thorough review of the area, but have no regulatory authority.

The absence of regulation leaves companies a free hand in determining what they publish, with the consequence that information is not generally comparable from company to company and is not audited. Most companies are moving towards addressing issues such as how they treat water, whether they emit gases, how they deal with recycling packaging and how they use natural resources in general. Some just publish a small note (see Nestlé example opposite), while others, such as British Telecom, issue a separate document with enormous detail.

Nestlé

Environment

During 1998 Nestlé continued its broad-based efforts for protection of the environment within its spheres of activity.

Using the framework of the Nestlé Environmental Management System, Nestlé carried out a comprehensive world wide factory environmental audit. The audit allowed a thorough evaluation of its key environmental accomplishments since the last such audit, as well as an inventory of its global environmental projects.

Results of the audit confirmed that water management, the reduction of air emissions and the improvement in solid waste recovery continue to be the top environmental priorities. Activities in these areas included diminished water consumption, the construction and expansion of waste water treatment facilities, specific projects targeted at the protection of the ozone layer, measures to reduce the greenhouse effect and solid waste management programmes that involved recycling and energy recovery. The audit clearly demonstrated Nestlé's continuous pattern of investment in specific environmental measures in its factories, an investment that has averaged 100m SFr annually. In addition substantial amounts were expended as part of regular capital investment projects and factory environmental operating costs. Examples of these additional expenditures included environmental aspects related to factory construction and renovation, environmental training of personnel and maintenance costs for waste water treatment facilities.

Commitment to environmentally sound business practices

During 1998 Nestlé continued its packaging source reduction efforts. Figures for 1991 to 1998 show that the Company, without compromising product quality, saved, on a world wide basis, close to 150,000 tonnes of packaging material, representing 250m SFr.

The achievements realised by Nestlé stand as clear evidence of its commitment to environmentally sound business practices. Furthermore, Nestlé participates actively in the work of several organisations dealing with this subject; for example, Nestlé is a founder member of the World Business Council for Sustainable Development (WBCSD) in Geneva, and contributes to the working group "sustainable development" in the town of Vevey.

Source: Nestlé Annual Report 1998, extract from Business Review

---

Should analysts be interested in this information? Well, yes, because viewed from a strictly capitalist standpoint, we are moving further into a political environment where governments are insisting that 'the polluter pays'. This means that any company which has caused pollution, intentionally or otherwise, may become liable to clean up the countryside and compensate people who are badly affected. Hidden pollution is therefore, aside from social considerations, very bad from an investor's point of view because it may mean a severe drain on future earnings. An extreme case in point is the settlements reached in the US between state governments and the tobacco industry for large payments to be made to compensate the government for healthcare costs caused by treating smoking-related diseases.

This brings us back to formal accounting. A potential clean-up or compensation liability should be addressed in compiling the financial statements as either the object of a provision or disclosure of a contingent liability. Some companies, and particularly oil companies, now provide for decommissioning costs alongside the depreciation of mineral resources. In other words, they now recognize that they cannot just close down a well and go away, they need to make good the land as far as possible. Since this is an estimable cost of using the mineral resource, it should be spread over the period when the asset is used. Increasingly we should expect this approach to be applied to factories as well.

There is some disagreement as to how such decomissioning provisions should be applied. The simple way is to charge an amount each year to the income statement and build a liability year on year. However, the IASC says that if there is a liability, full provision should be made from the start, but for the damage already done. As use of the site progresses, further provisioning should be done.

Intellectual capital

There are fashions in corporate evaluation as in everything else, and one of the current fashions is to consider the value of the 'intellectual capital' of a group. Essentially the argument is that while physical assets (such as a city centre sales location or an efficient factory) may be important for the group, intellectual assets (patents, brands, staff know-how, research and development, customer loyalty) are possibly even more so: you can build a new factory in a few months for a finite amount of money, but a brand takes years and the cost cannot be forecast reliably. Intellectual capital is even more important, obviously, in a service industry where it relates to the quality and nature of the service, which in turn is the product you are selling. Increasingly there is a perception that business now changes rapidly, and the ability to develop new products or adapt methods quickly is considered to be part of the intellectual capital of the group. Intellectual capital fits into the framework of analyst's concerns about assessing the quality of the management and the quality of the assets under their control.

How do companies convey this information? We discussed the difficulties of measuring intangible assets in a historical cost framework in Chapter 5. There are several problems. Firstly, a company incurs costs often over several years in product research, staff development and related areas, without being able to tie these costs to an identifiable asset (source of future cash flows) until towards the end of the process, so these costs are taken directly to the income statement. Secondly, where staff development is concerned, the company does not 'control' the asset: a trained person usually has the right to leave the company, so money spent training them cannot be regarded as an asset in accounting terms. Thirdly, a company may hire people who have the skills needed (who have themselves invested in their personal development by doing an MBA) and so there is no acquisition cost available to be capitalized.

Clearly traditional accounting does not provide the techniques for this kind of asset, and that is not surprising when you remember that financial reporting was developed in the nineteenth century. So far there is therefore no way of reflecting this through accounting measures in the annual report. However, it is an issue which some companies are trying to address internally and where some discussion should be expected somewhere in the annual report.

The Measurement and Management of Intellectual Capital: an introduction

It is recognised that the intellectual capital of a firm plays a significant role in creating competitive advantage, and thus managers and other stakeholders in organizations are asking, with increasing frequency, that its value be measured and reported for planning, control, reporting and evaluation purposes. However, at this point, there is still a great deal of room for experimentation in quantifying and reporting on the intellectual capital of the firm.

Source: IFAC Handbook 1999, extract from summary of study published in October 1998

Summary

In this chapter we have looked at a number of issues in supplementary disclosures. We noted that the fashion is for more and more disclosures, not only in the annual statements but also through the informal medium of investor and analyst briefings by the company. In particular we have looked at the problem of anticipating future costs, both in a general sense as provisions or disclosure of contingencies, and in the specific area of financial instruments and environmental costs.

Questions

1. Why is it important to management to manipulate the earnings figures so that the group appears to return steadily increasing profits?
2. Discuss why the existence of contingencies is important to the financial statement analyst, making reference to environmental issues and financial instruments.
3. Explain what is meant by intellectual capital and discuss what an analyst can do to make an assessment of the intellectual capital of a particular group.

15 International taxation

The object of this chapter is to give you a working overview of taxation. Generally speaking, governments have a bigger stake in companies than do shareholders (in terms of receiving cash flows from the company), and yet not all companies pay as much attention to tax minimization as they might, nor do company executives have a clear idea of where tax bites in a company's cost structure.

This chapter will first look at the different kinds of tax and how they are levied within a single jurisdiction, and then look at issues which specifically concern multinationals and cross-border activities.

Introduction

The number of taxes to which a company is subject varies enormously from country to country and depends partly upon political structure and partly upon historical precedent. In Europe a study for the European Commission found that in 1989 France had 76 different taxes and levies, while the lowest number (Spain) was 19 (Iain Stitt (1993) "Corporate taxation in the EC". *British Tax Review*, No. 2, 75). The way in which taxes are collected varies widely as well. From a company perspective, we can identify the main types of taxation which are 'costs' to the company (accountants would say that corporate income-based taxes are not a cost as such because they are only levied when there is profit, so they are a distribution of profit. However, assuming that we expect a company to be profitable, we should try to maximize after tax cash flows for the shareholders, and tax represents a negative flow):

1. social security;
2. local/regional taxes;
3. national taxes on profit.

Within the European Union, Value Added Tax (VAT) is a major source of tax revenue, and companies collect this for the state, but technically this is a tax on the consumer, not on the company, in the same way as sales taxes in the US and other countries.

Social security. Here there is a great difference between countries in the extent to which they levy contributions from employers and employees based on the amount of pay.

In Switzerland, for example, the deductions are relatively low, but the employee is obliged to take out compulsory private medical insurance, whereas in France the deductions are high, and relatively little is left to the individual. There is also a great variation in contributions to pension schemes, with some countries preferring a system in which the state plays a major role and others preferring to participate in private sector schemes. This means that in some countries payroll-based charges can amount to an additional 50 per cent on top of gross salaries, whereas in others the employee expects to pay more – and may expect a higher salary. Payroll-based taxes and contributions to pension schemes are generally accounted for in the financial statements as part of personnel cost, and are therefore invisible both to the external analyst and often the internal manager.

Local/regional taxes. Here again there is a wide variety of taxes and methods of collecting them. In federations, such as Germany or Switzerland, regional political units (Länder, Cantons) are able to levy taxes on corporate profits, as also are municipalities. This means that corporate income taxes may be split three ways: local municipality, regional political unit and federal government (and they are not necessarily calculated off the same profit base). All of these taxes, since they are profit based, will appear in the financial statements as a deduction from shareholder profit.

However, in other countries, there are different ways of channelling money to municipalities. In France they receive the proceeds from annual vehicle taxes, and also levy a tax which is based on the capital structure of the company. In the UK, municipalities receive tax based on the value of property occupied by a company in their jurisdiction. These are not income taxes as such and do not therefore normally appear in the income statement as a tax but as a cost of property or of running motor vehicles etc.

National profit taxes. These are the most visible part of company taxation. Governments use this kind of taxation both to raise revenue and to encourage (or to penalize) particular kinds of behaviour by companies. The calculation of profit is done according to tax rules, rather than accounting rules, but one of the most important shaping forces in accounting is the relationship between these and in particular the degree to which in any jurisdiction, the calculation of taxable profit is limited by what is in the published accounts.

In most countries, even those such as Germany or France which are reputed to have a very close relationship between accounting profit and tax profit, the calculation of taxes on profits is based on an approach where there is a reconciliation statement between accounting profit and taxable profit:

Accounting profit before tax

Add back: disallowed expenses such as entertaining, fines, excess depreciation, excess provisions

Deduct: special allowances for capital investment, environmental protection etc.

= Taxable profit

A particular problem in corporate taxation is that of the potential double taxation of dividends. Suppose a country levies 40 per cent corporate profit tax and then the company pays what is left as dividend to its shareholders, and that personal income tax is also 40 per cent. That means that the dividend (60 per cent of the original profit) will be subject to a second 40 per cent tax, which amounts to another 24 per cent of the original profit. The latter has therefore been taxed in total at 64 per cent. This is a major disincentive to investors and different countries find different solutions to the problem. One way is to tax profits which are to be paid to shareholders at a lower rate than those retained in the company. Another way is to give shareholders a tax credit with their dividend.

Value Added Tax is applied throughout the European Union and the European Commission in fact receives a small proportion (less than 2 per cent) of the proceeds of the national rate. Companies charge VAT to their customers and are themselves charged VAT on their purchases. However, a corporation separates out VAT received from customers and VAT paid to suppliers in its accounting and every month (or three months depending upon jurisdiction) pays the difference between the two to the state. Consequently, a company's accounts exclude VAT for reporting purposes, both inside and outside the company.

VAT is therefore not a tax as such upon companies, but it does bear upon them to an extent. Firstly, there is the administration of VAT which involves elaborate accounting systems to measure and control VAT payments. Secondly, there is the cost of maintaining the knowledge of staff and using outside experts to deal with changes and complex transactions. And thirdly, there is the cash flow problem. A company that sells on credit and is obliged to settle monthly with the VAT authorities will be in effect paying to the authorities VAT from customers which has been invoiced but which the customer has at that time not paid. There is a disguised cash flow effect which can increase a company's capital requirements considerably.

Deferred taxation

The fact that there are differences between the accounting measure of profit and the tax authorities' measure gives rise to an accounting problem if these differences are substantial. In effect there are two kinds of difference between accounting and taxable profit:

1. permanent differences;
2. reversing timing differences.

The permanent differences arise because, for example, the tax authorities do not accept some expenses as a deduction from profits. Examples of this would be fines, in some countries bribes, sometimes entertaining or what the authorities consider to be unnecessarily expensive consumption such as supplying managers with luxury cars or holding board meetings in holiday resorts. These are simply 'disallowed' and cause taxable profit for the year to be higher than accounting profit and do not call for any special accounting.

---

22 Deferred Income Taxes

Aggregate deferred tax amounts are summarized below:

December 31 (in millions)	1998	1997
Assets		
GE	$5,309	$4,891
GECS	5,305	4,320
Liabilities		
GE	5,059	4,576
GECS	14,895	13,286
	19,954	17,862
Net deferred tax liability	9,340	8,651

Source: General Electric 1998 Annual Report (extract)
www.ge.com

The reversing timing differences, however, present a difficulty. Some jurisdictions offer high tax depreciation at times, either just to encourage business to invest in general or to encourage a particular kind of investment which the government thinks is important (environmental protection, high technology etc.). If this accelerated depreciation can be claimed without using the high rate in the accounts, this gives rise to a reversing timing difference. The asset will be fully depreciated over its useful life in the accounts; however, the tax paid by the company will be artificially low early in the asset's life, but later the asset will be depreciated in the accounts with no tax deduction available.

To illustrate the problem let us look at an exaggerated model. Let us say that a company buys an asset in 20X1 for $10,000, intending to depreciate, for shareholder purposes, over two years, but the tax authorities will allow the whole depreciation in the first year. If the company's profit before depreciation is $25,000 in each year, the shareholder profit in both years would be $20,000 ($25,000 less $5,000 depreciation on asset). However, the tax computations would be:

20X1		$
Net profit before tax	20,000	
add back Depreciation	5,000	
deduct Special allowance	(10,000)	
Taxable profit		15,000
Tax due at 50 per cent		7,500
20X2		
Net profit before tax	20,000	
add back Depreciation	5,000	
deduct Capital allowance	—	
Taxable profit		25,000
Tax due at 50 per cent		12,500

Returning to the shareholder profit and loss account, the figures would be:

	19X1	*20X2*
	$	*$*
Net income before tax	20,000	20,000
Corporation tax	(7,500)	(12,500)
Net income after tax	12,500	7,500

The result of the timing difference is that the same net income before tax yields quite different results over the two years. So the question is: should that be reported to shareholders as given above, or should the tax saving in year 1 ($2,500 or 50 per cent of the depreciation difference) be set aside and carried forward to year 2 to offset against the year 2 tax charge and equalize the accounting charge for tax?

Broadly, current practice is that where there is a material timing difference, this should be provided for in the accounts. So in the case above, the income statement for 20X1 should be constructed:

Taxable profit		20,000
Taxation paid	7,500	
Deferred taxation provision	2,500	
Total tax		(10,000)
Profit after tax		10,000

The \$2,500 deferred tax provision will appear in the balance sheet at the end of 20X1. The following year the timing difference reverses and the provision is released to the income statement:

Taxable profit		20,000
Taxation paid	12,500	
less Provision	(2,500)	
Total tax		(10,000)
Profit after tax		10,000

For analytical purposes, all you need to know is that a deferred tax provision in the balance sheet represents the fact that profit for accounting purposes has in the past been higher than that for tax purposes and the provision is there to compensate for future taxation on that difference. Deferred tax will normally arise in individual company accounts in jurisdictions where the relationship between accounting profit and taxable profit is reasonably loose.

It should also normally appear in group accounts prepared according to IASC rules. Companies based in jurisdictions like Germany or France where there is a close relationship between accounting profit and tax should restate the individual company accounts for consolidation purposes. Excess depreciation or provisions which have been introduced for tax minimization purposes should normally be corrected during the consolidation process, and deferred tax provisions introduced if appropriate.

IAS 12 *Income Taxes* deals with the issue of accounting for deferred taxation. Its details are beyond the scope of this course, but essentially it addresses what it designates as 'temporary differences' between the balance sheet value of assets and liabilities and their tax value.

International taxation

The general rule in taxation is that a profit is taxed in the country where the transaction takes place, although this is obviously more complicated for cross-border trading and Internet sales. Generally it is then the country where the buyer resides which determines tax, even if for the moment Internet sales are largely untaxed. From a corporate perspective, tax is administered on a company-by-company basis, and calculated on individual subsidiaries' accounts, not on the group accounts as a whole. This is sometimes an issue that MBA students find bizarre. While the whole point of consolidated accounts is to look at the company as an economic whole, and from a management perspective one should never lose sight of the overall group, from a tax perspective, the focus is exactly the opposite: tax sees the group as a collection of more or less unconnected activities, and deals with it subsidiary by subsidiary.

Consequently, it is useful for a multinational to try to compartmentalize its activities within each tax jurisdiction by forming separate companies and retaining clear records of transactions for discussion with different tax authorities. As noted earlier, many corporations use worldwide systems for uniform internal accounting but then retain local specialists in each country (often in fact the auditor, where independence rules allow this) to recalculate the figures in line with local measurement rules and tax needs.

International business presents both threats and opportunities as far as tax is concerned. The fact that national tax authorities cannot go outside their jurisdiction enables the corporation to structure international transactions in the most tax efficient way. On the other hand, mishandling can cause a revenue to be taxed in two different countries, or an expense not to be accepted as a deduction from profit.

Tax planning by multinational corporations

Tax planning is essential in all strategic decisions because of the impact of tax on their worldwide operations. This takes in not only corporate profits taxes, but also personal taxes, social security charges and indirect taxes. Management will invariably wish to focus on tax rate risk and tax risk management.

Source: Terry Browne, Deloitte & Touche, extract from article in *Accounting & Business*, September 1998, p.13

Leaving aside tax havens, most countries have entered into double tax treaties with main trading partner nations. These deal with issues like the taxation of international transactions, the rules for withholding taxes on royalties, interest and dividends and similar items. So if a company is thinking about doing business in a country other than its main base, one of the first things to do is check whether there is a double tax treaty and what are its provisions.

The double tax treaty will normally have a section dealing with 'transfer prices'. These are the prices, often very difficult to calculate, at which goods and services change hands between subsidiaries of the same group. Artificially fixing the transfer prices is a way of determining where profits are taxed. Supposing a company makes a machine in Country A (tax rate 50 per cent) for a cost of $10,000 and sells it to a fellow subsidiary in Country B (tax rate 25 per cent) for $11,000. This subsidiary sells it in turn to a subsidiary in Country C (tax rate 40 per cent) for $18,000, and that subsidiary sells it to the customer for $20,000.

The taxable profit will be distributed:

	Profit	*Rate*	*Amount*
Country A	1,000	50	500
Country B	7,000	25	1,750
Country C	2,000	40	800
Total	10,000	30.5	3,050

The group has been able to reduce consolidated tax by artifically fixing the transfer prices and flowing the transaction through a low tax country. Of course, the tax authorities are well aware of this possibility, so the double tax treaty usually states that transfer prices must be 'at arms' length' (i.e. what an independent buyer would have to pay) or at market rates. It is not always easy to prove these prices and companies are well advised to reflect carefully on these issues because most tax jurisdictions can go back many years in a tax investigation, and levy penal rates of tax if they do not agree the basis of the transfer price. It remains, for all that, an interesting corner of profit management.

Related to this is the issue of what expenses can be charged by head office or other centres against subsidiaries. Typically a multinational has regional management centres which are not themselves revenue generating. Equally it has research and development activities which probably involve cost being incurred in one jurisdiction and subsequently a new product or process being exploited in other jurisdictions. The same is true of advertising – maintaining a worldwide brand is expensive and has effects everywhere. If your company takes advertising at (say) a football world cup in France which is televised all over the world, does the French subsidiary pay that, or head office, or who?

This is a problem for internal management purposes in terms of relating costs to revenues, but it is also a problem with the tax authorities. If your R&D is based in the UK but exploited in the US, the UK tax authorities are not likely to accept that the cost should all be offset against UK tax. But the US authority may refuse to accept any expenses either in the sense that the costs were not incurred in the US.

Transfer-pricing: the key international issue?

There is little doubt that (government tax) authorities have become more adept at countering the "profit-shifting" aspects of transfer-pricing practices and are strengthening their statutory powers with ever more extensive and complex legislation and regulations.

To strengthen the tax authorities' position, regulations typically introduce specific rules to determine arm's length prices and require that taxpayers maintain very extensive records documenting the methods used to determine their transfer prices (which often necessitates the employment of teams of both in-house and outside counsel, accountants and economists). Provision is made as well for the imposition of very stringent penalties in case of non-compliance.

Source: Richard Casna, editor, *International Tax Report*, extract from article in *Accounting & Business*, February 1998, p.30

Basically flows between subsidiaries in different countries are easiest when structured according to the tax treaty: transfer prices for goods and services (but may be subject to justification, which is not always easy), royalties for use of intellectual property (brands, product manufacturing processes) and interest (in relation to financing). All of these are, though, with the proviso that the company may need to persuade the tax authorities that the level of charge is justified.

Tax havens

Tax havens have a small place in the corporate world, but they may well be expensive to use (you usually need to work through a local lawyer or accountant) and other tax jurisdictions usually have extensive powers to stop you sheltering profits in a haven. For example, if the UK considers that you have a controlled foreign corporation (CFC) in a jurisdiction which is on its list of havens, it will feel free to tax you in the UK on the profits of that CFC. If you do not provide accounts for the CFC, it will simply estimate the profits and tax accordingly. Tax havens do not generally benefit from double tax treaties with other countries.

Tax havens typically offer low tax or flat rate tax for companies which are resident there but whose activities are external to the haven (hence 'off-shore' companies). These can be used legitimately and effectively by a multinational to provide international services such as finance or insurance to itself. For example, an offshore finance vehicle will borrow on the international markets (guaranteed by the group) and then lend to fellow subsidiaries.

The tax haven lends itself also to the Internet business and it is surprising that more companies such as Internet sales companies or those with international transactions such as tour operators do not site themselves in tax havens. The costs are not negligible, and therefore the throughput needs to be substantial to create a saving on tax after professional costs.

In recent years a new kind of tax minimization opportunity has appeared – what are known as 'offshore financial centres'. These are a near relative of the tax haven, but with the difference that they have double tax treaties with major trading countries – they have a foot in both camps, as it were. Like a tax haven, their object is to attract corporate business whose operations take place outside the financial centre. Unlike the tax haven, they levy corporate taxes on income, but these are at a level which is sufficiently high for the developed countries not to treat the financial centre as a haven, but sufficiently low so as to still to be attractive to companies. Dublin is a financial centre in this sense, and Botswana has just joined the club, hoping to attract business as a regional centre for multinationals operating in sub-Saharan Africa.

Summary

This has been a short tour through the rather strange land of corporate taxation. The principal points to retain are that individual companies pay taxes to governments in a number of different ways. These can impact substantially upon business costs and need to be thoroughly reviewed at the project stage, not left until a new operation is up and running. Corporate income tax is calculated in quite a complicated way, and is linked to accounting profit, but always with some differences. Where accounting profit and taxable profit differ greatly, companies must make an accounting adjustment called deferred tax which represents tax on these differences.

Tax is levied on a country-by-country basis, which calls for a good deal of expenditure of resources to compile tax date and negotiate. The fact that multinationals usually have transactions which run through several subsidiaries and different countries presents tax planning opportunities and some risks in that national tax authorities do not necessarily agree with the company's way of calculating profits, nor with that of other tax authorities. Multinationals can make a limited use of tax havens and offshore financial centres to reduce their taxation.

Questions

1. Is all the tax which a group pays visible in the financial statements?
2. ZZ consultants have won a contract from the Russian government to advise on small company accounting regulation and to provide training for government officials and educators. Some of the contract will be performed by staff in ZZ's Moscow office, but they will be helped by staff transferred from their offices in Germany, the UK and Switzerland. If the rate of corporate income tax in Russia is 80 per cent, in Germany 60 per cent, in the UK 35 per cent and in Switzerland 25 per cent, how would you advise them to structure their internal transactions? Should all the staff to be used be transferred to the Moscow office, or should Moscow be invoiced from other locations with staff flown in and out to meet specific assignments?
3. For what purposes may a tax haven be profitably used by a multinational group?

16 Auditing and corporate governance

The subject of auditing and auditors was covered in Chapter 2 of this book. The object of this chapter is to set out a little more background information concerning external audit and the framework of corporate governance as they impact upon multinational groups. The chapter does not bear directly on the techniques of financial statement analysis, but is intended to broaden the knowledge base of analysts in respect of the financial statements and the constraints on corporate reporting. It will deal first with the subject of corporate governance, then the audit of group accounts and related issues of independence, audit committees, and finally internal control.

Corporate governance

In a small or medium-sized business, the owners are very often also the managers of the business, and prior to the Industrial Revolution, most business was run this way. It was only in the nineteenth century that a major change took place, as a result of the Industrial Revolution, and businesses started to become much larger. This had two consequences: large companies were financed by larger numbers of shareholders and so were less and less dominated by individual or family shareholders, and the 'professional manager' started to appear. This gives rise to what is known as an 'agency problem' – the owners of the business ('principals' in the jargon) had to find means to ensure that those whom they appointed to run the business ('agents') did so in a way that matched with shareholders' needs.

There are a number of ways of addressing this problem. One of the most frequent in the Anglo-Saxon world is to give top managers contracts by which their salaries vary according to how well they meet key shareholder objectives, such as increase in share price, or return on equity. However, accounting and audit also play a highly significant role. Historically the accounting statements were a means through which professional managers reported to shareholders on what they had done with the company over a twelve-month period, and in many countries audit was introduced as a means whereby a representative of the shareholders checked the accuracy of the accounts on behalf of the shareholders. It is not clear that this was originally a very effective way of checking on managers, and the evolution of accounting regulation and the audit profession has in part been a response to the need to create transparency in the accounts and confidence in their accuracy.

In current times the agency problem has been broadened out into the concept of corporate governance, which asks not only are company managers acting in the interests of their shareholders, but are they acting in the interests of a much wider group known as 'stakeholders'? This is an important shift in focus and involves a cultural change in what is expected of companies and their management. What it means is that the company can no longer be seen as an isolated unit whose central task is to make money for shareholders, and whose other obligations can be summarized as simply to meet legal requirements in all other areas, if they cannot be got round. Increasingly society is saying that multinationals are extremely powerful and rich entities, many of them more so than the governments of the world's smaller or economically weak states, and they are able to escape control because their structure is international while law is basically constrained to national boundaries. Such companies must be constrained to take into consideration the public interest as well as that of their shareholders, and there must be transparent systems of corporate governance to see that this is done.

Different countries have different views about corporate governance, but there have been many reports in the 1990s dealing with different countries, such as Viénot in France, Cadbury in the UK and many others. These have been followed in 1999 by an OECD report which aims to provide a framework for corporate governance.

Stakeholders in corporate governance

A key aspect of corporate governance is concerned with ensuring the external flow of capital to firms. Corporate governance is also concerned with finding ways to encourage the various stakeholders in the firm to undertake socially efficient levels of investment in firm-specific human and physical capital. The competitiveness and ultimate success of a corporation is the result of teamwork that embodies contributions from a range of different resource providers including investors, employees, creditors and suppliers. Corporations should recognise that the contributions of stakeholders constitute a valuable resource for building competitive and profitable companies. It is, therefore, in the long term interest of corporations to foster wealth-creating cooperation among stakeholders. The governance framework should recognise that the interests of the corporation are served by recognising the interests of stakeholders and their contribution to the long run success of the corporation.

Source: Extract from *OECD Principles of Corporate Governance*, 1999

Independent directors

Good corporate governance practices are now considered to involve the presence in the central decision-making unit of the company of a number of external or independent directors. In a system such as that of Germany where large companies have two boards, an executive board and a supervisory board, this function already exists, with the supervisory board exercising oversight over what the executive directors are doing. In countries where a unitary board is the norm such as France, the Netherlands and Italy, the recommendation is that a board should include a proportion of non-executive, or independent, directors whose function is simply to attend board meetings on a regular basis and monitor corporate behaviour.

In the best companies this monitoring function offers an opportunity for the company to emphasize its ethical behaviour by appointing high-profile figures who are completely independent of the business. However, neither the dual board system nor the unitary board with independent directors is foolproof. Famously, the supervisory board of Metallgesellschaft in Germany were unaware of the dealings of its US subsidiary in oil futures which cost it many millions of dollars to unwind; the supervisory board of SEAT in Spain (a Volkswagen subsidiary) were given incorrect figures by the company. Michael D. Eisner, chief executive of Walt Disney, has been accused by some commentators of appointing his personal friends and business associates to be independent directors of Disney. A report on accounting frauds by SEC-registered companies identifies what it calls 'grey' directors which it defines as independent directors who have a business connection with either the company or its executive directors.

Fraudulent Financial Reporting: 1987–1997

Approximately 60 per cent of the directors were insiders or "grey" directors (i.e. outside directors with special ties to the company or the management). Collectively the directors and officers owner nearly 1/3 of the companies' stock, with the CEO/President personally owning about 17 per cent. Nearly 40 per cent of the boards had not one director who served as an outside or grey director on another company's board.

Source: From results of study into a sample of cases of fraud pursued by the SEC, published by the Committee of Sponsoring Organizations of the Treadway Commission 1999

Aside from generally monitoring what the company is doing, the independent directors are increasingly asked to participate in sub-committees to deal with particular tasks. The most important are the Remuneration Committee and the Audit Committee. The idea of the remuneration committee is that executive directors should not be in a position to fix their own salaries, and this should be done by independent directors who make comparisons with other companies and ensure that the package offered is in line with the market and the good of the shareholders and others. It is not clear how well this works either, and the existence of remuneration committees has not stopped major shareholder criticisms of some pay proposals.

Independent directors

A survey carried out by the NOP research group on behalf of Ernst & Young and the Institute of Directors has revealed that approximately a third of the companies interviewed have no non-executive directors on their board currently and 82 per cent of these have no plans to employ this valuable additional resource in the future.

The survey reveals that the majority (57 per cent) of non-executive and executive directors from UK companies interviewed believe that independent directors' contribution to strategy is one of their most important roles on the board. The second and third most frequently mentioned attributes, in terms of importance, were their knowledge and independence.

Source: Extract from press release issued by Ernst & Young, September 1999

The audit committee is supposed to act as an intermediary between the board and the external auditors (and possibly internal auditors as well) on the basis that auditors should not be reporting management failings directly to the managers potentially concerned. We will look at audit committees in more detail later in this chapter.

Institutional shareholders

It has been argued that part of the need for formal corporate governance frameworks arises from the fact that the major shareholders in large multinationals are typically financial institutions (banks, insurance companies, fund managers, pension funds etc.). Historically this kind of shareholder has considered that they should not intervene in the management of the company directly. They have taken the view that they are making an investment to get a return, and if that return is not delivered, they take their investment elsewhere. This kind of passive shareholder approach is blamed for creating an environment where company management felt they could do what they liked as long as the share price held up.

However, this situation is changing, partly because the investment industry has wanted to respond to the criticisms, and partly because the individuals who invest in pension funds and collective investment vehicles are increasingly wanting an assurance that their money is not being used to invest in companies with whose behaviour they do not agree. The personal finance press is increasingly vociferous in raising these issues, and individuals are increasingly demanding that their money goes into 'ethical' investments. As a consequence, institutional investors are drawing up codes of conduct for companies, and some are now asking company boards to sign up to a code of conduct before the investment fund will buy any shares. This is, of course, another sign of the change in society's values and increases the pressure on companies to address these issues.

Statutory audit

The independent auditor has always had a role to play in corporate governance, and never more so than now when the multinational has subsidiaries all over the world, and only the Big Five audit firms have similar organizations which can check on the existence and activities of these vast networks. Essentially, the signature of a Big Five audit firm on a multinational's audit report is taken to be the guarantee of the accuracy and validity of the financial statements, and an assurance that there is nothing nasty hidden behind the bland comments of the chairman. The investment market places a very heavy reliance on the auditor's assurance – the analyst may modify the figures to compare with other companies, may make all sorts of adjustments for forecasting purposes, but the very existence of all the company's assets, its activities and their legality, and the main board's control over these is attested to by the auditor.

In fact the audit of a multinational group is a very difficult task and one which carries with it a great deal of legal and moral responsibility. In essence the audit of a multinational is no different from that of an individual company, since the consolidated accounts are simply a re-working of the financial statements of all the individual companies that make up the group. However, it is more complicated in that the subsidiaries are working in different legal environments, and the more complex the accounting web, the easier it is to 'lose' transactions. The auditor of the group accounts is responsible for any error in the group audit, even if such an error has arisen because of a mistake by the auditor of a subsidiary. Equally, multinationals are under pressure to publish their results as soon as possible after the year end, which means that the process of auditing and agreeing the accounts of the individual subsidiaries may have to take place within two months of the year end, leaving a further month to consolidate and agree the consolidation adjustments.

This leads to a situation where the large audit firms like to be the exclusive auditor of a multinational and all its subsidiaries. Critics say this is simply to build up their fee base, which may be true, but it is also true that using several different firms of auditors is necessarily more expensive because they need to have meetings to liaise with each other, and necessarily more risky because there is no one with an overview of the whole group. The Bank of Credit and Commerce International (BCCI) is a famous example of a group which operated as two separate but related networks, each network audited by a different Big Five auditor. After the collapse of BCCI it became apparent that there had been a 'black hole' between the two networks which was used to conceal fraudulent or illegal transactions.

Typically the audit of a multinational is a continuing operation where one year's audit leads into the next, and if doubtful issues are identified one year, they may well be subjected to a more intensive scrutiny the following year and so on. The auditor will attempt to identify the areas of the group which have the highest audit risk (operations in a difficult trading and credit environment, such as Russia, high volume of cash transactions, poor control environment, poor local accounting systems, high volume of foreign currency transactions etc.) and devote most resources to checking these. The auditor will also each year select particular areas for special investigation. These might be selected in response to worries expressed by the group's internal audit or accounting units, or may be selected more or less at random so that even a low-risk part of the group is occasionally subject to an intense scrutiny.

Fortunately the rules for the conduct of an international audit are less likely to be radically different from country to country than for accounting. While audit rules may differ quite radically even between developed countries, there is a set of international audit rules put out by the International Federation of Accountants (IFAC – see Chapter 2) which are often used for multinational audits, and in particular when the accounting rules used are those of the IASC. Analysts should check the audit report carefully, however, to see what rules have been applied. The standard audit report should specify both what accounting rules have been applied by the company and what auditing rules have been used by the auditor in conducting the audit. Beware terms like 'have been prepared subject to professional standards' which do not specify which professional standards. While auditing standards are much the same in developed countries, they are not uniform, and in developing countries may be fairly rudimentary.

Issues in international audit

That brings us to a delicate subject in international audit – how much reliance should you place on the financial statements of companies headquartered in developing or newly industrialized countries? These have been the subject of quite a lot of criticism, mostly as a consequence of the financial crisis in South-East Asia in the late 1990s. Here it became apparent that a number of companies had had their financial statements audited by Big Five firms, but had either used local accounting standards with a low degree of transparency or used International Accounting Standards while not complying fully with their requirements – using what is known as 'IASC-lite' in the trade.

The role of accounting in the East Asian financial crisis

There is now growing agreement that the failure and near failure of many financial institutions and corporations in the east Asian region resulted from a highly leveraged corporate sector, growing private sector reliance on foreign currency borrowing, and lack of transparency and accountability. Since financial statements act as the most reliable and easily accessible vehicle for dissemination of enterprise-level information, lack of adequate accounting disclosures prevented investors and creditors from receiving timely and necessary information for choosing between successful and potentially unsuccessful enterprises.

Accounting disclosures by financial institutions and corporations in most of the East Asian countries do not follow or comply with international accounting standards.

Source: M. Zubaidur Rahman, extract from report published by United Nations Conference on Trade and Development 1998

It became clear that many relevant bits of information had not been disclosed to investors – in particular, issues such as unhedged loans in strong currencies to finance investments which would generate cash flows in weak currencies. This was an important cause of a flight from the Asian markets, and the economic depression and collapse of many companies which followed. These deficiencies in reporting and auditing raised a number of questions. Firstly, should the Big Five sign clean audit reports of financial statements which do not conform with high international standards? The Big Five pointed out that the accounts made it clear that local standards had been followed, and analysts should be reminded that the first thing to do when looking at a company report is indeed to check what rules have been applied. However, the market sentiment was rather that the Big Five should maintain certain minimum standards.

This in turn raises another issue – to what extent is an audit by the same Big Five firm the same the world over? or, put another way, are the Big Five firms uniformly run and directed? In fact the firms are not multinational companies with pyramid-style reporting and authority chains. They are networks of national partnerships or similar structures which work together through varying mechanisms, but which lack any formal or legal means whereby an international board, as it were, can impose its will on a national partnership on all questions. It is rather like running a franchise operation such as McDonald's where some outlets are directly owned by head office and some are franchises, both regional and local, but without the right to specify in detail what is sold or how it is prepared.

Independence

A perpetual policy issue in audit is the independence of the auditor. Of course, the value of the modern audit depends partly upon the technical skills of the auditor and partly upon the independence and ethical qualities of the auditor. Without the competence and the distance from the management of the company, the audit report is worthless.

In some countries, such as Germany and France, the governments take the view that independence can only be obtained if the auditor performs only audit for the client and has no other relationship with the management. However, in many other countries, including Switzerland, the UK and the Netherlands, the auditor is free to sell other services to the same client, although in the UK the company must publish details of how much it paid for the audit and what other fees it paid the auditor.

FTSE 100 group Audit Fees – UK top 20					
Company	Year end	Auditors	Audit fee £m	Other fees	
				UK £m	Non-UK £m
HSBC Holdings	31.12.97	KPMG	10.9	12.5	0
BP	31.12.97	E&Y	8.0	3.0	3.7
Unilever	31.12.97	PwC	7.0	20.0	0
BTR	31.12.97	E&Y	6.0	3.0	—
NatWest	31.12.97	KPMG	5.2	10.4	3.1
Siebe	04.04.98	KPMG	4.8	1.3	2.0
ICI	31.12.97	KPMG	4.7	11.4	0
Barclays	31.12.97	PwC	4.4	7.7	2.0
CGU		KPMG	4.2	1.9	3.8
SmithKline Beecham	31.12.97	PwC	4.1	1.5	4.8
BAT	31.12.97	PwC	4.0	1.0	0.9
Lloyds TSB	31.12.97	PwC	4.0	6.2	3.0
Tomkins	02.05.98	AA	3.5	0.8	2.4
P&O	31.12.97	KPMG	3.3	2.6	2.4
Allied Domecq	31.08.97	KPMG	3.0	3.0	0
Rio Tinto	31.12.97	PwC	3.0	0.1	0
GEC	31.03.98	D&T	2.6	2.7	0
Royal & Sun Alliance	31.12.97	PwC	2.6	2.7	0
Glaxo Wellcome	31.12.97	PwC	2.5	0.7	1.7
Rentokil	31.12.97	PwC	2.5	0.1	0

Source: Table published in *Accountancy* International edition, October 1998, p.17

There is a good deal of discussion about the effect of this on independence. Audit firms say that independence is a state of mind and does not vary directly with the commercial relationship. The Big Five also point out that they are bigger than many of their clients, and independence is much more a problem for a single partner firm than one with thousands of partners. However, there is also evidence that over time, audit partners come to identify fairly closely with their clients, and in this connection, the old firm of Coopers & Lybrand, for example, were sanctioned for having been too ready to listen to Robert Maxwell, whose companies they audited for many years.

In France the audit appointment is for six years, and a listed company must appoint two auditors. In Italy the appointment is for three years and may only be renewed twice, leading to a maximum of nine years for the audit engagement. However, auditors point out that statistically the most likely time for a fraud is when there is a new auditor – it takes time for a new firm to understand thoroughly the workings of a large multinational. There is clearly no magic solution to the independence problem, and the US has created an Independence Standards Board to review the issue in the US.

Internal control

As we have discussed before, internal control is the generic term for accounting systems which follow transactions in such a way as to minimize the opportunities for fraud and error and ensure that transactions are checked by different people. The existence of internal control is what leads managers to become frustrated with demands for supporting documentation and authorizing signatures when they wish to make payments. This is not to do with accounting staff being 'difficult' but to do with the internal control system whose function is to safeguard the company's assets. Auditors always make an assessment of what they call the 'control environment': Are there good systems in place? Are they applied seriously by the staff or disregarded? Are transactions generally accounted for correctly?

In large companies the internal control system is usually backed up by an internal audit team. Their job, which is becoming wider all the time, is first to ensure that internal control systems are followed, and then to investigate any failures and recommend system changes as necessary. They also have developed a wider brief which is to assess risks within the company and to assess the consequences of management decisions.

All these arrangements to safeguard the company have existed for a long time, but have taken on a new significance in the new corporate governance framework. It is particularly true of a large multinational that there are many parts of the group that senior executives never see. Decisions are passed up and down the management pyramid, but only an effective internal financial reporting system shows that those decisions are carried out, and only an effective internal control and audit environment ensures that the accounting is accurate and the risks being taken by the company are being measured.

Lufthansa

Risk management system implemented

As a globally active group which provides a wide range of services, Lufthansa is naturally exposed to diverse risks. The object of Lufthansa's risk management system is to avoid risks wherever possible or to render their consequences manageable through a set of appropriate instruments. In order to comply with the new Act on Corporate Governance and Transparency, Lufthansa last year elaborated a structured overview of the essential risks to which its business operations are exposed as the basis of an early warning system for identifying potential risks.

The Group's internal auditing department regularly audits the suitability and effectiveness of these instruments as an independent and objective body.

Source: Lufthansa Annual Report 1998, extract from Group Management report

---

A good system of internal control means that central management can be sure that they know what is going on in the company, and now in some countries the board of directors puts a note in the annual financial statements to the effect that they are satisfied with the system of internal control. As we have observed before, it is the absence of good internal controls which permits executives to carry out transactions against company policy and without the financial consequences being immediately visible, as Deutsche Bank, Barings and others can testify, and hence its importance in corporate governance discussions. There is no point in central management having the right policies in place if they are unable to monitor their application.

Audit committee

This brings us to the question of the audit committee. The idea of an audit committee originated in the US more than 20 years ago, and has spread slowly to Europe. Companies listed on American stock exchanges are obliged to have an audit committee, and this of itself means that European companies listed in the US have one. However, as the corporate governance movement has gathered pace, so has an indigenous insistence upon the merits of an audit committee in different European countries.

Committees of the Board of Directors in 1998

The Audit Committee consists of non-executive directors. Its responsibilities include the consideration of the financial statements and the internal control systems and the internal audit. The Committee meets in the presence of external auditors, the CFO and the Group Controller and, upon invitation, other senior executives. The Audit Committee was composed of the following members of the Board: Dr Edward Andersson, Joukjo K Leskinen and Robert F W van Oordt.

Source: NOKIA Annual Report 1998, Extract from note on Corporate Governance

---

Essentially, the idea is that the audit committee should provide a quasi-independent forum where those concerned with checking the accuracy and quality of the company's accounting and control should be able to meet with shareholder representatives (independent directors) to discuss these issues. In theory this is a fine idea, and helps encourage an open discussion about the group's effectiveness and protect the 'whistle-blower' from inside the company who is concerned about management fraud, ecological damage, tax fraud or whatever. It also helps preserve the independence of the external auditors from management. However, it depends upon the independent directors being willing to listen and to take action where they think this is necessary. Clearly in practice there is a risk that the audit committee will think it is there to defend the executives, or will not follow up the issues raised with the executives. In other words, the success of the audit committee is not guaranteed at all – it depends very much on the quality of the people concerned.

American concern about the effectiveness of the audit committee led to the chairman of the New York Stock Exchange and the chairman of the National Association of Securities Dealers (which runs NASDAQ) to form what they called a 'blue ribbon' committee in 1998 to review audit committees. This committee published a report in 1999 with a whole series of recommendations. These included that the members of the audit committee should have some degree of specialist knowledge of accounting as a minimum and that they should publish their own annual report within the group annual report, commenting on their meetings and giving their view on the financial statements and the audit.

Summary

The object of this chapter was to give you a certain amount of background information concerning, in particular, audit and internal control. This information should serve to make you better understand the context within which the financial statements have been prepared and some of the information that is published in the annual report. If, as an analyst, you have the opportunity to attend company investor briefings, you should not hesitate to ask companies about the independent directors, the composition and mandate of the audit committee and the degree of efficacy of the internal control system. These are all indications of the transparency of company management and their effectiveness.

Questions

1. What is the current state of the corporate governance debate in the country in which you are based? Try to identify from the different sources of regulation (stock exchange, government, accounting profession etc.) current guidance in your country.
2. Compare the audit committee disclosures of an American corporation (see SEC EDGAR database) with that of a company based in your country.
3. Do you think that the independence of auditors is an issue about which you should be concerned? What are the rules in your country?

Part Five

Advanced financial statement analysis

17 Financial statement analysis II

In this chapter you are going to deepen your analytical technique and should, by the end of it, know what other inputs are used by analysts to arrive at their opinions about companies. You should have learned new methods for comparing companies of different sizes and considered what is implied by the quality of a company's earnings, and also learned to use certain ratios as a clue to the strategic positioning of a company.

Introduction

The basic intention in this chapter is to take your analytical skills a stage further, introducing newer analytical tools and concepts which give further insights into a company and help with investment and other decisions.

The first issue is that, of course, accounting numbers are not the only input into the assessment of a company's prospects. Analysts use many other factors, mostly economic, about the state of the economies where the company trades, the state of the industry etc. to help predict future peformance. An example of this is provided by Moody's.

Moody's is one of a number of firms that offer a bond rating service – they assess the riskiness of individual companies and then publish their risk rating, which in turn impacts upon a company's cost of borrowing. Moody's use inputs from the following areas (not given in any priority ranking) in order to determine their risk rating:

Industry
Company
Capital structure
Sovereign risk
Bond instrument
Financial flexibility
Capital expenditure
Internal cash flow
Competitors
Use of debt capacity
Customers
Management risk appetite

Not all the information comes from financial statements! Moody's talk to company management and since they provide ratings for all large companies, talk to all the competing managements too, and therefore have a broad picture of competition and patterns of development. Moody's offer the following 'rating pyramid' which shows how they approach the rating decision:

Sovereign macro-economic analysis

↓

Industry sector analysis

↓

Regulatory environment
(national and global)

↓

Competitive trends
in sector

↓

Market position

↓

Quantitative analysis
financial statements
past performance
future projections

↓

Qualitative analysis
management
strategic direction
financial flexibility

↓

Rating

It is our intention within this book to provide some of the skills necessary for quantitative analysis, and you will draw from other books and courses insights into economics, finance, business strategy etc. which can be used to refine your analysis.

As far as accounting analysis goes, though, you should note the increasing use of investor briefings by companies as a means of obtaining explanations. Investor relations departments in large companies are generally also willing to respond to individual queries, provided that they know the analyst. In this context, the analyst carries out a series of technical measures, calculating ratios and so on, and uses the ratios to form a view about what is going on in the company, or to recognize that the expected patterns do not emerge, and further information is necessary to explain this anomaly. For example, if sales are increasing, you would expect the level of stock and receivables to increase as well. If this is not the case, you should ask the investor relations department to comment.

All expert users showed a clear desire to identify what drove cash flow and profits, together with the expert users' application of a mixture of systematic search and intuition for the likely answer. The systematic search followed the route of considering:

- the economy
- product market
- industry

- the business of the company
- quality of management; and
- quality of assets

Source: ICAS *Corporate Communications: views of institutional investors and lenders* Research Committee, Institute of Chartered Accountants of Scotland, 1999

Another point is that analysis frequently involves comparing companies in the same industrial sector. As a consequence the analyst gains insights into what are the typical financial structures and operating margins in the industry.

Common accounting base

When comparing two or more companies it may be necessary to adjust the statements because of accounting differences. Of course, there are often elements for which the analyst is unable to adjust because insufficient information is available, but the more one is comparing like with like, the more useful is the analysis. Many analysts try, when carrying out cross-sectional analysis, to eliminate any major accounting differences between companies, or for that matter, convert all companies to a common accounting base. The most obvious examples of this are reducing all revalued assets back to historical cost, or treating goodwill as an asset instead of writing it off. As discussed before, the first thing to do when analysing a company is to look at the note dealing with accounting policies. When comparing two different companies, you should compare their policies on major issues such as accounting for goodwill, depreciation rates, and valuation generally. You should also look at their provisions to see whether they are comparable.

The analyst can often usefully put pro-forma statements on to a spreadsheet, using an adjusted, common accounting base to make comparisons. Indeed this is a technique which is virtually essential when analysing the accounts of companies which are based in different countries. This is a subject which is beyond the scope of this book, but it is easy to see that common assumptions – or as near as the analyst can get – are essential to make valid comparisons.

Common size

Ratios have the characteristic that they do away with size considerations so that quite different companies may be compared. This may also be done by the preparation of 'common size statements' – these consist of profit and loss account and balance sheet expressed in percentages (i.e. profit and loss expressed as percentage of sales, balance sheet as percentage of total assets). For example, NEXT plc's 1992 balance sheet could be restated:

	Published £m	Common size %
Assets		
Fixed assets		
Tangible	113.9	22.4
Investments	8.6	1.7
Current assets		
Stocks	53.2	10.5
Debtors	218.6	43.0
Bank	114.3	22.4
	508.6	100.0
Liabilities and equity		
Creditors		
Trade and related	111.6	22.0
Short borrowing	201.3	39.6
Long borrowing	3.1	0.6
Provisions	24.1	4.7
Equity	168.5	33.1
	508.6	100.0

Quality of earnings

An analyst is looking for sustainable profit and growth of that profit. So a key question is to assess the extent to which the current earnings are subject to short-term influences or accounting manipulations. You should check for things like (a) changes of accounting policy or estimates; (b) pension holidays; (c) unusual asset disposals; (d) distortions caused by buying and selling subsidiaries (this is much helped where there is a requirement to disclose figures from continuing business as opposed to discontinued lines); (e) anything else which suggests that short-term results will not be replicated in the long term.

   This kind of subjective assessment of earnings is generally referred to as 'quality of earnings' and involves posing the question (as far as it is possible to tell) to what extent are the earnings revealed by the financial statements sustainable in future years?

Ebitda

This sounds like some strange mantra, and certainly some analysts can be heard chanting it at times, but this is simply a rough measure of operating cash flows. Ebitda stands for 'earnings before interest, taxation, depreciation and amortization'. While MNCs have largely harmonized their cash flow reporting and produce cash flow statements in line with IAS 7, and therefore provide operating cash flow data, some analysts prefer a measure drawn directly from the income statement. The idea is that the analyst is trying to assess trading cash flows before non-cash accounting allocations of cost (depreciation, provisions and amortization) and before returns to lenders and taxation. How much cash is the business generating on a day-to-day basis? This measure may be subject to technical criticism, but it has the advantage that it strips out – as far as possible, provisions are not necessarily highlighted, even if depreciation usually is – subjective accounting adjustments from the income measure and enables a more robust comparison of performance year on year or company to company.

Objectives of analysis

As we have discussed, there are many potential uses and users of annual financial statements, but for the immediate purpose of statement analysis we are addressing only the needs of the two main groups for whom the accounts are formally prepared: investors and creditors. These two groups are concerned with similar but different investment decisions about the company.

Investors (whether actual or potential) face a buy/sell/hold decision. They receive a return on their investment in the form of a flow of dividends and the difference between buying and selling price of the shareholding. There is no established pattern of behaviour amongst long-term shareholders as to whether they prefer income by way of dividends or by way of holding gain. (Clearly short-term holders are only interested in a speculative holding gain.) Finance theory suggests that shareholders should be indifferent, on the assumption that if a company restricts its dividend payments the share price will rise, so shareholders wanting cash flow can realize this by selling a part of their holding.

The evidence suggests that some companies pay high dividends in the belief that their shareholders want this, while others believe that shareholders prefer capital gains and restrict dividends (extreme case: Eurotunnel). The way in which unit trusts are sold suggests that fund managers believe these are different markets. Some companies attempt to satisfy both types of shareholder and offer the option of taking the dividend in the form of new shares.

Professional investors have varying points of view. US pension funds often look at dividend flows (over as much as a 50-year time horizon) while many UK brokers sell to institutional investors on the basis of expected holding gains. For example, Ian Hay Davison, chairman of Alexander Lang & Cruikshank, wrote the following:

> At 8.15 each weekday morning the security salesmen and analysts in my firm meet to consider the ideas that will be put to our 300 or so institutional customers during the day. Analysts responsible for following companies in various sectors of the market give their recommendations for specific shares: buy, hold or sell. It is these recommendations, together with similar conclusions reached at twenty or so other security houses, that collectively drive prices in the market. The single most important figure affecting the analyst's – and hence the market's – view is forecasted earnings per share. I know that accountants deplore the fact that judgements about the worth of a share turn largely on one number. Nonetheless that is what happens, and you and I know that it is accounting rules that determine earnings per share.

The way this works is that brokers expect the p/e ratio of a company to be stable (subject to economic changes, management changes etc.) and the market price to be a function of the forecast earnings and the p/e ratio (as discussed in Chapter 14).

For example, if a hotel company is forecast to have earnings per share of 20p, and a p/e of 12, its market price should be 240p. If an analyst who follows the hotel sector believes that the company is actually going to achieve significantly better than 20p, say 25p, this would mean that s/he would expect the price to rise to 300p, and the securities house would issue a buy recommendation to its clients. These recommendations can themselves move the market.

The professional investor will look at indicators which are predictors of future performance on the assumption that growth in profits will lead to high dividends or high share price rises. Clearly these indicators may be to do with the state of the economy, or based on some inside information (investor relations departments of large companies hold special briefings for brokers and institutional shareholders) about new products etc. However, this course is concerned directly only with the information which can be gleaned from the published financial statements, so while acknowledging that investors use many different information sources, we will concentrate on accounting information.

Growth in profits may be predicted from the accounts based on a number of factors such as evidence of management skill, or evidence of high investment. Other factors such as a high debt/equity ratio will provide indicators of some aspects of the degree of risk in investing in the company.

The investor wishes (a) to predict the level of future returns and (b) to evaluate these against competing investment opportunities in the light of the riskiness of the investment (the higher the risk, the higher the expected return to compensate for the investment).

The creditor (the supplier of loans rather than short-term trade credit) is also concerned with predicting performance but from a slightly different angle. The creditor's main risk is default risk but ordinarily the creditor will also be concerned to assure themselves that the company's likely future cash flows will be sufficient to meet interest payments and finally repay the debt. The creditor will have more interest in the financial structure and prospective cash flows of the company.

Broadly both investor and creditor will use much the same indicators, but the relative importance of specific indicators will be different. The indicators may also serve different purposes at different times. The investor may use indicators which lead to a buy decision. Having already bought a holding, the release of new accounting data will prompt a hold/sell decision. In making this decision the investor will look not only for the indicators of the future, but should also look for feedback into his or her own decision-making process. The investor will look to see how the company actually performed during the period an investment was held, as compared with the predictions made at the time of making the investment, to improve future predictions.

Strategic ratios

A recent development in financial statement analysis has been the attempt to develop ratios which will give insights to a company's strategic positioning in terms of the kind of analysis proposed by authors such as Porter or Peters. These authors identify ideas such as the life cycle of products and firms, whether the company operates in a market where entry is difficult (margins should be large) or entry is easy (margins are tight), whether its products are specialist, niche products (low volume, high margin) or bulk (high volume, low margin) and many other considerations. Again, the intention within this book is to provide financial statement inputs, and detailed discussions of business strategy should be looked for in specialist publications or courses.

Sustainable growth

This ratio measures internally generated growth potential. The ratio is calculated as:

$$\text{Growth} = \text{return on equity} * (1 - \text{Dividend payout ratio})$$

The dividend payout ratio is:

$$\frac{\text{Dividend}}{\text{Profit attributable to shareholders}}$$

Equity is, of course, equal to the net worth of a company, so the return on equity ratio would tell you by what proportion the company would grow if it retained its profits and reinvested them. This is then reduced by the dividend payout, since clearly the dividend involves returning cash to shareholders, to show the proportion of net worth retained in the company each year out of that year's earnings. This is described as 'sustainable growth'. It ignores the fact that depreciation has been charged in arriving at this figure because that is regarded as a surrogate for the cash outflow required to sustain the company at its present size.

Put another way, a company which is breaking even after depreciation charges (which reflect the economic life of the assets) should be able to replace its assets and stay the same size; a company which makes a profit (i.e. makes a positive return on equity) but pays it all out to shareholders by way of dividend will similarly stay the same size; but to the extent that a company has profits which are greater than the dividend, it will have internal growth potential.

This potential growth rate can be used as one basis of comparison. Clearly companies can also borrow, but ultimately that increases risk and is subject to fairly finite limits which link back to its equity base and the growth of that equity base. It is therefore a useful growth indicator to compare companies. If comparing companies within the same industry, one might predict that a company with a higher than average sustainable growth rate would be able to increase its market share.

ROI/Net margin/Asset turnover

There is a conventional relationship between some ratios (sometimes known as the Du Pont pyramid) which links ROI, net margin and asset turnover as follows:

$$\text{Net margin} * \text{Asset turnover} = \text{ROI}$$

This depends upon using certain definitions of these ratios:

$$\frac{\text{Profit before interest}}{\text{Sales}} * \frac{\text{Sales}}{\text{Total assets}} = \frac{\text{Profit before interest}}{\text{Total assets}}$$

In assessing the quality of the ROI measure, this should be decomposed into the two other ratios. Industries which are capital intensive are likely to have a low asset turnover ratio. However, such an industry is also usually characterized by high margins because it is difficult for new companies to enter the market. A company which is capital intensive but also has low margins well be on a declining trend in its life cycle.

Industries which have little capital involved will have higher asset turnover ratios. However, they will normally be highly competitive because of the lack of barriers to entry into the market and will therefore show lower margins.

Operational gearing

Another aspect of a company's competitive position is the flexibility of its cost structure: companies with high fixed costs cannot react easily to downturns and generally need to seek high market share to maximize their fixed capacity. Companies in the same industry but which organize themselves with higher variable costs are more flexible, but may need to site themselves in a high price niche rather than look for large market share.

This can be illustrated graphically. The convention in management accounting is that a company's costs are either fixed or variable in the short to medium term (this is an over-simplification, but useful for analytical purposes). Thus a company with high fixed costs would have the relationship between volume and profit shown in Figure 17.1.

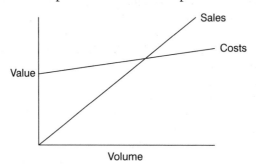

Figure 17.1 The relationship between volume and profit in a company with high fixed costs

Clearly, the higher the volume, the more profit, and such a company has some interest in reducing prices to gain market share, because that will lead to more than proportionately higher profits. Conversely, a company with low fixed costs and high variable costs is not very sensitive to volume changes and has much more interest in increasing prices. Such a company should therefore seek niche products, or highly differentiated products, where a small volume can be sold at high price.

From the point of view of the external analyst a way of assessing the operational gearing (ratio of fixed costs to total costs) is the ratio:

$$\frac{\text{Long-term assets}}{\text{Total asset}} \quad \text{or} \quad \frac{\text{Long-term assets}}{\text{Current assets}}$$

This assumes that the fixed cost element comes from plant costs (labour and materials being relatively variable). The high variable cost operator will buy semi-finished goods, for example, rather than process raw materials in house, so variable costs are higher and the asset base is lower.

Z scores

Some analysts like to use computerized models for assessing company performance. The best known in this kind of area are Altman in the US and Tafler in the UK. Essentially their technique consists of comparing the past financial statements of successful companies with those of similar but unsuccessful companies from which they derive a model against which to assess other companies. To give a simplified example, such a model typically works on a weighted series of ratios such as

$$0.2 \text{ ROE} + 0.5 \text{ Debt/equity} + 0.25 \text{ Current ratio} \geq 1$$

If a company scores below a certain value, it is deemed to be at risk. These models are known generically as 'Z scores' after Altman's original work. Such models may well be useful to audit firms and to banks to assess the viability of clients, and have the merit that they are an objective test. Critics on the other hand point out that the models are derived from statistical relationships which existed between particular companies in the past in particular industry sectors and particular economies and there is no guarantee that other companies at other times and in other circumstances will replicate the same relationships. The method does not, as it were, attempt to harness together data about actual economic circumstances as such.

It is a complex technique which is beyond the scope of this book. A number of proprietary versions are available on the market and there is an extensive research literature.

Shareholder value

An alternative approach to analysing statements is the concept of shareholder value, which appeared in the US during the 1980s but does not really have a generally agreed rationale or working methodology. Our intention here is to provide an introduction to the subject, which students can take forward when they study the related material in the finance literature. The underlying idea is that instead of looking at earnings per share and the p/e ratio to arrive at the value of a company, the analyst should look at the discounted present value of forecast earnings.

In principle the idea is excellent and in effect simply uses the definition of income which is used in economics. However, in practice the idea is more difficult because it involves forecasting future earnings over at least a ten-year horizon and determining the appropriate discount rate to use.

The basis normally used for imputing value in economics is the discounted value of the future cash flows that a project presents. You will normally cover the concepts of discounting and present values in the context of a finance or business statistics course. The essence is covered below.

Present value

Present value calculations are used in economics, finance and financial management to assign a value to future cash flows after adjusting for the time value of money. The essence of present value is that a rational person will prefer to have a receipt sooner rather than later because the money can be used to generate more money.

For example, if a company has a choice of receiving $1,000 now or $1,000 in a year's time, it would prefer to have the cash now because it could be invested and earn a return. If the money was put into risk free securities where it could earn 15 per cent, then $1,000 now would be worth $1,150 in a year's time.

Extending that, the $1,000 to be received after a year is worth $1,000/1.15 (or $870) today, because $870 invested today at 15 per cent would yield $1,000 in a year's time. Similarly, $1,000 to be received in two years' time is worth $1,000/(1.15*1.15) = $756 at present (i.e. compound interest at 15 per cent for two years would be $244).

By way of a simplified example, supposing that a listed company was forecast to have a life cycle of five years, the cost of capital for a company at that level of risk is 10 per cent and it is forecast to generate the following cash flows after meeting its operating costs:

	1 $m	2 $m	3 $m	4 $m	5 $m
Net cash flows	100	250	250	200	50
Discount factor:	.909	.826	.751	.683	.621
Present values	90.9	206.6	187.8	136.6	31.0

The present value of the company – or the shareholder value – is $652.9m. Supposing that it has 200m shares in issue, the share price should be ($652.9/200=) $3.26. If the actual share price is $2.70, then the investor should buy or hold, whereas if the actual market price was $3.50, the investor should sell (if holding shares) or simply not buy, on the basis in both cases that the share price will be likely to move towards $3.26.

If the management of the company are performing well, they will be increasing the future net cash flows of the company and therefore *increasing shareholder value*. The concept of shareholder value as a means of evaluating investments is very useful; however, the methodology involves a considerable amount of subjective inputs. These revolve around two key points: (1) the forecast cash flows of the company; and (2) the discount rate.

Forecast cash flows

The cash flow forecast needs to consider both the likely cash flows from existing operations and the capital expenditure necessary to renew existing equipment and expand capacity. The cash flow statement gives cash flows both from operations and outflows to pay interest and tax (the dividend stream is part of shareholder value, since this is being directed to the shareholder), the net after these is in effect the cash available for the shareholder or for reinvestment. In forecasting the future, it is necessary to make assumptions about the rate of inflation and the rate of real growth (which derive partly from observation of economic indicators and partly from an estimate of management's performance).

Estimating the capital expenditure rate is even more difficult. In the future, given a long time series of cash flow statements, it will be possible to produce a long-term average correlation between profit growth and investment growth. At this time, the analyst could take annual depreciation as a surrogate for maintaining existing equipment, and add to that a year-on-year change in net fixed assets and net working capital. The longer the time series, the more reliable an average figure would be.

Discount rate

There is an extensive literature on this subject. The discount rate should reflect the cost of capital as adjusted for inflation and the risk associated with the particular activities of that company. Alternatively, the analyst might use the weighted average cost of capital for the individual company.

There are many different formulations which might be used, both to forecast cash inflows (e.g. starting from forecast sales and using profit margins) and cash outflows, and the question of discount rate is contentious, since a small difference in discount rate usually gives a large difference in present value. However, it is a valuation model which best approximates the real cash flows of the company, and is particularly useful in cross-sectional analysis of companies in the same industry, since the same basic assumptions can be used.

Summary

In this chapter we have aimed to expand your knowledge of financial statement analysis and put it in closer touch with the actual practices of securities houses. We have looked at the evaluation model which examines the surrounding economic environment and we have looked at techniques such as common-size statements and accounting adjustments which can make financial information more directly comparable. We have seen that the analyst's forecast of earnings and the market p/e ratio are used to forecast the future share price and make buy/sell/hold decisions by investors.

We then went on to look at how financial statement analysis can give inputs into the strategic analysis of a company. We looked at a ratio for sustainable growth, as well as indicators of how capital intensive an industry is and its operating gearing. We looked also at the evolving concept of shareholder value.

Questions

Gloucester Gardens plc

You are an analyst working for an American investment bank, Insecurity International (II). You are called in by a junior associate in the Mergers and Acquisitions department to comment on a particular case.

II has been approached by a venture capital firm, Kindly Keep Repaying (KKR), which wants to dispose of a small investment in a company (Gloucester Gardens) which runs a chain of garden centres in South-West England. Gloucester Gardens (GG) started out as a nursery growing plants for direct sale to the public and also selling to the trade. Over a period of twenty years it first expanded its retail activities to sell a wide range of garden products beyond its own plants, and then took on more and more new retail units, supplied partly from its own nursery.

The company is now operated as two divisions: nursery and retail. All the output from the nursery is sold through the GG retail division, although for internal control purposes it is sold at market prices by the nursery division to retail.

The KKR representative says that GG is family run but the founder is nearing retirement and is quite interested to sell out, although his daughter is also involved in managing the business and would like to stay on and participate in the expansion of the business, assuming that some satisfactory package could be worked out. The family know that KKR is making this approach.

KKR thinks that the GG operation has potential as the basis of establishing a national chain of such centres, but thinks that the existing family management do not have the necessary expertise to grow any further. KKR would like to see their stake bought out by a major national retailer, possibly with the potential to slot the GG operation alongside a chain of out-of-town DIY or similar stores. KKR itself paid £1,400,000 for a 25 per cent stake in GG early in 1991 and is looking for upwards of £3,000,000 for its stake.

The M&A associate thinks that possible targets would include WH Smith (Do It All), Kingfisher (B&Q), Ladbroke's (Texas) or Sainsbury's (Homebase) and wants you to prepare an analysis of the figures for the last five years for GG for presentation to a potential client.

When the KKR representative has left, the M&A associate provides the attached figures and asks you to prepare a report for her to include:

(i)   an analysis of the company's investment and financing policy;
(ii) a review of its management as evidenced by the financial statements;
(iii) an executive summary, including your assessment of the situation and recommendations.

	1995 £'000	1996 £'000	1997 £'000	1998 £'000	1999 £'000
Profit and loss					
Sales	2,220.0	2,941.3	3,537.8	4,573.0	5,584.0
Cost of sales	1,344.7	1,766.8	2,105.0	2,697.4	3,262.5
Gross margin	875.3	1,174.5	1,432.8	1,875.6	2,321.6
Distribution	116.0	130.0	147.0	160.0	171.0
Administration	145.0	168.0	204.0	237.0	283.0
	614.3	876.5	1,081.8	1,478.6	1,867.6
Interest exp.	183.0	246.0	332.3	369.0	432.6
Disposal income	0.0	2.0	(4.0)	0.0	3.6
Profit before tax	431.3	632.5	745.5	1,110.6	1,438.6
Taxation	125.1	202.4	246.0	388.7	517.9
Profit after tax	306.2	430.1	499.5	721.9	920.7
Dividends	75.0	100.0	140.0	190.0	240.0
Retained	231.2	330.1	359.5	531.9	680.7
Balance sheets					
Fixed assets					
Retail premises	2,086.0	3,006.0	4,478.0	5,847.0	6,774.0
Depreciation	(208.8)	(284.0)	(395.9)	(542.1)	(711.4)
Nurseries	3,200.0	3,200.0	3,200.0	4,400.0	4,400.0
Depreciation	(624.2)	(730.9)	(837.6)	(984.3)	(1,131.0)
Plant and equipt	91.0	109.0	158.0	296.0	278.0
Depreciation	(56.4)	(68.0)	(82.8)	(142.0)	(146.4)
Vehicles	49.0	65.0	122.0	176.0	194.0
Depreciation	(19.7)	(28.6)	(46.9)	(90.9)	(96.3)
	4,516.9	5,268.5	6,594.8	8,959.7	9,560.9
Current assets					
Stock – retail	139.4	233.2	350.3	546.5	799.0
– nurseries	440.0	530.0	588.6	699.8	761.6
Debtors	111.0	147.1	212.3	320.1	446.7
Cash at bank	56.3	101.7	108.4	15.2	13.1
	746.7	1,012.0	1,259.6	1,581.6	2,020.4

ST creditors

Trade creditors	(269.0)	(353.4)	(484.1)	(701.3)	(880.9)
Dividend	(75.0)	(100.0)	(140.0)	(190.0)	(240.0)
Taxation	(125.1)	(202.4)	(246.0)	(388.7)	(517.9)
Overdraft	—	—	—	(182.2)	(182.8)
	(469.0)	(655.8)	(870.2)	(1,462.2)	(1,821.5)
Sub-total	4,794.6	5,624.7	6,984.2	9,079.1	9,759.8
LT creditors	(1,500.0)	(2,000.0)	(3,000.0)	(3,200.0)	(3,200.0)
Net assets	3,295.6	3,624.7	3,984.2	5,879.1	6,559.8

Capital

Ordinary shares	1,800.0	1,800.0	1,800.0	2,400.0	2,400.0
Share premium	784.0	784.0	784.0	1,547.0	1,547.0
Retained profit	710.6	1,040.7	1,400.2	1,932.1	2,612.7
Total equity	3,294.6	3,624.7	3,984.2	5,879.1	6,559.7

Analysis of fixed assets

1995

	Retail premises £'000	*Nursery premises £'000*	*Plant and equipt £'000*	*Motor vehicles £'000*	*Total £'000*
Cost: 1 Jan	1,369.0	3,200.0	82.0	26.0	4,677.0
Additions	717.0		24.0	31.0	772.0
Disposals	—	—	(15.0)	(8.0)	(23.0)
Cost: 31 Dec	2,086.0	3,200.0	91.0	49.0	5,426.0
Depreciation					
Balance 1 Jan	156.7	517.5	49.2	13.5	736.9
Disposals			(11.0)	(6.0)	(17.0)
Provision	52.1	106.7	18.2	12.2	189.2
Balance 31 Dec	208.8	624.2	56.4	19.7	909.1
NBV 31 Dec	1,877.2	2,575.8	34.6	29.3	4,516.9

1996

	Retail premises £'000	*Nursery premises £'000*	*Plant and equipt £'000*	*Motor vehicles £'000*	*Total £'000*
Cost: 1 Jan	2,086.0	3,200.0	91.0	49.0	5,426.0
Additions	920.0		32.0	28.0	980.0
Disposals	—	—	(14.0)	(12.0)	(26.0)
Cost: 31 Dec	3,006.0	3,200.0	109.0	65.0	6,380.0
Depreciation					
Balance 1 Jan	208.8	624.2	56.4	19.7	909.1
Disposals			(10.2)	(7.4)	(17.6)
Provision	75.2	106.7	21.8	16.3	220.0
Balance 31 Dec	284.0	730.9	68.0	28.6	1,111.5
NBV 31 Dec	2,722.0	2,469.1	41.0	36.4	5,268.5

1997

	Retail premises £'000	Nursery premises £'000	Plant and equipt £'000	Motor vehicles £'000	Total £'000
Cost: 1 Jan	3,006.0	3,200.0	109.0	65.0	6,380.0
Additions	1,472.0		83.0	72.0	1,627.0
Disposals	—	—	(34.0)	(15.0)	(49.0)
Cost: 31 Dec	4,478.0	3,200.0	158.0	122.0	7,958.0
Depreciation					
Balance 1 Jan	284.0	730.9	68.0	28.6	1,111.5
Disposals			(16.8)	(12.2)	(29.0)
Provision	111.9	106.7	31.6	30.5	280.7
Balance 31 Dec	395.9	837.6	82.8	46.9	1,363.2
NBV 31 Dec	4,082.1	2,362.4	75.2	75.1	6,594.8

1998

	Retail premises £'000	Nursery premises £'000	Plant and equipt £'000	Motor vehicles £'000	Total £'000
Cost: 1 Jan	4,478.0	3,200.0	158.0	122.0	7,958.0
Additions	1,369.0	1,200.0	138.0	54.0	2,761.0
Disposals	—	—	—	—	
Cost: 31 Dec	5,847.0	4,400.0	296.0	176.0	10,719.0
Depreciation					
Balance 1 Jan	395.9	837.6	82.8	46.9	1,363.2
Disposals					
Provision	146.2	146.7	59.2	44.0	396.1
Balance 31 Dec	542.1	984.3	142.0	90.9	1,759.3
NBV 31 Dec	5,304.9	3,415.7	154.0	85.1	8,959.7

1999

	Retail premises £'000	Nursery premises £'000	Plant and equipt £'000	Motor vehicles £'000	Total £'000
Cost: 1 Jan	5,847.0	4,400.0	296.0	176.0	10,719.0
Additions	927.0		46.0	56.0	1,029.0
Disposals	—	—	(64.0)	(38.0)	(102.0)
Cost: 31 Dec	6,774.0	4,400.0	278.0	194.0	11,646.0
Depreciation					
Balance 1 Jan	542.1	984.3	142.0	90.9	1,759.3
Disposals			(51.2)	(33.4)	(84.6)
Provision	169.3	146.7	55.6	38.8	410.4
Balance 31 Dec	711.4	1,131.0	146.4	96.3	2,085.1
NBV 31 Dec	6,062.6	3,269.0	131.6	97.7	9,560.9

Segment information

	1995 £'000	1996 £'000	1997 £'000	1998 £'000	1999 £'000
Nursery sales	1,100.0	1,325.0	1,415.0	1,620.0	1,700.0
Retail sales	2,220.0	2,941.3	3,537.8	4,573.0	5,584.0
Gross margin					
Nursery	220.0	265.0	283.0	324.0	340.0
Retail	655.3	909.5	1,149.8	1,551.6	1,981.6

18 Accounting values

The object of this chapter is to provide a few bridges towards further study of financial reporting. It may answer a few questions which have been lurking in the back of your mind; alternatively, it may give you an opportunity to bring some perspective to accounting issues.

Introduction

Probably one of the most important questions to think about is: do analysts routinely believe what they see in the accounts, and are they likely to be misled by the manipulations that companies may try?

This is a difficult question and there is much conflicting evidence. There is a body of thought called the Efficient Markets Hypothesis (EMH) which you may have come across in the finance literature. According to its definitions a strongly efficient (financial) market is one where the price of a security compounds all public information about the security. It follows from this that the market price is the best current price available, and that investors can only make a market rate of return if they have special knowledge.

Professional analysts and institutional investors are trying, through their analysis but also through their meetings with corporate investor relations staff, to gain special knowledge (either the result of their own special insights or the 'insider' information gleaned from the company) which enables them to form a more accurate picture than that in the market. Theoretically they are then in a position to make special profits either by buying securities which are currently under-priced, or by selling securities which are current over-priced. Views differ as to whether this special knowledge really exists, but it is not in analysts' professional interests to agree that taking the market price without research is an efficient way to invest!

This problem of special knowledge is linked also to the image of the company put out by the accounts. There is conflicting empirical evidence here, some of which shows that analysts have not noticed an accounting manoeuvre: for example, an accounting change which extended the depreciation lives of long-term assets would result in an apparent increase in profit. If the market were efficient, analysts would not change their valuation of the company, because there has been no change in its underlying economic position. If, on the other hand, analysts were fooled by the change, they would increase their valuation of the company because they would perceive it as more profitable. Some companies persist in carrying out such manoeuvres, which leads one to think that some preparers, at least, believe that analysts do not see a purely accounting manipulation for what it is.

Notions of value

Value is a very subjective idea, but managers sometimes think that it is more concrete, and talk about 'real' values ('what is X really worth?') when in fact value is something that can only be judged in relation to a particular framework. You have to specify the framework in order to be able to make a valuation; change the framework and you change the value as well.

In thinking about values, it is useful in the first place to distinguish between 'entry' values and 'exit' values. Entry values are those that relate to acquiring something (how much can you buy it for?), whereas exit values are those that relate to exploiting something, either by using it or by selling it.

Basic accounting is concerned above all with entry values. The value of an asset in the balance sheet is what it cost to buy it (historical cost). However, in more sophisticated accounting, one may also consider a second entry cost – what would it cost to buy an asset now, that was in the same age and condition as an existing asset? This is known as 'replacement cost'. Someone who is trying to value a company might approach it on the basis of what it would cost to acquire a similar bundle of assets at today's prices. That might be a current entry value. In an economy where there is rapid inflation, historical cost values soon become irrelevant, and replacement cost might be a more useful measurement approach in some circumstances.

Exit values are what benefits can be generated from owning the asset. From a company perspective that usually comes down to what cash flows can the asset generate? But in personal consumption one might consider that a purchase decision is an evaluation of the exit value of an asset against its entry value. Do I consider that the benefits I get from buying this computer (say) are greater than the cost of buying it?

Accounting uses exit values as a control only. So stocks must be held at the lower of cost (normal convention) or net realizable value (the exit value of the stocks), while long-term assets which are held for use rather than resale are held at cost unless the cash flows which are expected to be generated by their use are lower than cost. In both cases the exit value provides a ceiling for the carrying value of the asset, but that is the only way in which it is used in accounting.

An investor on the other hand is looking at a company and asking whether the price of the security is justified in the light of the cash flows which will accrue to the owner of the securities. In effect this is the assessment which the analyst is making – what are the future cash flows which the investment will generate (what are the exit values?) and do these justify paying the purchase price of the security (entry value)?

Measuring income

A related issue is the question of valuation focus. Is the analyst trying to measure future cash flows from the company's operations, or the value of the company's assets? We would say that the investor is interested in the future cash flows which the investor is going to receive (dividends plus growth in the market value of the company) and that the company's ability to deliver (increasing) annual profits is the surrogate which is used (it is assumed that if the company produces increasing profits these will generate positive cash flows which will be used for dividends and investment in capacity, which will be reflected in higher market value). The current stock exchange value of a listed company is held, therefore, to represent the present value of the expected future cash flows of the company, derived from its profits. The measurement focus that interests the analyst is the income statement.

However, many regulators deplore this approach. They point out that there are many changes in a company's economic circumstances which are not captured by the income statement, not least because a company reports income on a prudent, realized basis. As a result, a valuation based on income omits important information.

Historically, annual income was defined as the change in wealth from the beginning to the end of the year, which could be translated in accounting terms into using the balance sheet as the measurement focus instead of the income statement. As discussed at the beginning, much of European regulation derives from a seventeenth-century requirement for businesses to prepare an annual 'inventory' of their worth. There was a period of experimentation in the nineteenth century where the balance sheet was the focus of corporate reporting in a number of countries, where, to put it in a simple form, a railway company might have had the following balance sheets:

	1 Jan 1870	31 Dec 1870
Current value of track, buildings, rolling stock	100,000	135,000
Net current assets	20,000	30,000
Loans	(40,000)	(50,000)
Net worth	80,000	115,000

Difference in net worth = £35,000 = profit for year

This balance sheet approach to profit measurement is still occasionally to be found today, for example as the basis of corporate taxation in Germany, and consists essentially of valuing assets and liabilities at two separate dates, and treating the change in residual value as the gain or loss over that period. Companies in France and Italy may revalue assets in their balance sheet to current value, but the increase in value becomes immediately taxable. Notice that the measurement issue becomes the valuation of assets and liabilities at a given moment.

This approach gradually changed to one where historical cost was the basis and this privileged the measurement of profits arising from trading transactions as the main driver of the accounting model, with the balance sheet value of assets being simply a residual of historical costs which would be absorbed, in most cases, into future trading costs through the mechanism of depreciation. Historical cost accounting as it is currently practised is (a) transaction based, and (b) driven by the measurement of profit and loss. In this sense it requires a transaction for some asset or liability to be recognized – the balance sheet does not set out to reflect necessarily *all* the assets owned by a company, only those for which a purchase transaction exists.

There are a couple of points to bear in mind here. The most important is that in traditional accounting the income statement 'articulates' (as the jargon puts it) with the balance sheet. The income statement is an explanation of changes in the internal value of equity as a result of operations. The income statement explains a change in equity, but is also directly linked, through accruals, depreciation and provisions, to the balance sheet value of assets and liabilities. Balance sheet values and income statement values are not derived independently of each other. Consequently, regulators have to have a preference: either you measure balance sheet values independently on different dates and the difference is the profit or loss for the intervening period, or you measure income, and the balance sheet represents unabsorbed costs (assets) and anticipated expenditure (current liabilities) and financing.

This can create tensions because while valuing the balance sheet independently provides a coherent economic assessment of the company, it is difficult to check for accuracy and reliability and difficult to compare. An income statement approach is much more verifiable, which induces confidence amongst managers and tax gatherers, but fails to capture significant elements of company value

Comprehensive income

Anglo-Saxon standard-setters issued a consultative document in 1999 on the presentation of financial reports which suggests that the way forward in reporting involves trying to square the circle of reporting income on a transactional basis while reporting balance sheet values on a current or 'value to the business' basis. As discussed above, the traditional iteration of balance sheet and income statement requires a policy decision as to which approach is driving measurement. However, the suggestion is that the relationship should be made more flexible by the expansion of the income statement to include a section which recognizes underlying economic gains and losses.

The measurement of income would then work as follows:

Traditional transaction-based, historical cost realized profit

+ economic gains and losses

= comprehensive income

The balance sheet would then be largely drawn up according to current values, with the difference in value between balance sheets shown in the income statement either as a transactional or economic one, depending upon how it was generated.

The UK has already introduced the idea of an extension of the income statement with its Statement of Recognized Gains and Losses. It has stopped short of introducing current values in the balance sheet yet, but that is clearly seen as the way forward in the long term.

The UK idea of current value is known as value to the business and is based on a concept known as deprival value (Figure 18.1). This is what the loss to the business would be if it were obliged to forfeit the asset in question. Deprival value asks: if the asset were lost, what would the company do? Would it buy a replacement asset? If the answer to that question is yes, then replacement cost is the appropriate value to appear in the balance sheet. If the answer is no (perhaps the asset is no longer used, the product is not profitable etc.) then the balance sheet value is the present value of the future cash flows from sale of the asset or from remaining production (whichever is the higher).

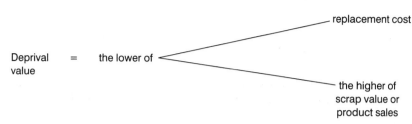

Figure 18.1 Deprival value

Essentially the application of this rule would normally provide a balance sheet value which is the cost of replacing the company's assets (and liabilities) at balance sheet date, subject to the proviso that unprofitable assets which would not be replaced are included at a lower value reflecting the cash flows expected to derive from the asset, either through use or sale. The assets are still therefore an entry cost (how much to buy the assets, not how much to sell) but at the same (current) value date.

The IASC on the other hand talks about 'fair value' which it defines as 'the amount for which an asset could be exchanged or a liability settled between knowledgeable, willing parties in an arm's length transaction'.

The beginning of the end of conventional accounting

IAS39 requires the presentation of many financial assets and liabilities at fair values. This particular revolution in accounting had taken years to arrange and the requirement to take gains to income relates only to trading and derivative items. However, in Warsaw, the IASC agreed two exposure drafts (on investment properties and agriculture) which propose to require approximately all investment properties and biological assets to be measured at fair value, with all gains and losses taken to income. This represents a dramatic increase in the use of fair values.

Agreement at the IASC on these moves would have been regarded as inconceivable even five years ago. The gradual triumph of fair values has been achieved partly by discussing the issues over and over again in the financial instruments project. Few Board representatives have any doubt that fair values provide more relevant information than cost for the conceptual framework's purpose of predicting future cash flows in order to make financial decisions.

Source: Chris Nobes, extract from article in *Accounting & Business*, September 1999

Obviously the major problem with moving to a basis of measurement other than historical cost is the loss of reliability in the measurements. This means that balance sheet values (and consequently some income statement values) would include a higher degree of subjectivity than they already do. In turn this puts pressure on auditors who become the sole arbiter of whether a value is "fair" or not, and potentially this reduces the comparability of financial statements. Against that, the user gets information which is more relevant in a fast-moving economy.

Business accounting has always been a tool at the service of the economy, and if the economy's information needs change, than accounting must change as well. By and large it has always done this in the past – the income statement was not produced in the nineteenth century, and virtually meaningless until the second half of the twentieth. The cash flow statement only came to be produced systematically and in more or less comparable format in the last decade of the twentieth century. Further change should therefore be expected, but regulators are slow to agree change, not least for the very good reason that the financial markets rely upon accurate data to channel investments to the businesses that can use them the most efficiently. When you start to mess around with the nature of the information, you risk a breakdown of the market, as the East Asian crisis showed.

Index